Lecture Notes in Computer S

T0238118

Commenced Publication in 1973
Founding and Former Series Editors:
Gerhard Goos, Juris Hartmanis, and Jan van Leeuwen

Erol Şahin   William M. Spears (Eds.)

Swarm Robotics

SAB 2004 International Workshop
Santa Monica, CA, USA, July 17, 2004
Revised Selected Papers

 Springer

Volume Editors

Erol Şahin
Middle East Technical University
KOVAN Research Lab, Dept. of Computer Engineering
Inonu Bulvari, 06531 Ankara, Turkey
E-mail: erol@ceng.metu.edu.tr

William M. Spears
University of Wyoming, Computer Science Department
Laramie, WY 82070, USA
E-mail: wspears@cs.uwyo.edu

Library of Congress Control Number: 2004117302

CR Subject Classification (1998): F.1, I.2.9, I.2.11, C.2.4, E.1, F.2.2

ISSN 0302-9743
ISBN 3-540-24296-1 Springer Berlin Heidelberg New York

Springer is a part of Springer Science+Business Media

springeronline.com

© Springer-Verlag Berlin Heidelberg 2005
Printed in Germany

Typesetting: Camera-ready by author, data conversion by Olgun Computergrafik
Printed on acid-free paper   SPIN: 11375661   06/3142   5 4 3 2 1 0

Preface

Swarm robotics can be defined as the study of how a swarm of relatively simple physically embodied agents can be constructed to collectively accomplish tasks that are beyond the capabilities of a single one. Different from other studies on multi-robot systems, swarm robotics emphasizes self-organization and emergence while keeping in mind the issues of scalability and robustness. These emphases promote the use of relatively simple robots, equipped with localized sensing abilities, scalable communication mechanisms and the exploration of decentralized control strategies.

With the recent technological advances, the study of robotic swarms is becoming more and more feasible. There are already a number of ongoing projects that aim to develop and/or control large numbers of physically embodied agents. In Europe, the CEC (Commission of the European Communities) has been funding swarm robotics studies through its FET (Future and Emerging Technologies) program. In USA, DARPA (Defense Advanced Research Projects Agency) has funded swarm robotics projects through its SDR (Software for Distributed Robotics) program.

Within this context, we set out to organize a meeting to bring together researchers in swarm robotics to review the ongoing studies, and to discuss and identify the research directions. Despite being the first meeting on the topic, our proposal to organize the workshop as part of the SAB 2004 (From Animals to Animats: Simulation of Adaptive Behavior) conference was enthusiastically accepted by the organizers, and Alfred Hofmann of Springer kindly agreed to publish the proceedings as a State-of-the-Art Survey in their LNCS (Lecture Notes in Computer Science) series. The Swarm Robotics Workshop was held on July 17, 2004, Santa Monica, CA, USA, after the SAB 2004 conference. We can confidently say that most of the prominent research tracks on swarm robotics were represented, and the workshop achieved the goals it set forth.

This volume contains 13 articles that were presented during the workshop which, we believe, provide a good review of the current state-of-the-art in swarm robotics studies. The first article is contributed by Gerardo Beni, who had coined the term *swarm intelligence* 15 years ago. In this article, Beni tells the story of how, and in what context, the term was conceived. He then describes the evolution of the term "swarm" applied to different domains, setting the stage for the term "swarm robotics." In a complementary follow-up to Beni's article, Şahin, in his article, proposes a definition for the term swarm robotics and puts forward a set of criteria that can be used to distinguish swarm robotics studies from the many other flavors of multirobot research. Balch's article reviews some of his early work on multirobot systems that are very relevant to swarm robotics approaches.

Dorigo et al.'s article provides a nice review of the SWARM-BOTS project, funded by CEC within FET. As part of this project, a mobile robot platform with the ability to connect to each other, called an *s-bot*, is developed. This platform and its physics-based simulations were then used to study self-organization and self-assembling behaviors, inspired from those observed in social insects. Payton et al.'s article reviews another project, funded by DARPA within SDR, describing their vision behind the "virtual pheromone" approach. They describe how a swarm of *pherobots* (mobile robots that can locally communicate with each other through directional infrared messaging) can be used to find survivors in disaster areas and guide the user towards them. Rothermich et al.'s article presents a review of another project, funded by the same source, on how a swarm of *swarmbots*[1] (mobile robots that can localize each other through "line-of-sight infrared communication") can perform collaborative localization in an unknown environment. Seyfried et al.'s article presents the vision of the I-SWARM project, funded by the CEC within the FET (Future and Emerging Technologies) program, which started in 2004. The I-SWARM project has a goal of designing a micro-robot of size $2 \times 2 \times 1$ mm that can be mass produced in thousands. The challenges of building micro-robots of that size are discussed.

Spears et al.'s article describes the "physicomimetics" framework, which relies on local control rules derived from physics, rather than ethology, and illustrates how this approach can be used to create solid formations for distributed sensing, liquids for obstacle avoidance, and gases for surveillance tasks. One advantage of this approach is the use of standard physics analysis techniques that allows the reliable control of the emergent behaviors by establishing correct parameter settings from theoretical first principles.

Martinson et al.'s article also focuses on the task of distributed sensing, and illustrates that, by exploiting a common reference orientation, orthogonal control rules can be developed that reduce the occurrence of local minima in the formation of lattices. Their control rules are a blend of ethological and physicomimetics-inspired behaviors. A nice aspect of their work is an illustration of robustness in the face of sensor noise.

Bayazıt et al.'s article reviews how roadmap methods can be integrated with simple flocking methods to generate guided behaviors such as exploring and shepherding. Winfield et al., in their article, introduce a new concept called "swarm engineering" to study how swarm intelligence-based systems (like swarm robotic systems) can be "assured of dependability." Lerman et al. review their work on the mathematical modeling of swarm robotic systems and discuss how such modeling would be of help in their analysis and design. The last article of the volume is another from Gerardo Beni. In his paper, Beni proves that "swarms with partial random synchronicity can converge in cases where synchronous or sequentially updated schemes do not." We believe that this result is very powerful, since it provides a rigorous support to the view that the swarm robotic approach has advantages over traditional centralized control approaches.

We would like to thank the SAB 2004 organizers Stefan Schaal, Auke Jan Ijspeert, Aude Billard, Sethu Vijayakumar, chairs, John Hallam and Jean-Arcady Meyer for giving us the opportunity to organize this workshop within the SAB

---

[1] The swarmbots have no relation with the SWARM-BOTS project described above.

conference; Alfred Hofmann of Springer for accepting to publish the post-proceedings of the workshop as a State-of-the-Art Survey in the Lecture Notes in Computer Science series; all the authors for submitting their papers; and the program committee members for providing timely and objective reviews which improved the quality of the articles in this volume. The program committee consisted of: Tucker Balch, O. Burçhan Bayazıt, Gerardo Beni, Marco Dorigo, Paolo Gaudiano, Alcherio Martinoli, David Payton, Cem Ünsal, Alan F.T. Winfield, and Joerg Seyfried.

Erol Şahin thanks Erkin Bahçeci, Levent Bayındır, Onur Soysal and Emre Uğur for helping him during the organization and the review process of the workshop and the preparation of this volume. Erol Şahin also acknowledges the travel support provided by TÜBİTAK (Turkish Science and Technical Research Council) and the support of the Department of Computer Engineering, Middle East Technical University (METU).

September 2004   Erol Şahin
                                                                    William M. Spears

Table of Contents

From Swarm Intelligence to Swarm Robotics

Gerardo Beni

Department of Electrical Engineering,
University of California, Riverside CA 92521, USA
beni@ee.ucr.edu

Abstract. The term "swarm" has been applied to many systems (in biology, engineering, computation, etc.) as they have some of the qualities that the English-language term "swarm" denotes. With the growth of the various area of "swarm" research, the "swarm" terminology has become somewhat confusing. In this paper, we reflect on this terminology to help clarify its association with various robotic concepts.

1 Introduction

This paper is meant as an introduction to a panel discussion on the use of various terms in current use, such as "swarm", "swarming", "swarm intelligence", "swarm optimization", "swarm engineering" and "swarm robotics". I will try to give some perspective by way of tracing, very imperfectly and subjectively, the evolution of some of these terms, hoping that, in looking at them, some robotics concepts may become clearer.

2 Why "Swarms"

About 20 years ago there was a significant interest in cellular automata; the interest diminished in the nineties until recently when the new book by Wolfram was published [1]. Wolfram gave some of the most important contributions to cellular automata theory in the early eighties. At that time, being interested in the topic of self-reproducing robots, I became interested in cellular automata since they can produce patterns of significant complexity starting from simple rules. Around the same time, Fukuda in Japan used the term "cellular robots" [2] to indicate groups of robots that could work like cells of an organism to assemble more complex parts. I used also the term "cellular robot" [3] but to indicate an extension, or a more general type, of cellular automaton. The extension was simply the fact that the units of the automaton were not operating synchronously nor sequentially and were moving and interacting dynamically. They were meant to represent a group of simple robots, self-organizing in new patterns.

With Jing Wang, we presented a short paper on cellular robots at one of the Il Ciocco conferences [4]. The discussion was quite lively and I remember Alex Meystel saying that "cellular robot" was an interesting concept, but the name was not appealing; a buzz word was needed to describe "that sort of 'swarm' ", as he put it. I agreed that the term "cellular robot" was not very

E. Şahin and W.M. Spears (Eds.): Swarm Robotic WS 2004, LNCS 3342, pp. 1–9, 2005.

exciting and, besides, it had already been used by Fukuda. By the way, also the term "cellular automaton" is probably not a very good choice. (May be part of the reason more people have not pursued that field is that it did not have a good buzz word.) Anyway, in thinking of how to call the "cellular robots" with a better term, I did not make any leap of imagination but simply used the word "swarm" that Alex had mentioned casually. There were some good reasons though. The fact is that the group of robots we were dealing with was not just a "group". It had some special characteristics, which in fact are found in swarms of insects, i.e., decentralized control, lack of synchronicity, simple and (quasi) identical members. Important was also the size, i.e., the number of units. It was not as large as to be dealt with statistical averages, not as small as to be dealt with as a few-body problem. The number of units was thought to be realistically of the order of $10^2 - 10^{<<23}$. So "swarm" was not just a buzz word but a term quite appropriate to distinguish that type of group.

Swarms were appealing as robotic systems since, compared to centralized systems designed for the same task, they had very simple components. Thus, the robotic units could be, in principle, modularized, mass produced, and could be interchangeable and maybe disposable. The second main (promised) advantage was reliability: since the swarm was in general highly redundant, the swarm could be designed to survive through many kinds of disturbances (possibly more severe than those considered in standard control systems); because of redundance, the swarm would have the ability to adapt dynamically to the working environment–another feature required for high reliability. It was also possible to envision the swarm as acting like a massive parallel computational system and thus carry out tasks beyond those possible to other type of robotic systems, either complex single robots or centralized groups of robots. (This is the main topic of section 4.)

While the swarm appeared as a very promising concept for robotics, Guy Theraulaz came to visit with us for a while and spoke about his work with insects [5]. It was clear that the concept of swarm was quite appropriate for insect societies. While roboticists tried to make the swarm do some prescribed tasks, the biologists tried to explain the behavior of insect societies as swarms. All the key qualities of swarms apply to insect societies: decentralized, not-synchronized, with quasi-homogeneous, simple units, not in "Avogadro-large" numbers. A key concept in their model of swarm was "stigmergy", i.e., communication by way of the environment. Ants communicate to other ants the "quality" of a path by marking it with pheromones so that a positive feedback mechanism ends eventually in most insects following the "best" path. This is an example of "swarm optimization", and in this particular area the concept of swarm has been most successful.

3   Why "Swarm Optimization"

While progress by roboticists in making swarms of robots do prescribed tasks has proceeded slowly, progress by biologists and other interested in optimization has been significant. It also seems entirely appropriate to use terms like "swarm optimization" to include algorithm such as Dorigo's [6] "Ant Colony Optimization" (ACO) algorithm and the "Particle Swarm Optimization" algorithm of Kennedy and Eberhart [7]. The word "swarm" here is appropriate because the algorithms are run asynchronously and in a decentralized fashion. They also mimic the stigmergic behavior of swarms of insects. This aspect of what swarms can do has been original to biologists and was not considered extensively by roboticists. The main departure is in the goal of the swarm. Roboticists were looking at the swarm as a constructor, a system to create patterns or some kind of ordered structures either internally, as self organization, or externally, as, e.g., self reproduction. Biologists instead were also looking at the swarm as a pattern analyzer, a system capable of recognizing the best way to do something. From this perspective the applications to stochastic optimization followed. Actually, besides foraging and related optimization problems, biologists were also looking at swarms of insects as creators of patterns since, e.g., in termite societies, swarms of termites build complex structures. The interest was in modeling how the swarm can build ordered complexity [8].

Looking at these various perspectives, it is not surprising if the concept of swarm appears more and more to be closely associated with systems capable of carrying out not just useful tasks but also "intelligent" tasks. From the robotic side, swarms self-organize into patterns. From the biological side they construct ordered patterns. The production of ordered patterns is a characteristic of intelligence. (Of course this is extremely simplified; in practice, robots can also manipulate objects and construct patterns, not just move around). Another is the recognition and/or analysis of patterns, which swarms do when they optimize a function. So, from all sides, we are led to look at the swarms as maybe doing something intelligent – "swarm intelligence".

4 Why "Swarm Intelligence"

"Swarm" and "swarm optimization" are appropriate terms to represent two well-defined concepts. The term "Swarm Intelligence" is more complicated to justify mainly because the term "intelligence" is very difficult to deal with [9–11]. A similar situation applies in Artificial Intelligence. As is well known, there is no satisfactory definition of intelligence. The concept is elusive. There are many qualities of intelligence, but, for any one of them, one can think of some non-intelligent system that has it. Dealing with robotics, we wanted to restrict the attention to some qualities of intelligence relevant to robotics.

One characteristic of intelligent behavior is the production of something ordered, i.e., unlikely to occur: an improbable outcome. Another is the fact that this outcome should not be predictable. A manufacturing machine produces a mechanical piece (ordered pattern, improbable outcome) but in a predictable way. We do not consider that machine intelligent. On the other hand the designer that produces the design of that mechanical piece is considered intelligent. Nobody knew what the designer would come up with. She was unpredictable. But of course just unpredictability is not intelligence; a roulette is not intelligent. It seems that somehow both unpredictability and the creation of some order are necessary to be able to speak of "intelligence".

In [12], we were thinking about this concept of intelligence in relation to the cellular robots and ended up calling it "swarm intelligence" (with no pretense of knowing what intelligence is). To get to that definition, in [12] we labored through a set of preliminary definitions, as follows.

Machine: an entity capable of mechanical behavior, i.e., of transferring and/or processing matter/energy.

Automaton: an entity capable of informational behavior, i.e., of transferring and/or processing information.

Robot: a mechanical automaton, i.e., an entity capable of both mechanical and informational behavior.

These three definitions are somewhat different from those in common usage but they help avoiding confusion since they contain only the two well-defined concepts of matter/energy and information. Strictly speaking, a "pure" machine cannot exist. A machine is always also an automaton since mechanical states contain information; in processing/transferring matter, a machine always also processes/transfers information (In contrast, an automaton can be a pure automaton since it operates on representations of states, not on physical states). Thus, in the definition of machine given above, there is the implied assumption that the information change is negligible with respect to the mechanical change produced by the machine.

An intelligent robot was defined as,

Intelligent robot (preliminary def. 1): a robot whose behavior (as defined below) is neither random nor predictable (as specified below).

Note that all the previous definitions apply to a generic entity regardless of its plurality, so they apply to groups of units as well. Groups of automata cannot be robots since they do not process matter/energy. But groups of pure (as defined above) machines can be robots since they can process information by changing mechanical states (e.g., by encoding information in patterns of the group). Thus intelligent robots can be built out of groups of pure machines. At this point the possibility of an intelligent robot made from a group of non-intelligent ones has been defined. However, the definition of intelligent robot still needs specifications. First, about "behavior", it is necessary to define the intelligent robot's behavior in terms of its relation to patterns of matter, i.e., arrangements of material objects, in contrast to arrangements of representations. In terms of patterns, there are two types of intelligent behavior: pattern analysis and pattern synthesis. The former can be accomplished by an automaton, the latter only by intelligent robots. Thus, the behavior specific to the intelligent robot was defined as the synthesis of material patterns. Thus,

Intelligent robot (preliminary def. 2): a robot capable of forming material patterns unpredictably (in the sense specified below).

At this point in [12] the concept of intelligent swarm could be formulated as:

Intelligent swarm (preliminary def. 3): a group of non-intelligent robots forming, as a group, an intelligent robot. In other words, a group of "machines" capable of forming "ordered" material patterns "unpredictably".

Note, in passing, that the swarm algorithms derived from foraging, such as the ACO algorithm and the PSO, are forms of pattern analysis behavior. The swarm finds an optimal pattern (e.g., path, function, etc.). Thus, the systems described by these algorithms are more swarm automata than swarm robots. On the other hand the termites' behavior in building structure is characteristic of the intelligent robot behavior defined above.

Most of the rest of [12] was a discussion of "unpredictability". Without a clear notion of unpredictability, the definition of intelligent swarm could be applied to trivial systems. For example, the definition could be satisfied by a mechanical "screen saver" that produces interesting patterns from a random algorithm. But picking at random some ordered patterns from a set is not the idea of unpredictability that suggests intelligence. Thus, anything that appears unpredictable simply because it is not accessible must be ruled out. Eventually the argument for unpredictability runs into the computational power of the system which is very appropriate, since the concept of intelligence has been often associated with computational power, as the Turing test, chess playing computers, and other AI arguments show. At this point we could further improve the definition of Intelligent Swarm as,

Intelligent swarm (preliminary def. 4): a group of "machines" capable of "unpredictable" material computation.

Unpredictability can be achieved if the system making the prediction is not capable of outrunning the system it is trying to predict. Now, if a system is capable of universal computation it cannot be outrun. In fact if one tries to predict a system which is capable of universal computation, one must use another universal automaton to simulate the first. Thus, the infinite time behavior of a system capable of universal computation is in general unknowable in any finite time: the problem is formally undecidable.

Our interest though was not so much in a system that is unpredictable at infinity, but at every step, or at least over a finite range of time; so, undecidability was not an entirely satisfactory choice for "unpredictability". We were looking for a system (the intelligent swarm) which cannot be predicted in the time it takes to form a new material pattern (of its own components). The issue is more one of tractability than decidability.

Normally one does not have a way of telling whether the method used for a particular computation is the most efficient possible. No clear lower bounds on the difficulty of computation have ever been established. The rate of computation is the issue. In general, once you have a system that is universal, you can make it to do any computation but the rate at which the computation is done is not obvious. In fact, without special optimization, a universal Turing machine will typically operate at some fixed fraction of the speed of any specific Turing machine that it is set up to emulate. Indeed, a priori, there can be great differences in the rates at which given computations can be done. However, it turns out [1] that a large number of universal systems can be made to emulate each other in a comparable number of steps. So, can a swarm be outrun? Certainly if is not properly designed. However, it is very plausible that the swarm can be designed so that no system capable of universal computation can outrun it. This is easy to see in the case of a Von Neumann architecture universal automaton versus a swarm.

To form the new pattern the intelligent swarm S would need to do (1) computations and (2) motions. The swarm does (1) and (2) in parallel. A universal automaton A trying to predict S must do (1) and simulate (2). We may assume that for S the time T_2 for (2) is much larger than for (1); but it is independent of N, the number of units in S, since the motions of the units may be assumed to occur in parallel. If A has a Von Neumann architecture the computation time scales with the number of states to be dealt with. If N is large enough this time will exceed T_2. So an automaton with von Neumann architecture could not predict the outcome of the intelligent swarm.

A more serious challenge to the intelligent swarm comes if A has a cellular automaton architecture and it is set up to simulate the intelligent swarm from its initial state. However, also in this case, A may not be able to outrun the swarm. The key is of course that the swarm be designed so as to be capable of universal computation. This is quite feasible since it has now become clear [1] that relatively simple (in terms of rules of evolution) systems are capable of universal computation. And swarms are actually generalization of cellular automata so there is no conceptual difficulty in thinking of a swarm capable of universal computation. The second key point is that in general, given a universal automaton, it is quite feasible to design it so that it cannot be outrun. This happens if, given a particular initial condition, an irreducible amount of computational work is required to find the outcome after a given number of steps of evolution. It is now considered likely that, asking about the possible outcome after a certain finite number s of steps of evolution of a universal system is a NP-complete problem. In other words, no Von Neumann or cellular automaton will ever be able to guarantee to solve this problem in a number of steps that grows only like some power of s.

So the intelligent swarm is unpredictable in the sense that it can be constructed as a computationally intractable system. Thus, the definition of intelligent swarm can be further refined as,

Intelligent swarm: a group of non-intelligent robots ("machines") capable of universal material computation.

Basically, the intelligent swarm [12], in terms of its unpredictability, is a particular instance of the principle of computational equivalence (and the concept of computational irreducibility) which Wolfram discovered in the '80s while working on cellular automata [13]. After the publication of [1], these concepts are becoming much clearer and more widespread. Which has further consequences for swarms. In fact, it now appears quite plausible that swarm intelligence is not just an interesting concept but something quite likely to be found in nature and quite feasible to engineer.

The whole point of defining the intelligent swarm was that one felt reassured of not studying a trivial system or a system that could easily be mapped into other well known systems. Swarm intelligence was an emergent property which led to systems of significant power in forming patterns of matter. The intelligent swarm could be a universal mechanical computer and as such unpredictable. It also showed that swarms were not just capable of doing what single robots do, but more capable. Thus, e.g., for defense applications, the swarm was inherently more promising (for this and other advantages) than the single robot, and, arguably, still is.

5 Why "Swarm Robotics"

The term swarm intelligence became more and more in use during the last 15 years and, as we have noted in sect. 2 and 3, generally with good justification. At the same time, the original application of the term (to robotic systems, sect. 4) did not grow as fast. One of the reasons is that the swarm intelligent robot is really a very advanced machine and the realization of such a system is a distant goal (but still a good research and engineering problem.) Meanwhile, it is already very difficult to make small groups of robots do something useful. Thus, there is not much reason to use a term (swarm intelligence) for much more modest groups of robots. It seems reasonable that terms such as "collective" robotics and "distributed autonomous robotic systems" should be used.

On the other hand, the use of labels such as "swarm robotics" or "collective robotics/distributed robotics" should not be in principle a function of the number of units used in the system. The principles underlying the multi-robot system coordination are the essential factor. The control architectures relevant to swarms are scalable, from a few units to thousands or million of units, since they base their coordination on local interactions and self-organization. The fact that only small groups of robots have been presented in most of the swarm robotics literature is a side effect of cost of robotic equipment and of the number of technologies involved to make robots working. Making a single mobile, autonomous robot working in a reliable way is already a big challenge nowadays, and even more so for a robotic swarm.

In biology, there is no such a mismatch between the term "swarm" and the systems one is looking at. First, because "swarm" is obviously the English-language word that describes some of the biological systems studied, regardless of whether or not what they do is intelligent. Second, because "swarm" is intuitively applicable to relatively large random systems that do something interesting. For example, "swarming" is used to describe mathematical solutions to some high order PDE [14]. Here it is clear that the term has a more distant relation to the concept of swarm as originally appeared in robotics (sect. 2); nevertheless it is a reasonable English language description when one looks at the patterns formed by the solutions of those PDEs, which resemble the paths of swarming fish or birds.

Swarm robotics [15], as a discipline, has attracted a significant number of research groups currently contributing to the field. An incomplete list of such groups includes: Caltech, Carnegie Mellon, Ecole Polytechnique Lausanne, Georgia Tech, Hughes Research Labs, MIT, Middle East Technical University, Riken, Texas A & M, Tokyo Institute of Technology, University of Alberta, UCLA, Universitat Karlsruhe, Université Libre de Bruxelles, USC, University of West England, University of Wyoming, Washington University.

Looking at applications, swarm robotics has by now accumulated a collection of "standard" problems which recur often in the literature. (This workshop itself describes a large array of such problems.) One group of problems is based on pattern formation: aggregation, self-organization into a lattice, deployment of distributed antennas or distributed arrays of sensors, covering of areas, mapping of the environment, deployment of maps, creation of gradients etc. A second group of problems focuses on some specific entity in the environment: goal searching, homing, finding the source of a chemical plume, foraging, prey retrieval, etc. And another group of problems deals with more complex group behavior: cooperative transport, mining (stick picking), shepherding, flocking, containment of oil spills, etc. This, of course, is not an exhaustive list; other generic robotic tasks, such as obstacle avoidance and all terrain navigation, apply to swarms as well.

Another aspect of swarm robotics that should be mentioned is "swarm control". Ultimately, after algorithms for task implementation have been devised, the practical realization requires robustness and this is the result of proper control. Swarm control presents new challenges to robotics engineers. The closest classic example, from the control engineering side, is perhaps formation control, e.g., the control of multi-robot teams or autonomous aircrafts or water vehicles. These studies lead to consider problems of asynchronous stability of distributed systems and are very much in line with the original drive toward swarm robotics. A brief review of these problems, as well as their relation to swarming in general, is given in the introduction section of a recent paper by Passino [16] whose work has focused on swarm robotics control.

In thinking about the actual realizations of swarms, it is important to mention also the new term "Swarm Engineering" coined by Alan Winfield and discussed in this workshop [17]. The notion goes beyond the control concepts of robustness and adaptation and brings about the issue of dependability in the actual realization of practical swarms. Generally, looking at swarm robotics and swarm engineering in a long range perspective, we may regard these notions as guiding paradigms toward the practical realization of systems capable of swarm intelligence as discussed in the previous section.

Overall, for the roboticist interested in engineering robotics swarms, all this nomenclature using the term "swarm" maybe a bit frustrating especially when trying to organize conferences to discuss swarm robotics problems. So, although defining terms is not one of the most creative activities, there is some valid justification in trying to describe more clearly the field of "swarm robotics". What is happening is a normal process of differentiation as fields grow. The success of the term "swarm" in various branches of science and technology is creating some confusion in understanding what type of swarm one is talking about; and so the need to separate various swarm areas has probably come. At the same time, looking at swarms themselves, we see that confusion (randomness) is an intrinsic reason for their power to do remarkable tasks. So, if at this time there is some confusion among swarm researchers, it may turn out to be a good thing.

Acknowledgement

The author thanks the referees for criticism and for many valid comments and suggestions, especially pertaining to the literature cited and the concept of intelligence and swarm robotics. The second paragraph of section 5 is taken almost verbatim from a referee's comment.

References

1. Wolfram, S. "A New Kind of Science", Wolfram Media (2002)
2. Fukuda, T., Nakagawa, S. "Approach to the Dynamically Reconfigurable Robotic System", Journal of Intelligent Robotic Systems, 1, (1988) 55–72
3. Beni, G., "The Concept of Cellular Robotic Systems", Proc. 3rd IEEE Int'l Symp. Intelligent Control, Arlington, VA, August 24–26 (1988) 57–62
4. Beni, G., Wang J., "Self Organizing Sensory Systems," in "Highly Redundant Sensing in Robotic Systems", Tou, J.T., Balchen, J. G., eds., Proc. of NATO Advanced Workshop on Highly Redundant Sensing in Robotic Systems, Il Ciocco, Italy (June 1988), Springer-Verlag, Berlin (1990) 251–262
5. Theraulaz, G., Pratte, M., Gervet, J., "Behavioural profiles in Polistes dominulus Christ wasp societies : a quantitative study", Behaviour, 113 (1990) 223–250
6. Colorni, A., Dorigo, M., Maniezzo, V., "Distributed Optimization by Ant Colonies", Proc. 1st European Conference on Artificial Life, 1992, 134–142
7. Kennedy, J., Eberhart, R.C., "Particle Swarm Optimization", in Proc. IEEE Int'l Conference on Neural Networks, 4 (Perth, Australia) 1995, 1942–1948
8. Theraulaz, G., Bonabeau, E., "Coordination in distributed building". Science, 269(4):686–688, (1995)
9. Parrish, J.K., Hamner, W.M., Eds., Animal Groups in Three Dimensions. Cambridge,U.K.: Cambridge University Press, 1997
10. Camazine, S., Deneubourg, J-L., Franks, N. R., Sneyd, J., Theraulaz, G., Bonabeau, E., Self-Organization in Biological Systems. Princeton, NJ: Princeton Univ. Press, 2001
11. Bonabeau E., Dorigo, M., and Theraulaz, G., "Swarm Intelligence: from natural to artificial systems", New York, NY. Oxford University Press (1999)
12. Beni, G., Wang, J., "Swarm Intelligence in Cellular Robotic Systems", Proceed. NATO Advanced Workshop on Robots and Biological Systems, Tuscany, Italy, Jun. 26–30 (1989)
13. Wolfram, S. "Undecidability and Intractability in Theoretical Physics", Physical Review Letters 54 (1985) 735–738
14. Topaz, C. M., Bertozzi, A. L., "Swarming patterns in a two-dimensional kinematic model for biological groups", SIAM J. Appl. Math., to appear (2004)
15. Dorigo, M., Şahin, E., "Swarm Robotics– special issue editorial", Autonomous Robots, 17 (2004) 2–3
16. Gazi, V., Passino, K. M., "Stability Analysis of Social Foraging Swarms", IEEE Trans.Syst. Man and Cybern -B 34 (2004) 539–557
17. Winfield, A., "Toward Dependable Swarms", this workshop

Swarm Robotics: From Sources of Inspiration to Domains of Application

Erol Şahin

KOVAN – Dept. of Computer Eng.,
Middle East Technical University, Ankara, 06531, Turkey
erol@ceng.metu.edu.tr
http://www.kovan.ceng.metu.edu.tr

Abstract. Swarm robotics is a novel approach to the coordination of large numbers of relatively simple robots which takes its inspiration from social insects. This paper proposes a definition to this newly emerging approach by 1) describing the desirable properties of swarm robotic systems, as observed in the system-level functioning of social insects, 2) proposing a definition for the term swarm robotics, and putting forward a set of criteria that can be used to distinguish swarm robotics research from other multi-robot studies, 3) providing a review of some studies which can act as sources of inspiration, and a list of promising domains for the utilization of swarm robotic systems.

1 Introduction

Swarm robotics is a novel approach to the coordination of large numbers of robots. It is inspired from the observation of social insects – ants, termites, wasps and bees – which stand as fascinating examples of how a large number of simple individuals can interact to create collectively intelligent systems. Social insects are known to coordinate their actions to accomplish tasks that are beyond the capabilities of a single individual: termites build large and complex mounds, army ants organize impressive foraging raids, ants can collectively carry large preys. Such coordination capabilities are still beyond the reach of current multi-robot systems.

2 Motivations for Swarm Robotics

Studies [1] have revealed that there exists no centralized coordination mechanisms behind the synchronized operation of social insects, yet their system-level functioning is robust, flexible and scalable. Such properties are acknowledged to be desirable for also multi-robot systems, and can be stated as motivations for the swarm robotics approach:

- **Robustness** requires that the swarm robotic system should be able to continue to operate, although at a lower performance, despite failures in the individuals, or disturbances in the environment. As anyone who tried to extinguish an ant raid into his kitchen would agree, social insects are extremely

E. Şahin and W.M. Spears (Eds.): Swarm Robotic WS 2004, LNCS 3342, pp. 10–20, 2005.

difficult to get rid of. This robustness can be attributed to several factors; First, redundancy in the system; that is, any loss or malfunction of an individual can be compensated by another one. This makes the individuals dispensible. Second, decentralized coordination; that is, destroying a certain part of the system will not deter the system's operation. Coordination is an emergent property of the whole system. Third, simplicity of the individuals; that is, in comparison to a single complex system that could perform the same task, in a swarm robotic system, individuals would be simpler, making them less prone to failures. Fourth, multiplicity of sensing; that is, distributed sensing by large numbers of individuals can increase the total signal-to-noise ratio of the system.

- **Flexibility** requires the swarm robotic system to have the ability to generate modularized solutions to different tasks. As nicely demonstrated by ants, in ant colonies individuals take part in tasks of very different nature such as foraging, prey retrieval and chain formation. During the foraging task, ants act independently searching for food in the environment; their search is partially coordinated by the pheromones laid in the environment. The prey retrieval task requires the ants to generate a force much larger than that of a single individual to drag a prey to the nest. When a large prey is discovered, each ant grip the prey with its mandible and pull it in different directions. The seemingly random pulls of ants are observed to be coordinated through the force integrated over the prey. In the chain formation task, ants form a physical chain-like structure that can extend beyond the reach of a single ant and exert large forces pulling together leaves. During the task, ants use their body as a medium of communication where ants in the chain act motionless with each ant gripping/holding the leg of other ants in the chain. In this task, coordination is achieved through the bodies of the ants. Swarm robotic systems should also have the flexibility to offer solutions to the tasks at hand by utilizing different coordination strategies in response to the changes in the environment.

- **Scalability** requires that a swarm robotic system should be able to operate under a wide range of group sizes. That is, the coordination mechanisms that ensure the operation of the swarm should be relatively undisturbed by changes in the group sizes.

Although we have presented the inspiration behind the swarm robotics approach, and described its envisioned properties as observed from natural systems, these by themselves are not sufficient to define the approach. In the next section, we propose a definition of the term, followed by a set of criteria to support the definition given.

3   Swarm Robotics

The term *swarm intelligence* was first coined by Gerardo Beni [2] as a "buzz word" to denote a class of cellular robotic systems (see [3] for a brief history). However, the term was embraced more by the social insect studies and by the optimization studies that used the social insect metaphor, losing much of its original robotics context [4]. During recent years, the term swarm robotics emerged as the application of swarm intelligence to multi-robot systems, with emphases on physical embodiment of the entities and realistic interactions among the entities and between the entities and the environment. In a sense, the term swarm robotics took the heir of swarm intelligence which moved on to cover a broader meaning.

Although, like every other newly coined term, swarm robotics will have a life of its own to claim its meaning, our observations indicate that such new terms run the risk of turning into buzz words that tend to be attached to existing approaches with little thought over whether it really fits or not. Such misuses, in time, can drift the term in every direction blurring the very point that made it novel. In an attempt to prevent this, we will propose a definition and a set of distinguishing criteria for the swarm robotics approach.

As our starting point, we propose the following definition for the term swarm robotics:

Definition 1. *Swarm robotics is the study of how large number of relatively simple physically embodied agents can be designed such that a desired collective behavior emerges from the local interactions among agents and between the agents and the environment.*

This definition by itself, however, is not sufficient to properly describe this newly emerging term. Within the multi-robot research only (see [5] and [6] for two rather out-dated surveys of the field), there already is a plethora of terms labeling different flavors of multi-robot research such as "collective robotics" [7, 8], "distributed robotics" [9], "robot colonies" [10], with often vague and overlapping meanings. Therefore, we would like to put forward a set of criteria for distinguishing swarm robotics research.

3.1 Autonomous Robots

As much as it seems obvious, we believe that the requirement that the individuals that make up the swarm robotic system be autonomous robots needs to be explicitly stated. That is, the individuals should have a physical embodiment in the world, be situated, can physically interact with the world and be autonomous. Sensor networks [11] that consist of distributed sensing elements, but with no physical actuation abilities, should not be considered as swarm robotic systems. Yet we believe that the studies on sensor networks are highly relevant for swarm robotics.

The metamorphic robotic systems [12, 13], in which units adhere to each other and can only move over each other by forming and disconnecting connections with other units can also be considered as swarm robotic systems as long as there exist no centralized planning and control centers.

3.2 Large Number of Robots

The study should be relevant for the coordination of a "swarm of robots". Therefore, studies that are applicable to the control of only a small number of robots and do not aim for scalability, fall outside swarm robotics. Although putting a number as a lower bound of group size is difficult to justify, and most would accept group sizes of 10–20 as "swarms". Despite the lowering cost of robots, maintainance and experimentation with large groups of robots will remain as a main obstacle. Therefore the issue of relevancy is mentioned to express that the field should be open to studies that are carried out with smaller group sizes, but with the vision/promise of scalability in sight.

3.3   Few Homogenous Groups of Robots

The robotic system being studied should consist of relatively few homogeneous groups of robots, and the number of robots in each group should be large. That is, studies that are concerned with highly heterogeneous robot groups, no matter how large the group is, are considered to be less "swarm robotic". For instance, studies on robosoccer teams mostly fall outside of swarm robotics since these teams typically consist of individuals whose different "roles" are assigned to them by an external agent prior to the operation of the team and hence they are highly heteregenous.

We agree that, the issue of homogeneity in a group of robots is not a trivial one. In [14] Balch proposed a metric, called the hierarchical social entropy, which can be used for this purpose. Yet, it is difficult to determine whether two individuals belong to the same group or not using a simple evaluation run in the *evaluation chamber* as proposed in [14]. This is due to two reasons: 1) the nonlinear inter-robot interactions will have a large affect on the behavior of the robots, and 2) probabilistic behaviors can make it impossible to obtain exact similar evaluation runs under exactly the same conditions.

3.4   Relatively Incapable or Inefficient Robots

The robots being used in the study should be *relatively* incapable or inefficient on their own with respect to the task at hand. That is, either 1) the robots should have difficulties in carying out the task on their own, and the cooperation of a group of robots should be essential, or 2) the deployment of a group of robots should improve the performance/robustness of the handling of the task. Collective retrieval of a large prey by ants is a good example to the first case where retrieval by a single ant would be impossible. Collective foraging of ants using pheromones laid on the ground for stigmergic communication create foraging patterns which are believed to improve their foraging performance [1]. Using a group of simple mobile robots, Sugawara et al [15] showed that signalling the discovery of an object in environments where objects are non-uniformly distributed can yield super-linear increases in the performance of the swarm.

It is important to note that this criterion does not impose any restrictions on the hardware and software complexity of the robots. The incapability and inefficiency of individual robots should not be taken in absolute terms, rather they should be seen relative to the task and be considered as a justification for the simplicity of robots.

3.5   Robots with Local Sensing and Communication Capabilities

The robots being used in the study should only have local and limited sensing and communication abilities. This constraint ensures that the coordination between the robots is distributed. In fact, the use of global communication channels within the robot group is likely to result in unscalable coordination mechanisms and would therefore act against the first criterion mentioned above. However, note that the global communication channels, which can be used as a means to download a common program onto the swarm, is acceptable, as long as it is not used for coordination among the robots.

We would like to warn the reader that the definition and the list criteria humbly expresses our current understanding of this newly emerging approach, as partially shaped by discussions held during the workshop. The reader should keep in mind that these criteria are not meant to be used as a checklist for determining whether a particular study is a swarm robotics study or not. Instead, they should be used as yardsticks for measuring the degree to which the term "swarm robotic" might apply. We hope that these views will act as a seed[1] for further discussion which will promote a better definition of "swarm robotics".

4   Sources of Inspiration

There are many research fields that can act as sources of inspiration for swarm robotics. First and foremost among them is the study of self-organization, which is defined [1] as "a process in which pattern at the global level of a system emerges solely from numerous interactions among the lower-level components of the system". In this sense, swarm robotics can be considered as the engineering and utilization of self-organization in physically embodied mobile swarms.

Studies of self-organization in biological systems show that an interplay of positive and negative feedback of interactions among the individuals is essential for such phenomena. In these systems, the positive feedback is typically generated through autocatalytic behaviors. The snowballing effect triggered by the positive feedback cycle is counterbalanced by a negative feedback mechanism, which typically stems from a depletion of physical resources in the system or the environment.

Studies that attempt to uncover the principles behind the emergence of self-organization in biological systems, often develop models that are built with simplified interactions in the world and abstract behavioral mechanisms in individuals. Self-organization models of social insects and animals have already been used as inspiration sources for many swarm robotics studies.

Below, we would like to draw attention to three other lines of research, which we believe, contain ideas that can act as inspiration sources. In our reviews, we tried to emphasize the ideas that, we consider, most relevant and inspiring for swarm robotics research.

---

[1] The discussion presented here extends from the views first put forward by Dorigo and Şahin in [16].

4.1   Unicellular Organisms

Some species of unicellular organisms, such as bacteria, myxobacteria, amoeba, are observed to display interesting examples of coordination. These organisms, which act independent of each other under favorable conditions (plenty of food, no antibiotics, etc.), are observed to display coordinated behaviors when times get hard.

Aggregation of Amoeba into Slime Mold. Aggregation is a highly observed phonemena in various life forms since it constitutes a pre-condition of most collective behaviors. One well known example of aggregation is observed during the formation of the slime mold by the *D. discoideum* from cellular *Dictyostelium* amoeba [1]. When the food is abundant in the environment, these amoeba feed and multiply with no signs of coordination among different individuals. When the food supply is depleted, however, the amoeba begins to aggregate forming complex spatial patterns. The aggregation process creates a slug, a multicellular organism which can move on a surface for some time, and then sporulate.

Studies have shown that the aggregation is governed by cAMP, a chemoattractant that is produced and released into the extracellular environment by the starving amoeba. It is shown that amoeba have two modes of cAMP secretion: oscillatory and relay. In the oscillatory mode, starving amoeba releases cAMP with a period of 5-10 minutes. In the relay mode, that is when the amoeba is hit by a cAMP pulse, the amoeba responds by a producing a larger cAMP pulse. The positive feedback of cAMP production cycle is bounded by the desensitization of cAMP receptors in high cAMP concentrations. This mechanism is shown [1] to generate spiral cAMP waves that propagate in one direction. The cAMP waves guide the cells towards the center of the spiral, which once begin to adhere to each other, create clumps that are difficult to disperse.

The amazing aspect of this aggregation process is its size; typically 10,000–100,000 cells aggregate to form the slime mold. Experiments on developing controllers for aggregation of mobile robots, which use sound or light for long range signalling, indicate that even aggregation of individuals on the order of 10's is very difficult [17]. The gap between the scales of aggregation suggests that stigmergic communication (which occurs through cAMP concentration in the extracellular environment of amoeba) is very important. Long range signalling modalities, such as sound and light, that are typical on mobile robots are not persistent in the environment as chemicals making them unusable for such stigmergic coordination. Two possible strategies to use stigmergy in swarm robotic systems exist. First, one can use embedded intelligent markers in the environment which can store stigmergic information and interact with each other to simulate physical diffusion like signal spreading. Gnats [18] or smart materials like those envisioned by the amorphous computing paradigm [19] can used for this purpose. Second, in a large swarm, some of the individuals can make themselves immobile and act as a stigmergic medium to guide the rest of the swarm. Although similar ideas were used in [20, 21] for route discovery and following, their use are rather limited and the idea needs to be exploited for other tasks as well.

Quorum Sensing and Communication in Bacteria. Recent studies of bacteria [22] started to reveal intricate communication mechanisms within bacteria colonies. Some species of bacteria are known to use quorum sensing to synchronize their actions: *Vibrio fischeri* produces light when its population reach a critical size, *Vibrio cholarae* delays the production of virulance factor in their host bodies until they reach a certain mass, possibly to ensure a successful infection by reducing the chance of immune system alert. Recent studies indicated that quorum sensing is done by the detection and production of extracellular chemicals called autoinducers that modulate gene expression. The discovery of different autoinducers and quorum sensing mechanisms in bacteria suggests that interactions between them can play an important role for the formation of complex structural organizations composed of multiple bacteria species.

Quorum sensing is a fundamental problem for swarm robotics that is yet to be faced. Therefore coordination mechanisms revealed in bacteria are very relevant. Although we would admit that the current state of the studies reviewed above, does not provide sufficient detail about these mechanisms yet, it is likely to do so in the very near future and therefore worth to keep an eye.

Information Exchange in Bacteria. It is observed [23] that "bacterial colonies can be far more resistant to antibiotics than the same bacteria living in suspension". It is thought that bacteria living in colonies form a genomic web and the enhanced robustness is due to the communication capabilities of bacteria through chemical signalling or the transfer of genetic material. The communication capabilities can be classified into two different categories: inducive and informative. In inducive communication, the (chemical) signal triggers a certain action within the cell. In informative communication, however, the message received is interpreted by the cell and the response is based on the current state of the cell and its history.

In real life, it is highly likely that some individuals of swarm robotic systems will discover certain hazards the hard way, through being destroyed by these hazards. Utilization of an information exchange mechanisms, inspired from bacterial communication, that can pass last-minute signals or codes to other individuals has the potential of improving the robustness of the swarm robotic systems in unknown environments.

4.2   Amorphous Computing

Amorphous computing, proposed by Abelson [19], sets its challenge as "How can prespecified, coherent behavior be engineered from the cooperation of vast numbers of unreliable parts interconnected in unknown, and time-varying ways?" This line of research considers "a system of irregularly placed, asynchronous, locally interacting computing elements" as a medium and aims to develop programming paradigms for translating a desired global pattern onto a finite set of rules to be executed by the elements. Their approach takes its inspiration from the morphogenetic processes in biological systems, such as tissue growth. In [24], Coore developed a programming language, called the growing-point language, which can be used to grow patterns in an amorphous medium through directed wave (message) propagation. Although there is no limitation on the mobility of the elements, work carried out so far has focused on immobile elements. Despite this, the programming paradigms developed in this line of research, we believe, are relevant for swarm robotics research.

4.3   Self-assembly of Materials

Self-assembly, defined as "the autonomous organization of components into patterns or structures without [external] intervention" [25], is of interest at different scales; Molecular self-assembly is useful for fabricating materials with regular structures (such as molecular and liquid crystals), nanoscale self-assembly stands as a promising method for building large numbers of micro electro-mechanical systems, meso- to macroscopic (objects with dimensions from microns to centimeters) self-assembly can aid robotic assembly process.

In [26], Whitesides and Boncheva argue that for successful molecular self-assembly the following characteristics be present; 1) the components should be designed for the desired structure, 2) the components should be mobile with respect to each other, 3) there exists an equilibrium of attractive and repulsive forces at the desired configurations of the components, 4) associations between the molecules should be reversible, allowing molecules to adjust their positions with respect to each other, 5) the environment should guide the interactions in the desired way.

Browsing through self-assembly literature, we discovered two other interesting ideas for swarm robotics research. One idea is the use of templates. It can scaffold the process reducing the defects in self-assembly. Another is the use of catalytic agents. Both ideas have the potential to improve the pattern formation performance in large swarm robotic systems and worth to be explored.

5   Domains of Application

Mass production of robots is essential for the deployment of swarm robotic systems. Advances in mechatronics technology have already started to shrink the size and costs of traditional autonomous robots. MEMS (Micro-Electro-Mechanical System) technology has been making impressive progress on the integration of mechanical, sensor, actuator and electronics components on silicon substrate opening the way to fully-autonomous micro-robots. As the mass produced robots, at macro, micro and nano levels, become available their cost will be relatively much cheaper (with respect to other single-robot solutions) making the individuals dispensible.

Below, we present a number of task domains where the swarm robotics would be applicable. We emphasize the properties of the tasks that make them suitable for swarm robotic systems, and provide a number of real-world problems as examples.

5.1   Tasks That Cover a Region

Swarm robotic systems are distributed sytems and would be well-suited for tasks that are concerned with the state of a space. Environmental monitoring (or tracking the well-ness) of a lake, would constitute a good domain of application. The distributed sensing ability of swarm robotic system can provide surveillance for immediate detection of hazardous events, such as the accidental leakage of a chemical. In dealing with this, a swarm robotic system would have two major advantages of sensor networks, which can also be considered as immobilized swarm robotic systems. First, in such a case, a swarm robotic system has the ability to "focus" on the location of problem by mobilizing its members towards the source of the problem. Such ability would allow the swarm to better localize and identify the nature of the problem. Second, the swarm can self-assemble forming a patch that would block the leakage.

5.2 Tasks That Are Too Dangerous

Individuals that create a swarm robotic system are dispensible making the system suitable for domains that contain dangerous tasks. For instance, clearing a corridor on a mining field can be cheaply accomplished by a swarm of robots. Unlike a single (more complex and expensive) "robotic de-miner" designed for the same task, the members of the swarm can afford being "suicidal" for carrying out their task by marching through the field. We would also argue that, a corridor that is marched by a swarm of robots would be safer than the one that is checked by the single "robotic de-miner" since the swarm robotics approach would physically walk over the mines, simulating the walk of the soldiers.

5.3 Tasks That Scale-Up or Scale-Down in Time

Swarm robotic systems have the power to scale-up or scale-down with the task at hand. For instance, the scale of an oil leakage, from a sunk ship, can increase dramatically as the tanks of the ship breaks down. A swarm robotic system which self-assembled to contain the initial spillage in a bounded area, can be scaled up by the "pouring" more robots into the area.

5.4 Tasks That Require Redundancy

The robustness of swarm robotic systems come from the implicit redundancy in the swarm. This redundancy allows the swarm robotic system to degrade peacefully making the system less prone to catastrophic failures. For instance, swarm robotic systems can create dynamic communication networks in the battlefield. Such networks can enjoy the robustness achieved through the re-configuration of the communication nodes when some of the nodes are hit by enemy fire.

6   Conclusions

In this paper we tried to define the newly emerging field of swarm robotics as a new aproach to the control and coordination of multi-robot systems. We stated the inspirations behind this approach, the desirable properties, and the requirements to clarify the defining characteristics of this approach in relation to other existing studies. However, the reader should note that like any other approach, this approach should not be seen to be applied in its pure "crystal" form to real problems. These clarifications are provided with the hope that it will guide the researchers to reveal the mechanisms behind, which can then be mixed with other approaches.

References

1. Camazine, S., Deneubourg, J.L., Franks, N., Sneyd, J., Theraulaz, G., Bonabeau, E.: Self-Organisation in Biological Systems. Princeton University Press, NJ, USA (2001)
2. Beni, G., Wang, J.: Swarm intelligence. In: Proc. of the Seventh Annual Meeting of the, Tokyo, Japan (1989) 425–428
3. Beni, G.: From swarm intelligence to swarm robotics. In Şahin, E., Spears, W., eds.: Swarm Robotics: State-of-the-art Survey. Lecture Notes in Computer Science, Springer-Verlag (in press)
4. Bonabeau, E., Dorigo, M., Theraulaz, G.: Swarm Intelligence: From Natural to Artificial Systems. Oxford University Press, New York, NY, USA (1999)
5. Dudek, G., Jenkin, M., Milios, E., Wilkes, D.: A taxonomy for multi-agent robotics. Autonomous Robots 3 (1996) 375–397
6. Cao, Y., Fukunaga, A., Kahng, A.: Cooperative mobile robotics: Antecedents and directions. Autonomous Robots 4 (1997) 1–23
7. Kube, C., Zhang, R.: Collective robotics: From social insects to robots. Adaptive Behavior 2 (1994) 189–218
8. Martinoli, A.: Swarm Intelligence in Autonomous Collective Robotics: From Tools to the Analysis and Synthesis of Distributed Collective Strategies. PhD thesis, DI-EPFL, Lausanne, Switzerland (1999) Nr. 2069.
9. Alami, R., Asama, H., Chatila, R., eds.: Proceedings of the Seventh International Symposium on Distributed Robotic Autonomous Systems (DARS'04), Toulouse, France (2004)
10. Arkin, R., Bekey, G.: Robot colonies - editorial. Autonomous Robots 4 (1997)
11. Akyildiz, I., Su, W., Sankarasubramaniam, Y., Cayirci: A survey on sensor networks. IEEE Communications Magazine (2002) 102–115
12. Chirikjian, G.: Kinematics of a metamorphic robotic system. In: Proceedings of IEEE International Conference on Robotics and Automation. (1994) 449–455
13. Yim, M., Zhang, Y., Lamping, J., Mao, E.: Distributed control for 3D metamorphosis. Autonomous Robots 10 (2001) 41–56
14. Balch, T.: Hierarchic social entropy: An information theoretic measure of robot group diversity. Autonomous Robots 8 (2000) 209–238
15. Sugawara, K., Sano, M.: Cooperative acceleration of task performance: Foraging behavior of interacting multi-robots system. Physica D 100 (1997) 343–354
16. Dorigo, M., E.Şahin: Swarm robotics - special issue editorial. Autonomous Robots 17 (2004) 111–113
17. Dorigo, M., Trianni, V., Şahin, E., Groß, R., Labella, T.H., Baldassarre, G., Nolfi, S., Deneubourg, J.L., Mondada, F., Floreano, D., Gambardella, L.M.: Evolving self-organizing behaviors for a swarm-bot. Autonomous Robots 17 (2004) 223–245
18. Balch, T., Bigio, V., Dodson, E., Irani, A., O'Hara, K., Walker, D.: Gnats: Characterization of and experimentation with a pervasive embedded network. In: Proceedings of the IEEE International Conference on Robotics and Automation (ICRA), New Orleans, LA, USA, IEEE (2004)

19. Abelson, H., Allen, D., Coore, D., Hanson, C., Homsy, G., Knight, T., Nagpal, R., Rauch, E., Sussman, G., Weiss, R.: Amorphous computing. Communications of the ACM **43** (2000) 74–82
20. Payton, D., Estkowski, R., Howard, M.: Compound behaviors in pheromone robotics. Robotics and Autonomous Systems **44** (2003) 229–240
21. Nouyan, S.: Path formation and goal search in swarm robotics. DEA for Universite Libre de Bruxelles (2004)
22. Bassler, B.: How bacteria talk to each other: regulation of gene expression by quorum sensing. Current Opinions in Microbiology **2** (1999) 582–587
23. Ben-Jacob, E.: Bacterial self-organization: co-enhancement of complexificatin and adaptability in a dynamic environment. Philosophical Transactions of Royal Society London A **361** (2003) 1283–1312
24. Coore, D.: Botanical computing: A developmental approach to generating interconnect topologies on an Amorphous Computer. PhD thesis, MIT Department of Electrical Engineering and Computer Science (1998)
25. Whitesides, G., Grzybowski, B.: Self-assembly at all scales. Science **295** (2002) 2418–2421
26. Whitesides, G., Boncheva, M.: Beyond molecules: Self-assembly of mesoscopic and macroscopic components. Proceedings of the National Academy of Sciences, USA **99** (2002) 4769–4774

Communication, Diversity and Learning: Cornerstones of Swarm Behavior

Tucker Balch

Georgia Institute of Technology, Atlanta, GA 30332, USA

Abstract. This paper reviews research in three important areas concerning robot swarms: communication, diversity, and learning. Communication (or the lack of it) is a key design consideration for robot teams. Communication can enable certain types of coordination that would be impossible otherwise. However communication can also add unnecessary cost and complexity. Important research issues regarding communication concern what should be communicated, over what range, and when the communication should occur. We also consider how diverse behaviors might help or hinder a team, and how to measure diversity in the first place. Finally, we show how learning can provide a powerful means for enabling a team to master a task or adapt to changing conditions. We hypothesize that these three topics are critically interrelated in the context of learning swarms, and we suggest research directions to explore them.

1   Overview

What is the relationship between communication, learning, and diversity in the context of robot swarms? We know already that different types of learning can impact the behavioral diversity of a learning robot team [1]. We also know that communication can improve robot team performance significantly. But communication adds cost and complexity to a robot system [2]. In spite of a substantial volume of work in each of these areas, there has been little, or no research that ties all three areas together.

The focus of this paper is to review fundamental research concerning robot teams in the areas of communication, diversity and learning. We hypothesize that robotic swarms will depend critically on research in each of these domains, and that successful systems will leverage results from each area. In fact, we suggest that it will be essential to consider all three issues at once. We propose new research directions that will serve to bring these domains together in the context of robot swarms.

The research we review here was primarily conducted with small teams of robots (from one to eight) and in simulation. These limitations were due primarily to experimental resource constraints that were present in the 1990s, but are largely absent in the 2000s: reliable robots are much less expensive now. We expect that the results from this earlier work will apply to swarms as well as they apply to teams.

E. Şahin and W.M. Spears (Eds.): Swarm Robotic WS 2004, LNCS 3342, pp. 21–30, 2005.

2   Communication in Robot Teams

Robot system designers must carefully consider each component of their design. The inclusion of sensors, actuators, or additional robots must be justified by contributing to efficient task completion. This becomes especially important in the case of robot swarms, which may include hundreds or thousands of agents – and thus multiplying cost substantially. The question is not simply whether or not to include inter-robot communication, but what type, speed, complexity and structure. How should these design decisions be made?

In the early 1990s Arkin [3] reported that successful task-achieving behavior can occur even in the absence of communication between agents. His work complements later research by Mataric that showed kin recognition can play an important role in robot team performance [4]. In particular, if robots can simply recognize their locations with respect to one another, they can perform better in in some tasks.

In the mid-1990s Balch and Arkin investigated how communication impacts multiagent robotic system performance [2]. We devised three societal robot tasks in which the performance in simulation of a team of robots was measured. For each task we evaluated three different types of communication. The experiments were designed so that performance for each type of communication can be compared across different tasks. In all, a six-dimensional space of task, environment, and control parameters was explored including: task, communication type, number of robots, number of attractors, mass of attractors, and percentage of obstacle coverage. The simulation results were supported by porting the control system to a team of Denning mobile robots. We focus on these results here.

2.1   Tasks for Communicating Robots

Our research focused on three tasks: **foraging**, **consuming**, and **grazing**. Foraging consists of searching the environment for objects (referred to as attractors) and carrying them back to a central location. Consuming requires the robot to perform work on the attractors in place, rather than carrying them back. Grazing is similar to lawn mowing; the robot or robot team must adequately cover the environment.

The forage task for a robot is to wander about the environment looking for items of interest (attractors). Upon encountering one of these attractors, the robot moves toward it, finally attaching itself. After attachment, the robot returns the object to a specified home base.

Figure 1a shows a simulation of two robots foraging for seven attractors and returning them to a home base. In the simulation, obstacles are shown as large black circles, attractors are represented as small circles, and the paths of the robots are shown as solid or dashed lines. They leave dashed lines as they wander, and solid lines when they acquire, attach, and return the attractors to home base.

Like forage, the consume task involves wandering about the environment to find attractors. Upon encountering an attractor, the robot moves toward it and

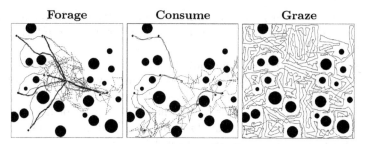

Fig. 1. Simulation of Forage, Consume, and Graze with two robots and seven attractors.

attaches itself to the object. Unlike the forage task, however, the robot performs work on the object in place after attachment. It is not necessary for the robot to carry the object back to home base. Applications for robots that can accomplish the consume task might include toxic waste cleanup, assembly, or cleaning tasks.

Figure 1b shows a simulation of two robots consuming seven attractors. Note that this task is performed in exactly the same environment as the forage task shown in Figure 1a. The robots leave dashed lines as they wander, and solid lines when they acquire and move to the attractors.

The graze task differs from forage and consume in that discrete attractors are not involved. Instead, the object is to completely cover, or visit the environment. Some familiar examples are mowing the lawn, sowing seed, and of course, cows grazing. The graze task for a robot is to search for an area that has not been grazed, move toward it, then graze over it until the entire environment (or some percentage of it) has been covered. It is assumed that the robot possesses some means to "graze" and that it grazes over a fixed "swath." The size of the task is dictated by the proportion of environment that must be covered before completion. Figure 1c shows a simulation of two robots grazing over 95% of the environment. The robots leave dashed lines as they wander, and solid lines when they graze. Grazing robots might be used to mow, plow or seed fields, vacuum houses [5], or remove scrub in a lumber producing forest.

2.2   Three Types of Communication

Three different types of communication were evaluated in this research. Using a minimalist philosophy, the first type, **no communication**, actually involves no direct communication between the agents. The second type, **state communication** allows for the transmission of state information between agents in a manner similar to that found in display behavior in animals [6]. The third type, **goal communication** requires the transmitting agent to recognize and broadcast the location of an attractor when one is located within detectable range.

In the case of no communication no messages are exchanged between the robots. However the robots are able to perceive the locations of nearby teammates (i.e. recognize their "kin"). When state communication is permitted, robots are able to detect the behavioral state (e.g. which behaviors are activated) of other robots. Although communication is often considered a deliberate act state communication is not necessarily "intentional" since information can be relayed by passive observation.

To take advantage of state information in reactive control, the behaviors for each task are modified slightly. From a robot's point of view, the most important states to look for in another robot are those where the other robot has found an attractor or an area to graze; that means that the other robot has found useful work. If the robot goes to the same location, it is likely to find useful work as well, or at least be able to assist cooperatively.

Goal communication involves the transmission and reception of specific goal-oriented information. Goal communication differs from the other two levels in that the sender must deliberately send or broadcast the information. A natural example of this type of communication is found in the behavior of honey bees. When a bee discovers a rich source of nectar, it returns to the hive and communicates the location with a "dance" which encodes the direction and distance from the hive to the source.

For reactive control, goal communication is implemented by modifying the behavioral assemblages in the same manner as described for state communication. However, a receiving robot moves directly toward the location of the attractor. The intent is that the agent may now follow a more direct path (beeline) to the attractor.

2.3   Results: The Impact of Communication and Stigmergy

Figure 2 shows a typical simulation run of two robots foraging for seven attractors with no, state, and goal communication. Inspecting the images from left to right reveals an apparent improvement in the "orderliness" of the robots' paths.

We compared the quantitative improvement in performance in all three tasks with communication to performance without communication. These results are summarized in the table below.

Forage
State vs No Communication 16%
Goal vs No Communication 19%
Consume
State vs No Communication 10%
Goal vs No Communication 6%
Graze
State vs No Communication 1%
Goal vs No Communication 1%

Specific conclusions we draw from these results are:

- Communication provides an important improvement in performance in forage and consume tasks.
- Communication doesn't help in the graze task.
- Goal communication does not provide much of an advantage over state communication in forage and consume tasks.

No Comm.   **State Comm.**   **Goal Comm.**

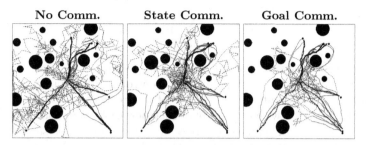

Fig. 2. Typical run for forage task with No (left), State (center), and Goal (right) Communication. The simulations required 5145, 4470 and 3495 steps, respectively, to complete.

Considering these results at a higher level, we observe that some tasks (in this case the graze task) enable a kind of communication through the environment: robots change the environment as they execute the task, and this change assists other robots in completing the task as well. Biologists refer to this as *stigmergy*. Since the time of this work was completed other roboticists have made similar observations and applied them to multi-robot tasks as well. In such tasks, explicit communication does not provide as much of an advantage.

3   Behavioral Diversity in Swarms

We now move to another important issue for swarm robotics – the advantages (or disadvantages) of heterogeneous teams. Most research in robot swarms has centered on homogeneous systems, with work in heterogeneous systems focused primarily on mechanical and sensor differences (such as Parker's work [7]). On the other hand, *behavioral* diversity refers to the situation where robots are mechanically identical, but differ according to their behavior.

In early work regarding behavioral diversity, the diversity of multirobot teams was evaluated on a bipolar scale, with systems classified as either *heterogeneous* or *homogeneous*, depending on whether any of the agents differ [8, 9, 7]. Unfortunately, this labeling doesn't tell us much about the *extent* of diversity in heterogeneous teams.

Heterogeneity is better viewed on a sliding scale providing for quantitative comparisons. Such a metric enables the investigation of issues like the impact of diversity on performance, and conversely, the impact of other task factors on diversity. *Social entropy*, inspired by Shannon's information entropy [10], is introduced as a measure of diversity in robot teams. The metric captures important components of the meaning of diversity, including the number and size of groups in a society.

To evaluate the diversity of a multirobot system, the agents are first grouped according to behavior (e.g. all red-collecting agents are placed in one group). Next, the overall system diversity is computed based on the number and size of the groups. Social entropy for a multirobot system composed of M groups is defined as:

$$H(X) = -\sum_{i=1}^{M} p_i \, \log_2(p_i) \tag{1}$$

where p_i represents the proportion of agents in group i.

An important limitation of simple social entropy as a diversity metric concerns its lack of sensitivity to the degree of difference between agents. As an example, consider that we have two robot societies, each composed of two groups of robots with the same number of robots in each group. In one society the two groups are not very much different – perhaps both groups are foraging robots and they both forage for the same type of attractor but in a slightly different manner. In the other society, however, the two groups are very much different: one group is a team of foraging robots, but the other group is a team of soccer robots. Their behaviors are substantially different. Simple social entropy would evaluate both systems as having the same degree of diversity. To address this issue we developed a slightly more complicated measure of diversity referred to as hierarchic social entropy. For more details, readers are referred to [1].

4   Learning and Diversity in Robot Teams

We now describe how social entropy can be employed experimentally to evaluate learning teams. We use simulated soccer and foraging tasks as domains for experiment. In both sets of experiments, the agents are provided a common set of skills (motor schema-based behavioral assemblages) from which they build a task-achieving strategy using reinforcement learning. The agents learn individually to activate particular behavioral assemblages given their current situation and a reward signal.

To foreshadow the results, we discovered that the diversity of a team depends critically on the form of the reward function used to train it. This begs the question that perhaps other factors may affect the level of diversity as well. We will address one of those (communication) later in the paper.

4.1   Learning Soccer

Soccer experiments were conducted by engaging an *experimental* learning team against a fixed opponent *control* team in soccer contests. Performance is evaluated as the total number of points scored by the learning team.

The learning teams were developed using the same behavioral assemblages and perceptual features as the control team. This approach ensures that the performance of a learning team versus the control team is due only to differences in policy. The control team's configuration uses a fixed selector for coordination. Learning is introduced by replacing the fixed mechanism with a selector that uses Q-learning instead. The Q-learner automatically tracks previous perceptions and rewards to refine its policy [11]. At each step, the learning module is provided the current reward and perceptual state. It learns over time to select the best assemblage given the situation.

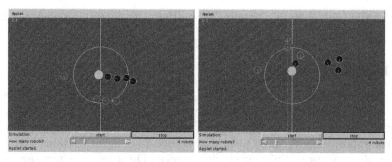

Fig. 3. Examples of homo- and heterogeneous learning soccer teams. In both cases the learning team (dark) defends the goal on the right. A homogeneous team (left image) has converged to four identical behaviors which in this case causes them to group together as they move toward the ball. A heterogeneous team (right) has settled on diverse policies which spread them apart into the forward and middle of the field.

The policy an agent learns depends on the reward function used to train it. One objective of this research is to discover how *local* versus *global* reinforcement impacts the diversity and performance of learning teams. Global reinforcement refers to the case where a single reinforcement signal is simultaneously delivered to all agents, while with local reinforcement each agent is rewarded individually. To that end, we consider two reinforcement functions for learning soccer robots:

- **Local performance-based reinforcement:** each agent is rewarded individually when it scores a goal, or is punished when it is nearest the ball when the team is scored against.
- **Global performance-based reinforcement:** all agents are rewarded when when the team scores, or punished when the team is scored against.

Experimental data were gathered by simulating thousands of soccer games and monitoring robot performance as the robot teams learned. The learning robots are evaluated on two criteria: task performance (score) and diversity of behavior.

When rewarded using the global reinforcement signal R_{global}, the learning teams out-scored the control team by an average of six points to four. This average includes the initial phase of training. When trained using the local reward R_{local}, the learning teams lose by an average of four points to six. In these soccer experiments, teams trained using global reinforcement perform best.

Two example teams, one homogeneous, the other heterogeneous, are illustrated in Figure 3. All members of the team on the left have converged to identical policies. In fact, *all* robots in the 10 locally-reinforced teams converged to the same "forward" policy used by the control team. All 10 teams converged to fully homogeneous behavior. $H(\mathcal{R}) = 0$ for the homogeneous teams trained using local reinforcement.

In contrast, all of the 10 globally-reinforced teams diversify to heterogeneous behavior. In all cases, the agents settle on one of three particular policies. All the teams include one robot that converges to the same "forward" policy used by the control team; they also include at least one agent that follows the same policy as the control team's "goalie." The other robots learn a policy similar to a mid-back role.

4.2 Learning Foraging

As in the soccer experiments, the approach in foraging experiments is to provide each agent a reward function that generates feedback at each movement step regarding the agent's progress, then to use that function over many trials to train the robot team. Again, Q-learning is used to associate actions with state. The learning agents are initialized with random Q-tables, thus random, poorly performing policies. Since each agent begins with a different policy, the teams are initially maximally diverse. They improve their policies using the reinforcement functions described below. Three reward functions were investigated:

- **Local performance-based reinforcement:** each agent is rewarded individually when it delivers an attractor.
- **Global performance-based reinforcement:** all agents are rewarded when any agent delivers an attractor.
- **Local shaped reinforcement:** each agent is rewarded progressively as it accomplishes portions of the task [12].

Full details on the formulation of these reward functions are provided in [1].

Agents are able to learn the task using all three types of reinforcement. A plot of the average performance for each learning strategy versus the number of agents on the team is presented in Figure 4. (In separate research, the performance of three different hand-coded systems was also evaluated [1]; performance of the best hand-coded system (a homogeneous strategy) is included in the graph for comparison).

The plot shows that, of the learning strategies, local performance-based and heuristic (shaped) reinforcement systems perform best. Performance in the globally reinforced system is worse than the other learning teams. Note that the performance plots for teams using local and shaped rewards are nearly identical and that one's confidence interval overlaps the other's mean value. Both also overlap the performance of the hand-coded homogeneous policy. In fact, there is no statistically significant difference between the homogeneous hand-coded systems and the best learning systems. Local and shaped reinforcement systems perform as well as the best hand-coded system.

5 Implications for Robot Swarms

The results across all these experiments suggest a number of implications for learning swarms. Namely:

- **Global rewards** tend to encourage diversity in a learning team.
- **Local rewards** encourage homogeneous teams.
- Which is best depends on the task. In some cases diversity is good, in others it is not.

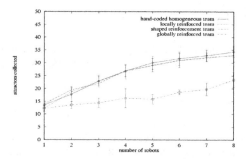

Fig. 4. Performance of foraging teams versus the number of robots on a team. The error bars indicate 95% confidence intervals.

We can also begin to answer the question of why behavioral diversity might be useful to a robot team (or swarm)? Our work and others' has shown that diversity becomes important when one or more of the following conditions exist [1, 8]:

- When individual robots cannot perceive the entire operating environment by themselves.
- When individual robots do not have enough program memory to hold an entire solution for the task.
- When communication bandwidth between robots is limited or it suffers from delays.

In these situations heterogeneous solutions can provide guarantees such as an assurance that necessary roles or locations will be assumed by at least one robot. In fact, in [13] we established conditions for tasks under which at least one optimal solution is heterogeneous.

When one considers all these results together it becomes clear that communication, learning and diversity are intimately related. As an example, consider how a noisy communication environment might impact the effectiveness of a particular learning algorithm for a robot swarm. Experiments indicate that for situations in which communications bandwidth is limited, diverse solutions are preferred. Furthermore, global rewards tend to encourage diversity. Accordingly a global reward system may be best in this case (this is speculation of course).

Communication, learning and diversity may be related in other ways as well. For instance, one method by which learning rates could be sped up for a team involve robots sharing their learning experiences. When using reinforcement learning, for example, a robot samples its sensors, selects an action, then receives a reward. Robots could share these <sense, act, reward> experience tuples by broadcasting them to one another. Essentially, the robots would hallucinate each others' learning experiences. Note however, that this kind of sharing would probably lead to homogeneous policies among the learners. But what if the task is best served by a heterogeneous solution?

The above suggestions are merely hypotheses. But they point to areas ripe for new work that will be critical for successful robot swarms.

Acknowledgments

Ronald Arkin provided intellectual and financial support for much of the research reviewed above. This research was funded by DARPA, ONR and Georgia Tech.

References

1. Balch, T.: Hierarchic Social Entropy: An Information Theoretic Measure of Robot Group Diversity. Autonomous Robots. **8(3)** (2000) 209–238.
2. Balch, T. and Arkin, R.: Communication in Reactive Multiagent Robotic Systems. Autonomous Robots. **1(1)** (1994) 27–52.
3. Arkin, R.: Cooperation without Communication: Multi-agent Schema Based Robot Navigation. Journal of Robotic Systems, **9(3)** (1992) 351–364.
4. Mataric, M. J.: Kin recognition, similarity, and group behavior. Proceedings of the Fifteenth Annual Cognitive Science Society Conference, (1993), 705–710.
5. MacKenzie, D.C. and Balch, T.: Making a Clean Sweep: Behavior Based Vacuuming. Working Notes of the 1993 AAAI Fall Symposium Instantiating Real-World Agents, (1993).
6. Moynihan, M.: Control, Suppression, Decay, Disappearance and Replacement of Displays. Journal of Theoretical Biology **29** (1970) 85–112.
7. Parker, L.: Heterogeneous Multi-Robot Cooperation. Massachusetts Institute of Technology Ph.D. Dissertation. Available as MIT Artificial Intelligence Laboratory Technical Report 1465 (1994).
8. Fontán, M. S., & Matarić, M. J.: Territorial multi-robot task division. IEEE Transactions on Robotics and Automation, **14** (1998) 815–822.
9. Coordinating mobile robot group behavior using a model of interaction dynamics. Proceedings, The Third International Conference on Autonomous Agents (Agents '99), (1999) 100–107.
10. Shannon, C. E., & Weaver, W.: Mathematical theory of communication. Univerisity of Illinois Press (1963).
11. Watkins, C. and Dayan, P: Q-Learning. Machine Learning, **8**, 279–292.
12. Mataric, M.: Reinforcement learning in the multi-robot domain. Autonomous Robots, **4(1)**, (1997) 73–83.
13. Zinkevich, M. and Balch, T.: Symmetry in Markov Decision Processes and its Implications for Single Agent and Multiagent Learning. International Conference on Machine Learning (2001) 632–642.

The SWARM-BOTS Project

Marco Dorigo[1], Elio Tuci[1], Roderich Groß[1], Vito Trianni[1],
Thomas Halva Labella[1], Shervin Nouyan[1], Christos Ampatzis[1],
Jean-Louis Deneubourg[2], Gianluca Baldassarre[3], Stefano Nolfi[3],
Francesco Mondada[4], Dario Floreano[4], and Luca Maria Gambardella[5]

[1] IRIDIA, Université Libre de Bruxelles, Belgium
{mdorigo,etuci,rgross,vtrianni,hlabella,snouyan,campatzis}@ulb.ac.be
http://iridia.ulb.ac.be/
[2] CENOLI, Université Libre de Bruxelles, Belgium
jldeneub@ulb.ac.be
http://www.ulb.ac.be/cenoliw3/
[3] Institute of Cognitive Science and Technology, CNR, Rome, Italy
baldassarre@ip.rm.cnr.it, s.nolfi@istc.cnr.it
http://gral.ip.rm.cnr.it/
[4] ASL, École Polytechnique Fédérale de Lausanne, Switzerland
{francesco.mondada,dario.floreano}@epfl.ch
http://lsa.epfl.ch/
[5] IDSIA, Lugano, Switzerland
luca@idsia.ch
http://www.idsia.ch/

Abstract. This paper provides an overview of the SWARM-BOTS project, a robotic project sponsored by the Future and Emerging Technologies program of the European Commission. The paper illustrates the goals of the project, the robot prototype and the 3D simulator we built. It also reports on the results of experimental work in which distributed adaptive controllers are used to control a group of real, or simulated, robots so that they perform a variety of tasks which require cooperation and coordination.

1 Vision

This paper introduces and illustrates the theoretical underpinning and the research agenda of the SWARM-BOTS project, a robotic project sponsored by the Future and Emerging Technologies program of the European Commission (IST-2000-31010). The aim of this project is the development of a new robotic system, called a *swarm-bot*, based on *swarm robotics* techniques.

Swarm robotics is an emergent field of collective robotics that studies robotic systems composed of *swarms* of robots tightly interacting and cooperating to reach their goals [1]. Swarm robotics finds its theoretical roots in recent studies of animal societies, such as ants and bees. Social insects are a valuable source of inspiration for designing collectively intelligent systems comprising many agents.

E. Şahin and W.M. Spears (Eds.): Swarm Robotic WS 2004, LNCS 3342, pp. 31–44, 2005.
© Springer-Verlag Berlin Heidelberg 2005

Despite noise in the environment, errors in processing information and performing tasks, and no global information, social insects are quite successful at performing group-level tasks. Based on the social insect metaphor, swarm robotics emphasises aspects such as decentralisation of the control, limited communication abilities among robots, use of local information, emergence of global behaviour and robustness [2].

The work carried out within the SWARM-BOTS project is directly inspired by the collective behaviour of social insects colonies and other animal societies, and in particular it focuses on the study of the mechanisms which govern the processes of *self-organisation* and *self-assembling* in artificial autonomous agents. In order to pursue these objectives, a new type of robot, referred to as *s-bot*, has been developed. Hardware development runs in parallel with the development of distributed adaptive architectures that make the *s-bots* capable of autonomously carrying out individual and collective behaviour by exploiting local interactions among the *s-bots* and between the *s-bots* and their environment.

The *s-bots* are mobile robots with the ability to connect to and to disconnect from each other [3, 4]. A *swarm-bot* is defined as an artifact composed of a swarm of assembled *s-bots* (see Figure 1). *S-bots* have relatively simple sensors and motors and limited computational capabilities. Their physical links are used to assemble into a *swarm-bot* able to solve problems that cannot be solved by a single *s-bot*. In the *swarm-bot* form, the *s-bots* are attached to each other and, when needed, become a single robotic system that can move and reconfigure. Physical connections between *s-bots* are essential for solving many collective tasks. For example, *s-bots* can form pulling chains to retrieve a heavy object (see Figure 1a). Also, during navigation on rough terrain, physical links can serve as support if the *swarm-bot* has to pass over a hole larger than a single *s-bot* (see Figure 1b), or when it has to pass through a steep concave region. However, for tasks such as searching for a goal location or tracing a path to a goal, a swarm of unconnected *s-bots* can be more efficient.

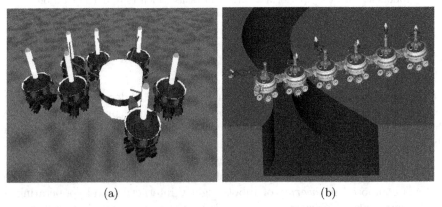

(a)   (b)

Fig. 1. Graphic visualisation of how the rigid gripper can be used to connect in a secure way *s-bots* among themselves so that they form a *swarm-bot* for (a) retrieving heavy objects or (b) passing over holes.

The design and realisation of both the hardware and the software of such a robotic system represents the scientific challenge of the SWARM-BOTS project. In what follows, we first give a brief description of the robot hardware, and of the experimental methodology employed to develop the *s-bots* controllers (see Section 2). Then, in Section 3 we describe the results of several experiments in which controllers have been designed to allow the *s-bots* to autonomously perform a variety of individual and collective behaviours in partially or totally unknown environments. Discussion and conclusions can be found in Section 4.

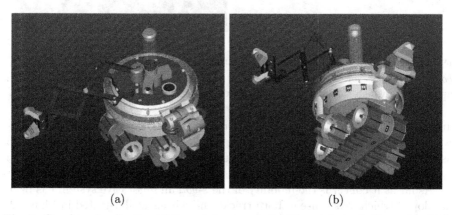

(a)   (b)

Fig. 2. Graphic visualisation of the *s-bot* concept. (a) The main body (turret), which has a diameter of 116 mm, is equipped with passive and active gripping facilities, sensors and electronics. (b) The lower body (traction system) is equipped with tracks and hosts the batteries.

2   The Hardware and the Simulation Environment

The construction of a number of artifacts (30-35) capable of self-assembling and self-organising represents one of the most significant scientific challenges faced by the SWARM-BOTS project. In subsection 2.1, we briefly describe the hardware of the *s-bots*, with particular reference to its sensor and motor apparatus. A more detailed description of the hardware components can be found in [5]. In subsection 2.2, we briefly introduce the main features of swarmbot3d, a simulation environment employed to design the software which controls the *s-bots*[1].

2.1   The *s-bot*

An *s-bot* is the basic elementary unit of the *swarm-bot* (see Figure 2). Each *s-bot* is a fully autonomous mobile robot capable of performing simple tasks such as autonomous navigation, perception of the environment and grasping of objects. In addition to these features, one *s-bot* is able to communicate with other *s-bots*

---

[1] Details regarding the hardware and simulation of the *swarm-bot* can also be found on the project web-site (www.swarm-bots.org).

(a)   (b)

Fig. 3. Pictures of *s-bots* transporting an object that can not be moved by a single *s-bot*. (a) A *swarm-bot* comprising four s-bots pulls an object. (b) Three *s-bots* pull/push an object to which they are directly attached.

and physically connect to them, thus forming a so-called *swarm-bot*. A *swarm-bot* is able to perform tasks in which a single *s-bot* has major problems, such as exploration, navigation, and transportation of heavy objects on rough terrain (see Figure 3).

As far as it concerns the mobility of the *s-bot*, an innovative system has been developed which makes use of both tracks and wheels as illustrated in Figure 2. The wheel and the track on a same side are driven by the same motor, building a differential drive system controlled by two motors. This combination of tracks and wheels is labelled *Differential Treels*© *Drive*[2]. Such a combination has two advantages. First, it allows an efficient rotation on the spot due to the larger diameter and position of the wheels. Second, it gives to the traction system a shape close to the cylindrical one of the main body (turret), avoiding in this way the typical rectangular shape of simple tracks and thus improving the *s-bot* mobility.

The *s-bot*'s traction system can rotate with respect to the main body by means of a motorised axis. Above the traction system, a rotating turret holds many sensory systems and the two grippers for making connections with other robots. In particular, each *s-bot* is equipped with sensors necessary for navigation, such as infrared proximity sensors, light and humidity sensors, accelerometers and incremental encoders on each degree of freedom. Each robot is also equipped with sensors and communication devices to detect and communicate with other *s-bots*, such as an omni-directional camera, coloured LEDs around the robot's turret, and sound emitters and receivers. In addition to a large number of sensors for perceiving the environment, several sensors provide each *s-bot* with information about physical contacts, efforts, and reactions at the interconnection joints with other *s-bots*. These include torque sensors on most joints as well as traction sensors to measure the pulling/pushing forces exerted on the *s-bot*'s turret.

---

[2] Treels is a contraction of TRacks and whEELS.

S-bots have two types of possible physical interconnections for self-assembling into a *swarm-bot* configuration: rigid and semi-flexible. Rigid connections between two *s-bots* are established by a gripper mounted on a horizontal active axis (see Figure 2). Such a gripper has a very large acceptance area allowing it to realize a secure grasp at any angle and, if necessary, allowing it to lift another *s-bot*. Semi-flexible connections are implemented by a gripper positioned at the end of a flexible arm actuated by three servo-motors.

2.2   The Simulation Environment: Swarmbot3d

Swarmbot3d is a 3D dynamics simulator of our multi-agent system of cooperating robots, based on the SDK Vortex^{TM} toolkit[3], which provides realistic simulations of dynamics and collisions of rigid bodies in 3D. Swarmbot3d provides *s-bot* models with the functionalities available on the real *s-bots* (see [5] for details). It can simulate different sensor devices such as IR proximity sensors, an omnidirectional camera, an inclinometer, sound, and light sensors.

A fundamental feature of the swarmbot3d simulator is that it provides robot simulation modules at different levels of detail. In particular, it provides a hierarchy of four *s-bot* reference models with increasing levels of detail. The less detailed models have been employed to speed up the process of designing neural controllers through evolutionary algorithms. The most detailed models have been employed to validate the evolved controllers before porting them on real hardware. The advantages of such a simulation environment are multiple: it works as an aiding tool for accurately predicting 3D kinematics and dynamics of a single *s-bot* in a *swarm-bot*; it has been employed to evaluate possible new options for hardware parts; it represents a "plastic" world model which allows the design of new experimental set-ups in 3D; it has been employed to quickly evaluate new distributed control ideas before porting them to the real hardware. Furthermore, the simulator provides on-line interactive control during simulation, useful for rapid prototyping of new control algorithms. Swarmbot3d allows to handle a group of robots either as independent units or in a *swarm-bot* configuration, which can be thought of as a graph, in which each node represents a connected *s-bot*. The connections can be created and released dynamically at simulation time. Connections may be of a rigid nature giving to the resulting structure the solidity of a whole entity.

3   Results

In this section, we briefly summarise the methods and the results of experimental work in which controllers have been designed to allow the *s-bots* to autonomously perform a variety of individual and collective behaviours in partially and totally unknown environments. These basic behaviours represent different lines of investigation which are pursued in parallel, and are focused on: 1) aggregation; 2) coordinated motion; 3) collective and cooperative transport of a prey item;

---

[3] Critical Mass Labs, Canada, (www.criticalmasslabs.com).

4) exploration; 5) adaptive task allocation; 6) navigation on rough terrain; 7) functional self-assembling. These research lines have been identified by looking at the kind of requirements that either a single *s-bot* or an aggregation of *s-bots* must fulfil in order to successfully perform the tasks involved in a complex scenario. The latter requires a swarm of up to 35 *s-bots* to transport heavy objects from their initial location to a goal location in an environment which presents difficulties of various nature, such as obstacles and holes on the ground. Moreover, the weight and/or size of the objects to be transported are such that these objects can not be transported by a single *s-bot* (see Figure 4).

To be capable of accomplishing the scenario, the *s-bots* must be equipped with controllers that allow them to successfully navigate in a totally or partially unknown environment in order to find and retrieve a target. The *s-bots* must also be capable of aggregating and self-assembling in a *swarm-bot* formation. The *swarm-bot* might be of fundamental importance for passing over a hole larger than a single *s-bot*, or to retrieve objects that can not be transported by a single *s-bot*. Finally, a group of *s-bots* should be capable of adaptively allocating resources to different tasks to be carried out either sequentially or in parallel. For example, if two heavy objects must be transported, a group of *s-bots* must be capable of splitting into two sub-groups each of which formed by the number of *s-bots* appropriately chosen with respect to the nature of the object the group aims to transport. The following subsections illustrate the research activities concerning the development of the basic behavioural capabilities above mentioned.

3.1   Aggregation

Within the SWARM-BOTS project, aggregation is of particular interest since it stands as a prerequisite for other forms of cooperation. For instance, in order to assemble into a *swarm-bot*, *s-bots* should first be able to aggregate. Several experiments have focused on the design of scalable aggregation behaviours by means of sound signalling (see [6, 7] for details). Artificial neural networks shaped by evolutionary algorithms control the behaviour of a homogeneous group of *s-bots* (i.e., within a group, all the *s-bots* share the same controller). During the evolutionary phase, the groups are randomly placed in a square arena. The agents are equipped with a simulated speaker that can emit a tone for long range signalling. *S-bots* can perceive the intensity of sound using three sound sensors that simulate three directional microphones. The *s-bot* controller takes as input the state of the *s-bot* proximity sensors, and the state of the sound sensors. Two output nodes control the *s-bot*'s motors. Controllers that exploit sound to let a group of *s-bots* aggregate are evolved using a fitness function that selectively rewards those groups which minimise the average distance of all the *s-bots* from the group centre of mass.

The evolved controllers show quite robust aggregation strategies. In particular, the *s-bots* exploit the sound signal both to get closer to each other, and to remain aggregated. In general, all evolved strategies rely on a delicate balance between attraction to sound sources and repulsion from obstacles, the former

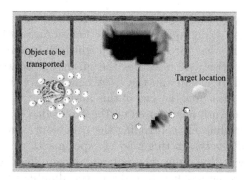

Fig. 4. The scenario: a swarm of up to 35 *s-bots* must transport a heavy object from an initial to a goal location. The cylinder on the left side represents the object to be transported; the landmark on the right side represents the target location where the object has to be transported. The four *s-bots* between the cylindrical object and the target location form a path which logically connects the former to the latter. This path is exploited by other *s-bots* to move back and forth between the target location and the object to be retrieved. Also visible are two types of obstacles: walls and holes.

being perceived by sound sensors, the latter by proximity sensors. A qualitative analysis of the evolved controllers reveals that different replications result in slightly different behaviours. In particular, the evolved solutions differ mainly in the behaviour of *s-bots* when they are close to each other.

Further evaluation tests concerning scalability of the evolved solutions have shown that controllers evolved for groups of four *s-bots* can successfully bring forth aggregation in groups with a higher number of *s-bots* (up to 40 *s-bots*). The best scalable strategy was the one in which the controller creates an aggregate that moves across the arena. This is a result of the complex motion of *s-bots* within the aggregate, which in turn is the result of the interaction between attraction to sound sources and repulsion from obstacles. The slow motion of the aggregate across the arena leads to scalability, as an aggregate can continue to move joining solitary *s-bots* or other already formed aggregates, eventually forming a single cluster of *s-bots*.

3.2   Coordinated Motion

Coordinated motion represents another basic ability for a *swarm-bot* formed of connected *s-bots* that, being independent of each other in their control, must coordinate their actions to choose a common direction of motion. The coordinated motion ability is essential for an efficient motion of the *swarm-bot* as a whole, and it is achieved mainly through the exploitation of the information coming from the traction sensor, which is placed at the turret-chassis junction of an *s-bot*. The traction sensor returns the direction (i.e., the angle with respect to the chassis' orientation) and the intensity of the force of traction (henceforth called "traction") that the turret exerts on the chassis. Traction is caused by the movements of both the connected *s-bots* and the *s-bot*'s chassis. Note that the turret of each *s-bot* physically integrates the forces that are applied to the *s-bot* by the other *s-bots*. As a consequence, the traction sensor provides the *s-bot* with an indication of the average direction toward which the group is trying to move as a whole. More precisely, it measures the mismatch between the directions toward which the entire group and the *s-bot*'s chassis are trying to move. The intensity of traction measures the size of this mismatch.

Our experimental work has focused on the evolution of artificial neural networks capable of coordinately controlling the behaviour of a *swarm-bot* (a collection of assembled *s-bots*). In this kind of experiments, the problem that the *s-bots* have to solve is that their wheels might have different initial directions or might mismatch while moving. In order to coordinate, *s-bots* should be able to collectively choose a common direction of movement having access only to local information (see Figure 5). Each *s-bot*'s controller (i.e., an artificial neural network), takes as input the reading of its traction sensor and other sensor readings, and sets the status of the *s-bot*' actuators.

The results show that evolution can find simple and effective solutions that allow the *s-bots* to move in a coordinate way independently of the topology of the *swarm-bot* and of the type of link with which the *s-bots* are connected (flexible or rigid). Moreover, it is shown that the evolved *s-bots* also exhibit obstacle avoidance behaviour (when placed in an environment with obstacles) and object pulling/pushing behaviour (when assembled to or around an object, see Figure 6), and scale well to *swarm-bots* of a larger size (see [8, 9] for details).

3.3   Collective and Cooperative Transport of a Prey Item

By taking inspiration from the behaviour of ants, the SWARM-BOTS project aims to build autonomous agents which by solely relying on local information, are capable of cooperatively and collectively carrying objects which can not be

(a)   (b)

Fig. 5. (a) Four physically linked *s-bots* forming a linear structure. The line between two *s-bots* represent the physical link between them. The white line above each *s-bot* indicates the direction and intensity of the traction. (b) Eight *s-bots* connected by rigid links into a "star formation".

moved by a single agent. The members of a group have to coordinate their actions to achieve the desired outcome. In particular, due to the nature of the object (i.e., its shape, dimension, and weight) the *s-bots* might be required to connect to each other in *swarm-bot* formation and/or to the object itself for transporting it (i.e., gripping the object with the fixed gripper, see Figure 7).

In a series of experimental works, artificial neural networks have been evolved to control the actions of a single homogeneous group of *s-bots* which is required to pull and/or push an object in an arbitrarily chosen direction. During the evolutionary phase, the *s-bots* are located in a boundless arena, in the proximity of objects of various shape, dimension, and weight. Only indirect communication through the environment can be exploited to attain coordination. The evolved controllers exhibit rather good transport performances. Certain controllers show scaling properties: they can be applied to larger groups of *s-bots* to move bigger and heavier prey objects. However, the controllers' performances are very sensitive to the size of the prey (see [10]).

A follow-up work focused on the self-organisation of *s-bots* into assembled structures and on the transport of heavy prey by groups of assembled *s-bots* to a target. To facilitate the process of assembling, the *s-bots* are provided with the ability to detect team mates; in addition, the presence of assembled structures is favoured by the fitness function employed. The best evolved controller proved fairly robust with respect to different combinations of size and shape of the prey (see [11]).

Recently the situation has been studied in which some *s-bots* are given the opportunity to localise the transport target, while the others (called the *blind* ones) are not. To enable a blind *s-bot* to contribute to the group's performance, it has been equipped with sensors to perceive both whether or not it is moving, and traction forces on its turret. For group sizes ranging from 2 to 16, it has been shown that blind *s-bots* make an essential contribution to the group's per-

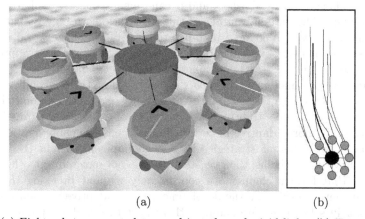

(a)   (b)

Fig. 6. (a) Eight *s-bots* connected to an object through rigid links. (b) Traces left by the *s-bots* (thin lines) and the object (thick line) during 150 simulation cycles. The gray and black circles represent the initial positions of the *s-bots* and of the object.

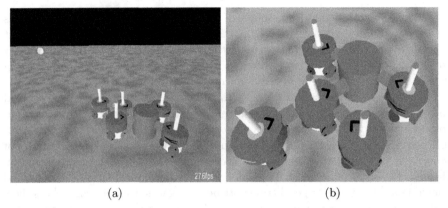

(a)   (b)

Fig. 7. (a) *S-bots* connected to each other and to an object. (b) A closer view on the connections.

formance. For the best evolved solution the performance scales well with group size, making possible the transport of heavier prey by larger swarms of blind and non-blind *s-bots* (see [12]).

3.4   Exploration

This subsection illustrates the mechanisms employed by the *s-bots* to efficiently explore a partially or totally unknown environment. Our approach is based on the exploitation of the collectivity, and it requires that some *s-bots* – referred to as *s-bot* beacons – be capable of positioning themselves in the environment in order to work as beacons for other *s-bots* – referred to as *s-bot* explorers – that move back and forth from a starting position to a goal location. The *s-bot* beacons should form a chain which connects different locations that cannot be perceived at the same time by a single *s-bot*. In this way, a path between a goal and a home location is established, and it can be subsequently exploited by the *s-bot* explorers. The main advantage of this exploration strategy is that it does not require the *s-bots* to create a map-like representation of the world.

The status of these experiments, in which a behaviour-based approach is employed to design the *s-bots* controllers, is still preliminary. However, simply by varying two parameters of the *s-bots* controller (i.e., the probability of each single agent to become a beacon and the probability of a robot beacon to become an explorer) it is possible to bring forth a variety of exploration strategies each of which results more adaptive in certain types of environment than in others. Up to date, two different strategies have been implemented. In the simplest setup, we have static chains: the *s-bots* beacons do not move. In the other setup, the *s-bots* that form a chain move coordinately without breaking the chain. We are currently working on the development of an adaptive mechanism which autonomously sets these parameters with respect to the characteristics of the environment experienced by the *s-bots*.

3.5   Adaptive Task Allocation

Task allocation and division of labour are two important research areas within collective robotics. Previous studies have shown that small groups of robots might perform a collective task better or not worse than a larger group. However, this efficiency loss can be avoided if large groups of robots are equipped with an adaptive task allocation mechanism which distributes the resources of the group with respect to the nature of the task and the diversity among the individuals of the group. Within the SWARM-BOTS project we are obviously interested in designing an adaptive task allocation mechanism which allocates to each task a sufficient number of *s-bots* without reducing the efficiency of the entire group. In particular, we have been working on a mechanism which adaptively tunes the number of active agents in a foraging task: that is, searching for objects and retrieving them to a nest location. The agents, controlled by a behaviour-based architecture, use a simple adaptive mechanism which adjusts the probability of each agent to be a forager with respect to the current success rate of the individual on the task. Owing to this simple adaptive mechanism, a self-organised task allocation is observed at the global level. That is, not all the agents end up being active foragers. The same mechanism is also effective in exploiting mechanical differences among the robots inducing specialisation in the robots' activities. More details are given in [13, 14].

3.6   Navigation on Rough Terrain

Navigating on rough terrain is an important feature for an adaptive autonomous system, that can open many possible application scenarios, like space exploration or rescue in a collapsed building. Within the SWARM-BOTS project, several experiments have been run on an instance of the family of navigation on rough terrain tasks, that is, hole avoidance. A *swarm-bot* is required to perform coordinated motion in an environment that presents holes too large to be traversed. Thus, holes must be recognised and avoided, so that the *swarm-bot* does not fall into them. The difficulty in this task is twofold: first, *s-bots* should coordinate their motion. Second, *s-bots* have to recognise the presence of a hole, communicate it to the whole group and re-organise to choose a safer direction of motion. The results demonstrate that the evolved controllers (i.e., artificial neural networks) manage to efficiently manoeuvre a *swarm-bot* in the proximity of holes in the ground. Evolution is able to produce a self-organising system that relies on simple and general rules, a system that is consequently robust to environmental changes and to the number of *s-bots* involved in the experiment. The evolved strategies strongly rely on the traction forces produced by those *s-bots* that feel the presence of a hazard (see [15] for details).

3.7   Functional Self-assembling

These studies focus on the design of controllers for a group of *s-bots* required to connect to each other, each time environmental contingencies prevent a single *s-bot* to achieve its goal [16]. We refer to this capability as functional self-assembling, since the self-organised creation of a physically connected structure has to be functional to the accomplishment of a particular task.

The complexity of functional self-assembling resides in the nature of the individual mechanisms required to bring forth the coordinated movements that lead firstly to the formation of the assembled structure, and subsequently to the collective motion of the assembled structure.

In a preliminary set of studies, we have focused on the evolution of neural controllers for self-assembling *s-bots* required to solve a simple scenario. In particular, we have investigated a scenario which requires the *s-bots* to approach a light source located at the end of a corridor. Assembling is required to navigate in a "low temperature" area in which a *swarm-bot* can navigate more effectively than a group of disconnected *s-bots*. When located in the low temperature area, the aggregation of the *s-bots* should facilitate the subsequent assembling through their gripper element. This experimental setup allows us to investigate the basic mechanisms that underpin functional self-assembling.

The results of our empirical work show that integrated (i.e., not modularised) artificial neural networks can be successfully synthesised by evolutionary algorithms in order to allow a group of *s-bots* to display individual and collective obstacle avoidance, individual and collective phototaxis, aggregation and self-assembling. To the best of our knowledge, our experiments represent one of the first works in which (i) functional self-assembling in a homogeneous group of robots has been achieved and (ii) evolved neural controllers successfully cope with a complex scenario, producing different individual and collective responses based on the appropriate control of the state of various actuators triggered by the local information coming from various sensors.

4   Discussion and Conclusions

In this paper we have illustrated the most important features of a novel robot concept, called *swarm-bot*. A *swarm-bot* is a self-organising, self-assembling artifact composed of a variable number of autonomous elementary units, called *s-bots*. As illustrated in Section 2, each *s-bot* is a fully autonomous agent capable of displacement, sensing and acting based on local information. Moreover, the self-assembling ability of the *s-bots* enables a group of agents to execute tasks that are beyond the capabilities of the single robot.

As far as it concerns the hardware, the presence of many of such autonomous entities that can self-assemble in a single body and disband any time the union is no longer required, makes the system extremely versatile and robust to failures. Contrary to the *swarm-bot*, other robotic systems composed of small elementary units capable of reconfiguring themselves are less versatile and less robust, due to the fact that each unit has no or very limited mobility, very limited sensing capabilities, and acts often under the control of a central unit (see [17–19]).

As far as it concerns the *s-bots'* controllers, we have developed them making an extensive use of artificial neural networks shaped by evolutionary algorithms. The solutions found by evolution are simple and in many cases they generalise to different environmental situations. This demonstrates that evolution is able to produce a self-organised system that relies on simple and general rules, a system that is consequently robust to environmental changes and that scales well with the number of *s-bots* involved in the experiments.

References

1. Dorigo, M., Şahin, E.: Swarm robotics – special issue editorial. Autonomous Robots **17** (2004) 111–113
2. Bonabeau, E., Dorigo, M., Theraulaz, G.: Swarm Intelligence: From Natural to Artificial Systems. Oxford University Press, New York, NY (1999)
3. Şahin, E., Labella, T.H., Trianni, V., Deneubourg, J.L., Rasse, P., Floreano, D., Gambardella, L.M., Mondada, F., Nolfi, S., Dorigo, M.: SWARM-BOT: Pattern formation in a swarm of self-assembling mobile robots. In: Proceedings of the IEEE International Conference on Systems, Man and Cybernetics, IEEE Press, Piscataway, NJ (2002)
4. Mondada, F., Pettinaro, G.C., Kwee, I.W., Guignard, A., Gambardella, L.M., Floreano, D., Nolfi, S., Deneubourg, J.L., Dorigo, M.: SWARM-BOT: A swarm of autonomous mobile robots with self-assembling capabilities. In Hemelrijk, C., Bonabeau, E., eds.: Proceedings of the International Workshop on Self-organisation and Evolution of Social Behaviour, Monte Verità, Ascona, Switzerland (2002) 307–312
5. Mondada, F., Pettinaro, G.C., Guignard, A., Kwee, I.V., Floreano, D., Deneubourg, J.L., Nolfi, S., Gambardella, L.M., Dorigo, M.: SWARM-BOT: A new distributed robotic concept. Autonomous Robots **17** (2004) 193–221
6. Baldassarre, G., Nolfi, S., Parisi, D.: Evolving mobile robots able to display collective behaviour. Artificial Life **9** (2003) 255–267
7. Trianni, V., Groß, R., Labella, T.H., Şahin, E., Dorigo, M.: Evolving aggregation behaviors in a swarm of robots. In Banzhaf, W., Christaller, T., Dittrich, P., Kim, J.T., Ziegler, J., eds.: Proceedings of the Seventh European Conference on Artificial Life. Volume 2801 of Lecture Notes in Artificial Intelligence., Springer Verlag, Berlin, Germany (2003) 865–874
8. Baldassarre, G., Nolfi, S., Parisi, D.: Evolution of collective behaviour in a team of physically linked robots. In Günther, R., Guillot, A., Meyer, J.A., eds.: Proceedings of the Second European Workshop on Evolutionary Robotics (EvoWorkshops2003: EvoROB). Volume 2611 of Lecture Notes in Computer Science., Springer Verlag, Berlin, Germany (2003) 581–592
9. Dorigo, M., Trianni, V., Şahin, E., Groß, R., Labella, T.H., Baldassarre, G., Nolfi, S., Deneubourg, J.L., Mondada, F., Floreano, D., Gambardella, L.M.: Evolving self-organizing behaviors for a swarm-bot. Autonomous Robots **17** (2004) 223–245
10. Groß, R., Dorigo, M.: Evolving a cooperative transport behavior for two simple robots. In Liardet, P., Collet, P., Fonlupt, C., Lutton, E., Schoenauer, M., eds.: Artificial Evolution – 6th International Conference, Evolution Artificielle, EA 2003, Marseille, France, October 2003. Volume 2936 of Lecture Notes in Computer Science., Springer Verlag, Berlin, Germany (2004.) 305–317
11. Groß, R., Dorigo, M.: Cooperative transport of objects of different shapes and sizes. In Dorigo, M., Birattari, M., Blum, C., Gambardella, L.M., Mondada, F., Stützle, T., eds.: Proceedings of ANTS 2004 – Fourth International Workshop on Ant Colony Optimization and Swarm Intelligence. Volume 3172 of Lecture Notes in Computer Science., Springer Verlag, Berlin, Germany (2004) 107–118

12. Groß, R., Dorigo, M.: Group transport of an object to a target that only some group members may sense. In et al., X.Y., ed.: Proceedings of PPSN-VIII, Eighth International Conference on Parallel Problem Solving from Nature. Volume 3242 of Lecture Notes in Computer Science., Springer Verlag, Berlin, Germany (2004) 852–861

13. Labella, T., Dorigo, M., Deneubourg, J.L.: Efficiency and task allocation in prey retrieval. In Ijspeert, A., Murata, M., Wakamiya, N., eds.: Proceedings of the First International Workshop on Biologically Inspired Approaches to Advanced Information Technology (Bio-ADIT2004). Volume 3141 of Lecture Notes in Computer Science., Springer Verlag, Heidelberg, Germany (2004) 32–47

14. Labella, T., Dorigo, M., Deneubourg, J.L.: Self-organised task allocation in a swarm of robots. Technical Report TR/IRIDIA/2004-6, Université Libre de Bruxelles, Belgium (2004) To appear in the 7th International Symposium on Distributed Autonomous Robotic Systems (DARS04), June 23-25, 2004, Toulouse, France.

15. Trianni, V., Nolfi, S., Dorigo, M.: Hole avoidance: Experiments in coordinated motion on rough terrain. In Groen, F., Amato, N., Bonarini, A., Yoshida, E., Kröse, B., eds.: Intelligent Autonomous Systems 8, IOS Press, Amsterdam, The Netherlands (2004) 29–36

16. Trianni, V., Tuci, E., Dorigo, M.: Evolving functional self-assembling in a swarm of autonomous robots. In Schaal, S., Ijspeert, A., Billard, A., Vijayakamur, S., Hallam, J., Meyer, J.A., eds.: From Animals to Animats 8. Proceedings of the Eight International Conference on Simulation of Adaptive Behavior (SAB04), MIT Press, Cambridge, MA (2004) 405–414

17. Yim, M., Duff, D.G., Roufas, K.D.: PolyBot: a modular reconfigurable robot. In: Proceedings of the 2000 IEEE International Conference on Robotics and Automation (ICRA 2000). Volume 1., IEEE Press, Piscataway, NJ (2000) 514–520

18. Castano, A., Shen, W.M., Will, P.: CONRO: Towards deployable robots with inter-robot metamorphic capabilities. Autonomous Robots 8 (2000) 309–324

19. Khosla, P., Brown, B., Paredis, C., Grabowski, B., Navarro, L., Bererton, C., Vandeweghe, M.: Millibot Report. Report on millibot project, DARPA contract DABT63-97-1-0003, Carnegie Mellon University, Pittsburgh, Pennsylvania, USA (2002)

Pheromone Robotics
and the Logic of Virtual Pheromones

David Payton, Regina Estkowski, and Mike Howard

HRL Laboratories, LLC, Malibu, CA 90265, USA
{payton,regina,mhoward}@hrl.com
http://www.hrl.com

Abstract. Using the biologically inspired notion of 'virtual pheromone' we describe how a robot swarm can become a distributed computing mesh embedded within the environment, while simultaneously acting as a physical embodiment of the user interface. By virtue of this simple peer-to-peer messaging scheme, many coordinated activities can be accomplished without centralized control.

1 Vision

We envision a robotic system where the system itself is not a single robot or even a team of robots, but rather, a superorganism of many small and simple autonomous elements acting together as a unified whole. The challenge in realizing such a system lies in developing a suitable medium for interaction between elements and in deriving the appropriate modes of information exchange such that large-scale complex coordinated actions can occur from the cumulative effects of many simple local interactions. This paper describes a biologically inspired concept for such an interaction medium and a software infrastructure for controlling the local information exchange between elements.

Imagine a future scenario in which a rescue team enters an unfamiliar building after a disaster, and needs to quickly locate survivors. A rescue worker opens a jar containing thousands of microscopic MEMS-based robots [9] and tosses them into the room. Interacting only locally with their neighbors, these robots use attraction/repulsion behaviors to quickly disperse into the open spaces. A robot, upon detecting a survivor, emits a message signaling the discovery. This message is relayed locally between neighboring robots, propagating only along unobstructed paths, producing a "virtual pheromone" gradient as it is propagated as illustrated in Figure 1. Ultimately, the message makes its way back to the entrance where rescue team members can now follow the gradient to the survivor. To do this, the robots themselves serve as a distributed display of guideposts leading the way along the shortest unobstructed path.

Ultimately, swarms of small-scale robots should be able to achieve large-scale results in tasks such as surveillance, reconnaissance, hazard detection, path finding, payload conveyance, and small-scale actuation [9]. The challenges to reaching this goal lie as much in the technology for controlling and coordinating the

E. Şahin and W.M. Spears (Eds.): Swarm Robotic WS 2004, LNCS 3342, pp. 45–57, 2005.

Fig. 1. A pheromone gradient produced by dispersed robots directs a user toward a disaster victim.

actions of thousands of entities as it does in the technologies for miniaturization. We address these issues of coordination and control by borrowing from techniques used by ants and termites.

Inspired by the chemical markers used by these insects for communication and coordination, we have developed a form of messaging we call a 'virtual pheromone,' implemented using simple beacons and directional sensors mounted on each robot. Like their chemical counterparts, our virtual pheromones facilitate simple communication and emergent coordinated movement between robots while requiring minimal on-board processing. Unlike chemical pheromones, virtual pheromones also transform a robot swarm into a distributed computation grid embedded in the world. This grid can be used to compute nonlocal information about the environment such as shortest paths and choke points in ways that are foreign to insect colonies. Our goal is to apply these techniques in a manner that is applicable to future robots with extremely small form factors and is scaleable to large, heterogeneous groups of robots as well. The remainder of this paper describes our mobile platforms and some of the unique hardware we use to produce virtual pheromones within a swarm of small robots. We also describe some of the software building blocks we use to manipulate virtual pheromones and to influence robot behavior. These logical building blocks provide a means to construct a variety of compound operations at the local level that allow complex group operations to emerge from local interactions.

Fig. 2. A pherobot swarm disperses to fill open spaces within a building.

2   The Swarm Robotic Environment/Methodology

Our swarm robotic environment consists of 20 custom-made pheromone robots, or 'pherobots.' Pherobots have a specially designed infrared communications ring that facilitates both inter-robot communication and obstacle detection. The pherobots are designed to perform cooperative tasks with minimal computing power, so we use a PalmV PDA as the main control computer. Use of a PDA provides a convenient combination of computing platform, display device, and user input device. Additional onboard processors handle real-time communications and mobility tasks. An additional coded beacon on each robot enables them to transmit data to an augmented reality display that allows users to visualize pheromone gradients superimposed over their surroundings. A swarm of pherobots is shown below in Figure 2.

Our approach is characterized by three key concepts: Virtual Pheromones provide a diffusive local-neighborhood interaction mechanism by which the robots communicate and coordinate. World-Embedded Computation is a technique for performing many graph-theoretic algorithms in a distributed fashion, without requiring a centralized intermediate representation. World-Embedded Display is a method for obtaining information from a swarm by using each robot as a display element embedded in the physical world. These concepts will be described in the next three subsections.

2.1 Virtual Pheromones

In nature, chemical pheromones and pheromone gradients are used extensively by insects to produce sophisticated organized group activity that emerges out of the simple interactions between individuals [1],[4],[6],[8],[11]. To arrive at properties similar to chemical pheromones, we implement virtual pheromones via optically transmitted signals from each robot that may be propagated in a relay-type fashion. Atop each robot is a set of eight radially-oriented directional infrared receivers and transmitters as shown in Figure 3. These allow a robot to transmit and receive messages directionally relative to its current orientation. The communications PIC, which manages all message traffic into and out of these devices, allows simultaneous receipt of eight distinct 10-bit messages, one from each receiver. If multiple messages should impinge upon a single receiver, a message collision is detected based on a parity check, and no message is recorded. When messages are properly received, they are tagged with the corresponding intensity and orientation of the received signal. These intensity and orientation values play an important role in both obstacle detection and in determining distance and direction to neighboring robots.

Infrared was chosen as the preferred medium of transmission for several reasons: it is directional, it propagates by line of sight, it is easily modulated, and it loses intensity with increased distance from the source. Directionality is needed to encode pheromone gradients, line-of-sight propagation is needed to assure that pheromone gradients do not pass through walls, modulation is needed to encode pheromone type and other data, and distance drop-off provides a means for robots to estimate their distance to the sender.

Our virtual pheromones are encoded through discrete messages consisting of a type field, a hop-count field, and a data field. The type field allows us to encode a large number of distinct pheromone types. Typically, pheromone messages are received, modified, and then retransmitted in their modified form. One of the most common ways a pheromone message is modified is through alteration of its hop-count field to create a pheromone gradient. In this computation, each robot, upon receipt of a virtual pheromone message, decrements the hop-count field and retransmits the message in some or all directions. If a robot receives the same type of pheromone from multiple directions, only the message with the highest hop-count value is used. Any pheromone messages of the same type received with hop-count values equal to or less than the hop-count already transmitted are ignored. Just as in the insect world, the sender of a pheromone message never needs to be concerned with which robots will receive a message or whether it has been properly received. These propagation rules are illustrated with a team of six robots in Figure 4.

Unlike chemical pheromones, our virtual pheromones are tied to the robots themselves rather than to locations in the environment. In addition, since virtual pheromones are propagated as symbolic messages, pheromone gradients may be altered without the need for physical movement of the robots. Despite the fact that a robot's virtual pheromone transmissions are received only by nearby neighbors, the relay mechanism allows any single message to propagate

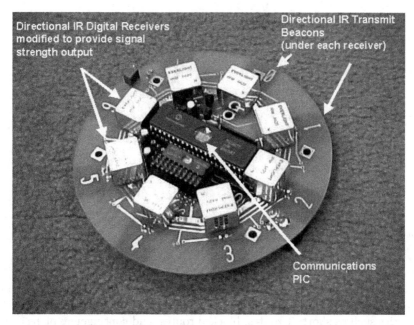

Fig. 3. A transceiver for virtual pheromones provides directional line-of-sight communications between robots.

quickly throughout an entire swarm of robots. If an originating source for a virtual pheromone moves, or if the environment changes, the gradient will adjust quickly, without the characteristic persistence of chemical pheromones. We can even envision implementing various ant algorithms using the messaging system alone, without any need for the robots to move. In this sense, our robot collective can truly become a distributed computing grid with each node providing local sensing, and connectivity between nodes revealing information about the topology of traversable paths. These properties are very important for enabling what we call world-embedded computation.

Our underlying communications mechanism is capable of modeling various aspects of chemical pheromones used by insect colonies, such as diffusion by means of message relaying and evaporation by means of systematic decrementing of all hop counts if the originating source is not sustained. Typically, we sustain an originating source by periodically retransmitting the pheromone message. Neighboring units receiving this message will then perform their operations on the message and retransmit, thereby rippling the message wave front throughout the swarm.

2.2   World Embedded Computation

Our use of virtual pheromones offers a new way to analyze an environment's geometry and identify salient features. Over the past decades, approaches to path planning and terrain analysis have focused primarily on single or parallel

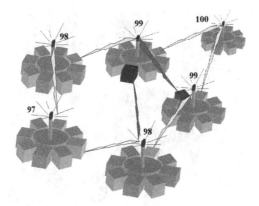

Fig. 4. Virtual pheromones are relayed with a lower hop-count by each subsequent robot.

processor solutions operating on an internal map containing terrain features [17]. Our approach externalizes the map, spreading it across a collection of simple processors, each of which determines the terrain features in its locality. Global properties such as shortest routes, blocked routes, and contingency plans can be computed in a robust, distributed manner, with each member of the population of simple processors contributing a small piece of the result.

Figure 5 illustrates the difference between our world-embedded approach and conventional approaches. In conventional methods, information about terrain or mobility features is extracted by sensors and then translated into a symbolic model such as a map. It is this symbolic representation that is then processed to obtain information about the terrain such as finding minimum cost paths.

Using world-embedded computation with our pherobots, there is no distinct step of map generation. Instead, the robots act as a distributed set of processors embedded in the environment, performing both sensing and computation tasks simultaneously. At the heart of this approach is the realization that communication pathways can double as a means of sensing obstacles and that many algorithms for computing properties of a map may also be performed as distributed computations within our robot swarm. For example, the fundamental message propagation rules we use for our virtual pheromones exactly mimic the wavefront computation used in Dijkstra's shortest path algorithm [7]. Because our computation is embedded in the world, however, this also means that the computation itself can directly affect the positioning of the robots, thereby guiding the acquisition of additional information.

While modification of hop counts is common in many ad-hoc networking systems, our approach is distinguished by the fact that we are explicitly seeking to exploit node connectivity to tell us something about the environment. In our approach, when a robot receiving a pheromone message modifies that message for retransmission, it does so for the purpose of incorporating information regarding the properties of the physical environment across the latest transmission hop. This can be as simple as updating a hop count or as complex as incorporating

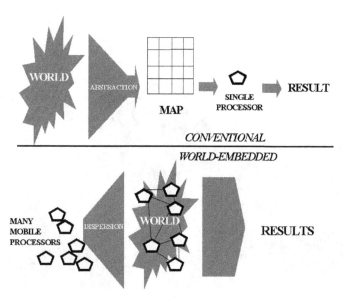

Fig. 5. In contrast to conventional map-based approaches to terrain reasoning, our approach is based on sending the processors out into the world, i.e. the world is its own map.

factors such as received signal strength, locally sensed terrain properties, or interactions with other received pheromone types. The propagation of the signal between successive pairs of robots provides, at each step, a local summary of the nonlocal properties along the path.

2.3   World-Embedded Display

Although our robot swarm can compute a great deal without the use of maps, we still must somehow convey this information back to a user. As it turns out, a rich source of information about the environment can be provided even with robots that have no explicit representations or maps of their locale. To do this, we transform our robot swarm into a distributed display embedded within the environment [5]. In effect, each robot becomes a pixel within a much larger display space so that any robot only has to send the user a small amount of information related to its location. The robot's position within the environment provides the remaining context needed for interpreting the meaning of the transmitted information.

Our concept of a world-embedded display is obtained using an augmented reality (AR) system [2] to present information to the user. A video camera mounted on the user's head, as shown in Figure 6, receives coded infrared signals from each robot. These signals are tracked, decoded and then displayed in a head-mounted display so that information such as gradient arrows appear overlaid on top of the individual robots. Taken collectively, a user sees these arrows as a gradient field [20] leading toward a hidden objective as illustrated in Figure 1.

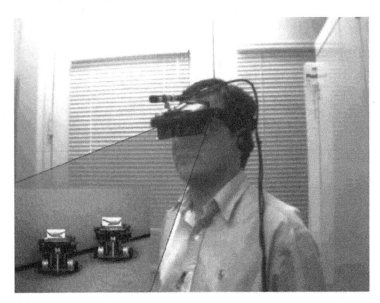

Fig. 6. Coded infrared signals are decoded into arrows for overlay onto a real scene. These are visible via the augmented reality head-mounted display system with camera.

3   Results

Using our swarm of 20 pherobots, we have demonstrated a variety of coordinated robot behaviors that combine robot locomotion with pheromone logic. We began with a set of primitive behaviors such as dispersing a swarm into an open space, generating virtual pheromone gradients, and following a gradient toward its source. We have also been able to demonstrate more complex behaviors that use these primitive behaviors as a basis. Some of the more sophisticated of these are behaviors for hiding and for distributed resource allocation.

Our distributed resource allocation technique provides a good example of how multiple primitive swarm behaviors can be combined to obtain fairly complex emergent behaviors from the swarm [22]. We begin with a swarm of robots with heterogeneous capabilities. For example, some robots may be suited for acoustic sensing while others are better suited for motion sensing. A resource allocation problem arises when it becomes desirable to bring together several robots at a particular location to combine information from their different sensors. Ideally, only the right number and combination of robots will come to the intended location, and no central coordination will be required.

Our demonstration illustrates our technique for distributed resource allocation by first dispersing a swarm of robots, each identified with one of three different capabilities: acoustic sensing, motion sensing, or neutral. During the dispersal phase, robots simply move away from each other and from obstacles [21] such that they fill the available space while remaining in contact with their neighbors. This is done either by modeling repulsive forces that push each robot away from its neighbors, or preferably, by modeling attractive forces that draw each robot toward open spaces. If a robot wanders too far from the swarm, it will be attracted back toward other robots until it gets within a predetermined range to its closest neighbors.

At some point, a detection will be triggered from one robot, requiring confirmation of the detection from another robot of the complementary type. The detecting robot first initiates a pheromone gradient that attracts all robots with a complementary sensor. All robots attracted to this pheromone then transmit a second pheromone type, adding to the data field an indication of how many hops they are from the source of the attracting pheromone. All attracted robots then treat this second pheromone as an inhibitor if they are further from the attracting source than another attracted robot. Since this inhibiting signal is transmitted throughout the swarm, only one robot will not be inhibited and be able to make its way toward the source. Of course, should this robot become disabled, the next closest robot will immediately take over because it now will no longer be inhibited. This provides a very robust methodology for any number of resources to be made to converge upon a location where they may then work together on a task.

4   Discussion and Outlook

Extending our techniques for virtual pheromones and world-embedded computation beyond the basic 2D world of our current implementation presents challenges in many different areas. The issues arise primarily in the areas of transitioning to denser grids of smaller robots and to more complex 3D spaces. With larger numbers of smaller robots, there is a potential mismatch between the scale of features that will be significant to the robots and the scale of features that will be of interest to a human user. Certainly, we don't want small pebbles or other objects on the floor to appear as insurmountable obstacles. Likewise, we don't want the robots to topologically link two rooms in a building simply because of a small mouse hole in the wall between them. Dealing with such potential incompatibilities between the scale of the robot network and the scale of the user will be an important area for development of distributed algorithms that allow reasoning about spatial extent as well as topology.

When we consider 3D spaces, similar issues arise. In some cases, perfectly ordinary topological connections between spaces could easily be missed because they involve small changes in elevation that end up looking like obstacles to a set of robots. Problems such as this might be overcome by using a different communications medium which is not strictly line-of-sight, but which is still blocked by major obstacles and walls. If robots are made to fly or operate underwater, then we truly have a 3D problem. In such cases, our algorithms would still be applicable, but the pheromone messaging system would have to operate in a spherical pattern rather than a circular pattern.

Ultimately, the aspect of this work that we consider most important is not the specific implementation of robots, but the underlying principles we use to organize their interactions. It is easy to imagine any number of nonrobotic applications where the concept of using the communication medium between distributed elements is used both for exchanging information and for sensing features of the environment. In so doing, it is likely that communication models such as our virtual pheromones will help facilitate the design of distributed algorithms that take advantage of such information.

5   Related Work

Several related efforts in robotics have been driven by some of the same biological inspirations that lie behind our own work. Many have sought to emulate behaviors of natural systems such as ant foraging, sorting, or cooperative transport [3, 12, 14, 24]. In Lewis and Bekey [15], a concept is described by which a swarm of nanorobots might be organized using diffusion of distinct chemical markers to perform tasks such as removal of a tumor. Of particular note is their idea of guidepost nanorobots that transmit a chemical marker of one type in response to detecting another. These guideposts are used both to extend the range of a diffused chemical marker as well as to focus robot movement around an axis of advance toward a detected tumor. In some ways, this use of guidepost robots to relay chemical markers is similar to our own use of robots to relay a virtual pheromone message.

In Werger and Mataric [27], robots themselves were used as a physical embodiment of a pheromone trail by forming into a contiguous chain. In this case, a pheromone trail could adapt to changing conditions through physical modification of the robot chain. In our work, a combination of robots and their communication serves to maintain an embodiment of pheromone trails. Our robots, however, are more like a substrate upon which pheromones can propagate rather than an actual embodiment of the pheromones. This allows a more rapid dispersion of pheromone messages, and enables a variety of pheromone types to be used.

In the somewhat different domain of distributed sensor networks, versions of message diffusion that are similar to our virtual pheromone concept can be found [13, 16]. Intanagonwiwat et al [13] introduce the idea of directed diffusion. This technique uses strictly local neighbor-to-neighbor communication to find efficient paths for information flow within a network of distributed sensor nodes. A request for information from a sink generates a gradient throughout the network. Information supplied by a source flows along the gradient back to the sink along multiple paths. The network reinforces the most efficient paths to eliminate redundant information flows. Although the general methods of diffusion used here are similar to our own work, there are some interesting differences. Since this work focuses on information transfer, the mechanism for establishing diffusion gradients is expressed in terms of requested data rates and rates of information updates. This provides a useful means for reinforcing the best paths for information flow, but it would probably not be as useful for creating a topologically meaningful gradient field toward an objective. McLurkin [16] uses a combination of pheromone messages that produce diffusion gradients and agent messages that hop from node to node in a directed fashion. This proves to be an effective combination for establishing message relay networks, position estimation, edge detection, and path projection within a distributed sensor network. It is notable that Intanagonwiwat and McLurkin both rely on explicit one-to-one communication between nodes. This means that each node must have a unique identity, which may be impractical for extremely large numbers of nodes. This requirement could probably be eliminated by use of a directional communication scheme comparable to ours. Directional communications and sensitivity of the communications medium to local environmental features are important aspects of our approach that enable our robots to perform world-embedded computations that make our virtual pheromone gradients correspond to physical paths. These aspects are absent from the above two approaches.

Parunak, et al [18, 19] employ a repelling pheromone approach in which robots leave virtual trails and are attracted to areas that have little or no pheromone. The pheromone concentrations dissipate and diffuse over time, so areas are searched periodically with some probability. Pheromone concentrations are stored and tracked by "place agents" that may be implemented in memory or in physical unattended ground sensors. Like their approach, we use digital pheromones to implement properties of potential fields. But our approach has taken digital pheromones much farther by using properties of the transmission of pheromone messages to implement specialized computations about the environment. Parunak [19] also mentions role allocation by means of a bidding process where matches are made based on the closest source with the right capabilities but there are not enough details for a thorough comparison.

Spears and Gordon [25] use a circular 'potential well' around particles to draw them to within a fixed range of each other, similar to the way we keep pherobots at a uniform spacings. But they point out a subtle distinction between a potential fields approach and the type of velocity vector combination used by an approach like ours. The former may be analyzed by conventional physics methods, which they do in [26]. Also they assert that the former can mimic natural physics phenomena more easily.

Acknowledgments

This work is supported by the Defense Advanced Research Projects Agency under contract N66001-99-C-8514. Any opinions, findings, and conclusions or recommendations expressed in this material are those of the authors and do not necessarily reflect the views of the Defense Advanced Research Projects Agency.

References

1. Aron, S., Deneubourg, J., Goss, S., and Pasteels, J. "Functional Self-Organization Illustrated by Inter-Nest Traffic in Ants: The Case of the Argentine Ant," in Biological Motion, eds. W. Alt and G. Hoffman, Springer-Verlag, Berlin, pp. 533–547, 1990.
2. Azuma, R., Hoff, B., Neely III, H., Sarfaty, R. "A Motion-Stabilized Outdoor Augmented Reality System," Proceedings of IEEE VR '99 (Houston, TX, 13–17 March 1999), 252–259.

3. Beckers, R., Holland, O. E., and Deneubourg, J., "From local actions to global tasks: Stigmergy and collective robotics." In Brooks, R. and Maes, P., editors, Artificial Life IV, Proceedings of the Fourth International Workshop on the Synthesis and Simulation of Living Systems. MIT Press, 1994.

4. Bonabeau, E., Dorigo, M., and Theraulaz, G., Swarm Intelligence: From Natural to Artificial Systems. New York, Oxford University Press, 1999.

5. Daily, M., Cho, Y., Martin, K. Payton, D. "World Embedded Interfaces for Human-Robot Interaction" in Proceedings of the 36th Annual Hawaii International Conference on System Sciences (HICSS'03)

6. Deneubourg, J. and Goss, S. "Collective Patterns and Decision-Making," Ethology, Ecology, and Evolution, 1:295–311, 1984.

7. Dijkstra, E.W. "A Note on Two Problems in Connection with Graph Theory," Numerische Mathematik, Vol 1, 1959, pp. 269–271.

8. Dorigo, M., Maniezzo, V., and Colorni, A., "Ant System: optimization by a colony of cooperating agents," IEEE Transactions on Systems, Man, and Cybernetics–Part B , vol. 26, No. 2, pp. 29–41, 1996.

9. Flynn, A.M. "Gnat Robots (And How They Will Change Robotics)," In Proceedings of the IEEE Microrobots and Teleoperators Workshop, Hyannis, MA, 9–11 November 1987. Also appeared in AI Expert, December 1987, p. 34 et seq.

10. Gage, D.W. "Command Control for Many-Robot Systems," In The Nineteenth Annual AUVS Technical Symposium (AUVS-91), Huntsville AL, 22–24 June 1992. Reprinted in Unmanned Systems Magazine, 10(4):28–34.

11. Goss, S., Beckers, R., Deneubourg, J., Aron, S., and Pasteels, J. "How Trail Laying and Trail Following Can Solve Foraging Problems," In Behavioral Mechanisms of Food Selection, ed. R. Hughes, Springer-Verlag, Heidelberg, Germany, pp. 661–678, 1990.

12. Holland, O. and Melhuish, C., "Stigmergy, self-organisation, and sorting in collective robotics." Artificial Life, 5:2, 2000.

13. Intanagonwiwat, C., Govindan, R., and Estrin, D. "Directed Diffusion: A Scalable and Robust Communication Paradigm for Sensor Networks," In Proceedings of the Sixth Annual International Conference on Mobile Computing and Networks (MobiCOM 2000), August 2000, Boston, Massachusetts.

14. Kube, C., and Zhang, R., "Collective Robotics: From Social Insects to Robots" in Adaptive Behavior, Vol. 2, pp. 189–218, 1994.

15. Lewis, M.A., and Bekey, G.A. "The Behavioral Self-Organization of Nanorobots Using Local Rules," In Proceedings of the 1992 IEEE/RSJ International Conference on Intelligent Robots and Systems, Raleigh, NC, July 7–10, 1992.

16. McLurkin, J., "Algorithms for distributed sensor networks," In Masters Thesis for Electrical Engineering at the Univeristy of California, Berkeley, December 1999.

17. Mitchell, J.S.B., Payton, D., and Keirsey, D. "Planning and Reasoning for Autonomous Vehicle Control," International Journal for Intelligent Systems, Vol. 2, 1987.

18. Parunak, H., Purcell, M., and O'Connell, R., "Digital pheromones for autonomous coordination of swarming UAVs" Proceedings of First AIAA Unmanned Aerospace Vehicles, Systems, Technologies, and Operations Conf., Norfolk, VA. AIAA (2002).

19. Parunak, H., Brueckner, S., and Odell, J., "Swarming Coordination of Multiple UAV's for Collaborative Sensing," in 2nd AIAA Unmanned Unlimited Systems Technologies and Operations Land and Sea Conference and Workshop & Exhibit, San Diego, CA, 15–18 Sept 2003.

20. Payton, D.W. "Internalized Plans: A Representation for Action Resources," Robotics and Autonomous Systems, 6(1), 1990, pp. 89–103. Also appearing in: Designing Autonomous Agents, ed. Pattie Maes, MIT Press, Cambridge, Mass. 1991, pp. 89–103.
21. Payton, D., Daily, M., Hoff, B., Howard, M., Lee, C. "Pheromone Robotics" in SPIE Symposium on Intelligent Systems & Manufacturing, Boston, Mass., November 5–8, 2000.
22. Payton, D. Estkowski, R., Howard, M., "Compound Behaviors in Pheromone Robotics" in Robotics and Autonomous Systems, 44(3–4): 229–240, 2003.
23. Reif, J. and Wang, H., "Social potential fields: A distributed behavioral control for autonomous robots." In K. Goldberg, D. Halperin, J.-C. Latombe, and R. Wilson, editors, International Workshop on Algorithmic Foundations of Robotics (WAFR), pp. 431–459. A. K. Peters, Wellesley, MA, 1995.
24. Russell, R., "Mobile robot guidance using a short-lived heat trail," Robotica, vol. 11, no. 5, pp. 427–431, 1993.
25. Spears, W. and Gordon, D., "Using Artificial Physics to Control Agents," IEEE International Conference on Information, Intelligence and Systems, 1999.
26. Spears, W., Spears, D. and Heil, R., "A Formal Analysis of Potential Energy in a Multi-agent System," Formal Approaches to Agent-Based Systems, 2004.
27. Werger, B.B., and Mataric, M.J. "Robotic food chains: Externalization of state and program for minimal-agent foraging," In Proceedings of the Fourth International Conference on Simulation of Adaptive Behavior: From Animals to Animats 4, MIT Press, 1996, pp. 625–634.

Distributed Localization and Mapping with a Robotic Swarm

Joseph A. Rothermich, Ihsan Ecemis, and Paolo Gaudiano

Icosystem Corporation, Cambridge, MA 02138, USA
{jr,ihsan,paolo}@icosystem.com

Abstract. We describe a project where behaviors of robot swarms are designed and studied for use in a distributed mapping domain. Behaviors are studied in both simulation and physical robots. We discuss the advantages and challenges of swarm robotics, in general and specific to our research. Software implementations and algorithms are introduced, as well as methodologies for the creation and assessment of swarm behaviors.

1 Introduction

This paper summarizes our achievements in a research effort supported under DARPA's Software for Distributed Robotics (SDR) program[1]. The overall goal of the SDR program is to perform a building-clearing mission: a swarm of robots enters a building whose layout is not known. The robots then disperse through the building and attempt to locate an object of interest. Once the object has been located, the swarm remains in the building to protect the item of interest until friendly forces arrive. This research was inspired by Doug Gage's vision of a swarm of simple, inexpensive robots collaborating to carry out exploration and mapping tasks [6, 7].

Icosystem is an applied research company that focuses on using principles of swarm intelligence and complexity science [3, 2, 8]. Our task in this project was to develop distributed algorithms that allow simple robots to execute key portions of the SDR building clearing mission. This includes not only the creation of distributed algorithms, but also improving our understanding of how and when these algorithms should be used, and qualities of the algorithms that impact their effectiveness.

We are trying to build foundations for a quantitative methodology that will facilitate practical applications of swarm intelligence to distributed robotics. This section lists some fundamental questions we are trying to answer about swarm robotics. Following is a brief overview of our approach, related work, and a high level description of some specific algorithms we have designed.

---

[1] This work was supported in part by DARPA contract NBCHC030042. Any opinions, findings and conclusions or recommendations expressed in this material are those of the author(s) and do not necessarily reflect the views of DARPA or the Department of Interior-National Business Center (DOI-NBC).

E. Şahin and W.M. Spears (Eds.): Swarm Robotic WS 2004, LNCS 3342, pp. 58–69, 2005.

1.1   Problem Description

The concept of swarming is generating significant interest as a methodology for the control of large groups of vehicles, epecially unmanned air and ground vehicles (UAVs and UGVs). While there seems to be general agreement that swarms can somehow afford a high degree of robustness and flexibility, little has been done to demonstrate systematically if and when a swarm approach to the control of unmanned vehicles is in fact superior to alternative approaches, or even desirable at all [7].

During a recent conference on 'Swarming and Network Enabled C4ISR', leaders from government, industry, and academia discussed applications of swarming to a variety of problems ranging from tactical maneuvers to logistics and network communications. The ample time dedicated to defining the term "swarm" and discussing potential applications stood in stark contrast with the paucity of quantitative results from real-world applications obtained under realistic conditions. Given the increasing interest in swarming concepts for military and industrial applications, it is imperative that future efforts focus on quantification of results and on a clarification of what exactly swarming can and cannot do. This is particularly important in the area of controlling large groups of UAVs and UGVs, where recent technological advances and cost reductions make swarming applications a near-term possibility.

We have identified a number of pressing questions that, by and large, have not yet been addressed satisfactorily. We have grouped these questions into six sets. The first set of questions centers on the general issue of when, or if, swarms should be used: What missions are particularly well suited for swarms? Are there missions that can only (or should not) be tackled with swarms? Are there indices or metrics that can be used to evaluate the "swarmability" of a mission? How do the stated success criteria of a mission influence the choice of control rules?

The second set of questions revolves around the functionality of individual robots and how this impacts swarm performance: How do the sensory, communication, and mechanical characteristics of individual robots affect the types of missions that the swarm can carry out? Are there sensors that are particularly well suited for swarm applications? How does sensor accuracy impact swarm performance? How does performance degrade as a result of individual failures?

Having established the characteristics of individual robots, the third set of questions focuses on communications: How should robots communicate with one another and with an operator? Do swarms require massive communications bandwidth? Can decentralized control strategies function well in spite of unreliable communications?

The fourth set of questions aims to an understanding of how the emergent behavior of swarms can be reconciled with the tight control requirements of a typical military mission: How can humans control a swarm efficiently and effectively? What level of control must an operator exert on individual robots? What information must the robots convey back to the operator? Is it possible to quantify the number of operators needed for a given swarm on a given mission? Can multiple operators share the load of controlling a swarm?

The fifth set of questions focuses on the quantification of swarm performance and efficiency: How is swarm performance measured and success quantified? How does performance depend on swarm size? Does software complexity increase or decrease when using swarms? Is the eventual performance increase of using a swarm offset by concomitant increases in cost?

Finally, the ability of a swarm to complete a mission may depend heavily on the environment in which the mission is carried out: How can the complexity of the environment be quantified? Is it possible to estimate accurately the required swarm size and functionality as a function of environment complexity for a given mission type?

This chapter describes a specific project that begins to address some of these issues in the context of real mobile robots performing a real-world task. The next section describes some related work in the general areas of robotic swarms and multi-robot control. This is followed by a description of our approach, the algorithms we developed, and some representative results. The chapter closes with a summary and discussion.

2   Related Work

Collective robotics, multi-robot systems, distributed robotics and swarm robotics are some of the terms that have been used to describe systems involving multiple robots. With few exceptions, work in these fields has existed only for about ten years. In fact, the technology required to assemble a sizable team of unmanned vehicles is only now becoming available. Much of the work on collective robotics to date has been qualitative in nature. The few examples of research with a strong quantitative component have typically been applied to tightly defined tasks that are amenable to direct analytical solution. In this section we summarize some of the work that is most relevant to this research.

A few publications have reviewed work in distributed robotics. Cao, Fukunaga and Kahng [4] have provided an extensive review of cooperative mobile robotics. A recent book by Balch and Parker [1] also provides useful overviews and examples of robot team applications. The journal Autonomous Robots is preparing a special issue on Swarm Robotics [5].

In terms of specific research projects, Matarić [17] is considered a pioneer in the study of collective robotics. She used a modified Reinforcement Learning algorithm to control a group of four robots performing a coordinated task, such as foraging. Her research was later extended to larger groups, and investigated other forms of control. [18] provides a good review of some of her work, which is considered seminal in the field of collective robotics.

Martinoli and colleagues [16] have done extensive research on autonomous collective robotics using the Khepera robotics platform (K-Team SA, Switzerland). As part of his research, he collaborated on the development of a laser-based positioning system, and a conducting floor that supplies power to the robots. Under normal conditions, the Khepera receives power through a tether, which renders multi-robot experiments virtually impossible. This system was used by Martinoli for various applications of swarm intelligence systems to autonomous collective robotics, and by other researchers, including for instance [13] developed a system of 12 Khepera robots to study task allocation in a foraging problem. One of the problems with this work is that the system they used would be difficult and costly to replicate. The Khepera robot, especially if equipped with wireless communications, costs thousands of dollars. The system developed by Krieger and Billeter included a custom-designed surface covered in copper to provide a continuous flow of power to the Kheperas.

Hayes [10] recently reported some simulation results using the Webots simulator. Hayes defines a metric to quantify performance of a team of robots during a search mission, which consists of finding a single target located at a random position in a square area. A team of simulated robots is released at the center of the area. The author derives analytical expressions to estimate the cost of searching the area as a function of team size (1–80 robots) under two different search strategies: a random strategy, in which each robot simply moves randomly around the area, and a coordinated strategy, in which the robots partition the space into equal-sized areas. He then performs Monte Carlo simulations and reports results, showing a good match to the data under the random search strategy. Unfortunately he does not report simulation results for the coordinate strategy. We believe part of the reason is that his analytical estimation effectively assumes that the robots start out already spread out uniformly. If the robots had to start from a single point and spread out, the results would undoubtedly differ from the analytical prediction. While the results are somewhat limited and the specific task overly simplistic, Hayes' quantitative approach should be commended. Of particular interest is his concept of calculating the cost of carrying out a mission, which he defines as a weighted sum of the time to find the target, the distance traveled by each robot, and the number of robots. This particular formulation of cost is limited, but it shows some interesting ways in which multiple criteria can be combined to derive a single performance metric, which may be more robust or meaningful than a single, directly measurable variable.

A task that has received significant attention, and that will be crucial for the proposed work, is collaborative mapping. If more than one robot is navigating an area, how can the various robots interact so as to construct the map more efficiently? Several approaches to this problem have been proposed in the literature. One class of approaches focuses on combining mapping information between multiple robots using probabilistic approaches [11, 22].

A different class of approaches uses information about the relative position between robots to propagate information or estimate positions and distances. For instance, Rekleitis and colleagues [19, 20] propose a method whereby two robots can observe one another and determine their relative positions. By taking turns at moving, one robot acts as a fixed landmark, and the other can compare its relative position to estimate its location in the environment more accurately than through dead reckoning (odometry). A related approach, proposed by Kurazume and colleagues [14, 15] uses multiple robots to perform triangulation. These authors have proposed several variants of what they call Cooperative Positioning System (CPS): in short, three robots take turns so that at any time one robot moves between two others, using triangulation to determine its position with a high degree of accuracy. By taking turns, the robots can navigate through an environment while maintaining a highly accurate estimate of localization even over very long distances. A third, related approach has been proposed by Howard and colleagues [12]. These authors also use the measured relative positions between robots for accurate localization. In this case, the formalism used to determine relative position is maximum likelihood estimation. In all three cases, the authors have shown some promising results using both simulated and real robots. With the exception of Howard et al., it is not clear how well the proposed approaches will scale with swarms of increasing size. Furthermore, the results are generally limited to one or few specific examples. Extending these approaches to larger swarms, and performing systematic evaluations of the sensitivity of the system to parameter variations, will be crucial in determining which, if any, of these proposals is likely to be applicable under realistic scenarios with variable swarm sizes.

3   Methodology

We now turn to a description of the methodology we employed for this project. Our effort combines software simulation as well as implementation on real robots. Our approach is to leverage and extend an existing robotics simulation tool. On top of this we are building a swarm control tool for swarm level communication, control and visualization. In addition, we are emulating specific hardware for the robots that we are using. Algorithms that are tested in simulation are then moved to physical robots to be evaluated.

In particular, our software simulation tool is the Player/Stage simulator developed at USC and HRL [9] (source available at sourceforge.net). This is an open source robotics development tool consisting of two distinct packages: *Player* provides a network interface to robots and sensors. It contains device drivers that allow control algorithms written in any programming language to control the sensors and hardware of robots. *Stage* is the simulation engine that allows multiple robots to interact with a simulated environment and device models. The power in the Player/Stage model is that the same control algorithms written for the Stage simulation environment can work directly on real robots using the Player drivers.

We have developed a tool that we call the Swarm Operator Control Center, or SOCC, designed as a Player/Stage client. SOCC will be described in detail in a separate paper, but we summarize here its main functional characteristics. SOCC allows the operator to control the swarm as a whole or to control individual robots manually. A behavior or a pre-defined combination of behaviors can be selected via the user interface. The user is able to monitor swarm behaviors online and offline using SOCC's visualization tools. Since the code is written for simulated hardware devices, the code can be transferred to real robots with minimal effort. On a technical level, it is written in C++ with the Qt GUI development library. SOCC features self-generating code, auto thread handling, widget creation, video capture and logging, and enables full automation of Stage and creates a socket communication to the Player/Stage simulator.

For this project, we used iRobot's *Swarmbot* hardware platform [21]. iRobot kindly allowed us to use their facilities and provided us with the technical support necessary to implement our algorithms. Swarmbots are small, limited sensor robots. The Swarmbots do not have accurate range sensors for the detection of obstacles, but they can localize one another through line-of-sight infrared (IR) communications.

This robot measures approximately 15 × 15cm and is capable of moving at a maximum speed of approximately 40cm/sec (configurable). Its sensor and actuator payload includes a wrap-around bump skirt that can activate one or more of eight bump sensors; four IR transmitter and receiver pairs (one at each corner) that are used primarily for communications and reciprocal localization; three LEDs that can be programmed to emit user-defined light patterns; and a speaker. The robot runs on four wheels and through a differential drive mechanism (skid steer). On-board radio and camera modules are also available, but were not used in this project.

The IR sensors are at the heart of the Swarmbot's communications system, which operates on a 4Hz transmit cycle. During each cycle, each Swarmbot broadcasts a few bytes of information, some set by the operating system (e.g., the Swarmbot's ID and its transmission power level), and a few other bytes configurable by the user. When a Swarmbot receives a transmission from another Swarmbot, it can use an intensity lookup table to determine the range of the transmitting Swarmbot. By interpolating the intensity as observed from two different IR receivers, it is also possible to establish the bearing of the transmitting Swarmbot. The transmission power can be set to several levels, resulting in communications ranges varying from about three feet to over 15 feet. It is also possible to use the IR as a crude form of obstacle detection by using reflections of a robot's own ID.

The biggest challenge for our project was to overcome some of the limitations of the Swarmbot's sensors, communications and CPU. Importantly, the Swarmbot platform is not designed for the type of accurate localization that we want to achieve, though it is perfectly adequate for distributed, emergent behaviors of the types demonstrated successfully by iRobot's team. We had to overcome limitations in three general areas: (1) memory is limited to about 600KB of RAM, (2) limited communication bandwidth of about 60 user-defined byte/sec, and (3) high levels of sensor and communication noise. Much effort was aimed at removing sources of systematic noise, e.g., rejecting range and bearing information from robots at or near the corners, or adding checksums to our user-defined data bytes. Details will be provided in a future full-length publication.

4   Overview of Algorithms

As we mentioned in Section 1 the goal of the SDR program is to perform a building-clearing mission where neither the layout of the building nor the location of the object of interest is not known. After we studied Swarmbot's sensors and built our infrastructure to overcome their limitations, we focused on the solution of three problems: collaborative localization, dynamic task allocation, and collaborative mapping, which are the key elements of the building-clearing mission.

4.1   The Collaborative Localization Algorithm

As each robot moves around the environment, it looks for landmarks (stationary robots) within its IR range. The landmarks are constantly broadcasting data packets containing their global position (X,Y) and heading. Each moving robot can estimate the relative range and bearing of each landmark, and combine this with the broadcasted information to estimate its own position in a global frame of reference. Furthermore, each robot can make some use of odometry to improve its localization.

At the core of our algorithm is a method for assigning confidence values to: (1) individual IR readings from landmarks, (2) the overall localization estimate based on the cumulative IR readings from multiple landmarks, (3) the odometry, and (4) overall localization estimates based on the combination of IR and odometry. Each of these values is normalized in the range [0.0,1.0].

Odometry confidence decreases with distance moved, and is dropped dramatically if the robot is bumped or makes a sharp turn. Individual landmark confidence is uniform to about 100cm and then decays linearly to a range of about 150cm. Estimates from multiple landmarks are combined proportionately to the confidence of each landmark. Finally, odometry is combined with IR estimates on the basis of their respective confidence values.

One key to successful localization is to collect data from multiple landmarks and to weight more heavily those data received from more reliable landmarks. However, when the size of the environment to be traversed is significantly larger than the range of the reciprocal localization mechanism, it is not possible to have a large number of stationary robots at known positions. If all robots are moving, errors in absolute positioning will accrue quickly, even though the relative localization between robots can remain accurate. The proposed solution is to let the robots take turns at moving and being stationary, and to do so in such a way that the swarm as a whole moves forward, while maintaining accurate global positioning information. In the next section we describe the dynamic task allocation algorithm we devised as a solution to this problem.

4.2   The Dynamic Task Allocation Algorithm

In the work of Rekleitis and colleagues [19, 20] and of Kurazume and Hirose [14, 15] experiments were limited to teams of three or at most four robots, and movements were controlled by letting the robots take turns based on some pre-specified strategies. We decided to extend this work to allow for large swarms, possibly over one hundred. This requires a decentralized algorithm that does not rely on predefined strategies for robot movement and which will not be sensitive to the failure of individual robots.

The task allocation algorithm is based on two components: the first determines if a robot is allowed to move based on constraints such as having the required number of landmarks in sight, distance from landmarks, and quality of localization information. For instance, a robot acting as a landmark should not begin to move if there are sufficient landmarks around it (in which case it would not be able to localize itself accurately), or if there are nearby moving robots that may be relying on it for their localization. Likewise, if a robot is moving, it should only stop and become a landmark if it has sufficiently good localization data from current landmarks; it should also avoid becoming a landmark if it is too close to another landmark, which could interfere with swarm movements, and may lead to reduced localization accuracy.

The second component calculates a robot's *desire to move* based on strictly local data. The desire to move can be suppressed or enhanced by neighbor robots based on factors including distance to landmarks, number of nearby moving robots, etc. The core idea is that robots compete with one another to determine who has the greatest desire to move. Competition depends in large part on the robot type (Landmark or Moving), distance, and each robot's current desire to move. In addition to distance-dependent, inter-robot factors, all robots take into account the swarm's general heading and compete most strongly with robots ahead of them; hence the robots that are toward the back of the swarm (relative to the swarm heading) will have the highest desire to move.

For this work we defined the interactions between robots as follows as shown on Figure 1. A landmark inhibits the desire to move of the nearby landmarks (top left). On the other hand, it excites the nearby moving robots because it does not want them to stop and be landmarks (bottom right). This prevents having landmarks very close to each other. At large distances though it inhibits the moving robots because we don't want them to break away from the swarm or get out of the range of the IR communication. For a moving robot the interactions are the opposite: It inhibits close landmarks while exciting farther landmarks (top right). This way those landmarks can move and join the moving robots. Finally two moving robots excite each other at close distances (bottom left) so that they move farther apart.

At each time step we updated the desire to move of a robot through:

$$I(t+1) = (1.0 - r)\, I(t) + r + \sum_{i=1}^{N} w\, I_i\, f(d) \tag{1}$$

where I is the desire to move of the robot that we are updating, r is the decay rate (typically 0.005 in our experiments), w is the interaction weight (typically 0.05 in our experiments), and f is the interaction function that depends on the current tasks of the robots and the distance d between them. The sum is over all the neigbors seen at time t. Note that when the swarm had a general heading we multiply the interaction functions by a directional term. Figure 2 shows desire-to-move interactions on an actual swarm from our experiment.

Taken together, these factors tend to generate a smooth forward progress, whereby some robots act as landmarks while other robots move past them, then the front robots become landmarks and the robots in the back migrate forward through the swarm.

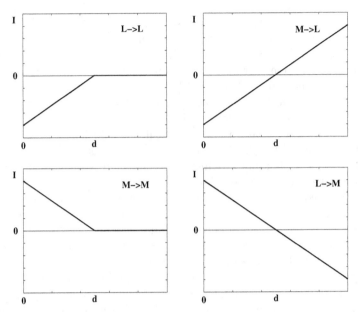

Fig. 1. Functions used for robot interactions.

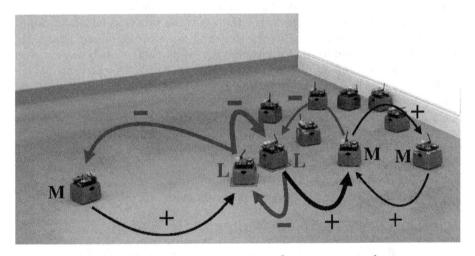

Fig. 2. Robot desire-to-move interactions shown on an actual swarm.

4.3 Collaborative Mapping

We combined all of the elements described above to allow the Swarmbots to create maps of their environment. Because the Swarmbots lack range sensors, we used the IR communications system to measure empty space between the robots. At each time step, each moving robot estimated its location as described above. If its localization confidence was sufficiently high (based on a predefined threshold), the robot kept track of its position and the position of each landmark whose IR readings individually had sufficiently high confidence. At the next IR cycle, it would perform the same calculations. If another good point was found, the robot formed a triangle with the landmark at its vertex, and its own two positions as the base. The triangles were then used to draw a map in the robot's memory. Landmarks also drew maps in a similar fashion, but only using information from moving robots from which they got high-confidence readings. As localization was done in global coordinates, each robot's map was also in global coordinates. However, each map was based on what the robot "saw" during its movements, so different robots could have different maps. Combining these maps results in a complete picture of what was seen by the swarm.

Figure 3 illustrates two examples of maps built in this fashion. In the first case (a), a group of 10 robots was instructed to move straight ahead. Robot movement was controlled by the dynamic task allocation algorithm described earlier. At the time shown in Figure 3, the robots had covered a distance of approximately 5m (nearly an order of magnitude greater than the reliable sensory range at the power levels we used).

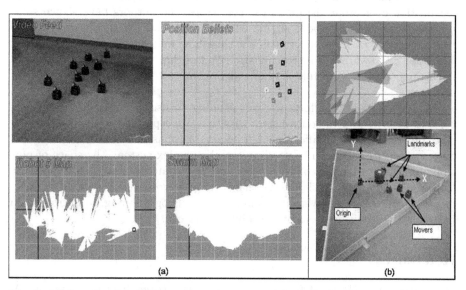

Fig. 3. (a) Localization and mapping along a straight hallway. (b) Mapping triangle shaped area with object in center.

The top left panel shows a video capture of the robots; the top right shows the position where each robot "thinks" it is; shading indicates the confidence each robot has in its localization estimate, with darker shading representing lower confidence. There is a clear agreement between the real and estimated positions of the robots. The bottom left shows the map built by one of the robots during the movement, while the bottom right shows the swarm map, obtained simply by superimposing maps from all ten robots. In the second example (b), a triangle shaped area is mapped. The top picture shows the combined maps from the robots and the bottom photograph shows three landmarks and two moving robots. The obstacle in the middle of the area is visible in the combined map.

5 Discussion

We have presented an overview of a research project in which we created a system for collaborative mapping using a swarm of small robots equipped with simple sensors. Our project is a working demonstration of the vision first put forth by Gage [6], demonstrating that collaborative techniques can be used to overcome the limitations of individual robots.

Significant other work has been done in the study of task allocation in natural and artificial systems. For instance, Bonabeau [3] provides an extensive description of task allocation, and summarizes some relevant work. We are not aware of other implementations of dynamic task allocation for landmark-based localization.

As mentioned earlier, other groups have proposed methods for collaborative localization over large distances. In these cases, the authors have shown some promising results using both simulated and real robots. With the exception of Howard et al's work, however, it is not clear how well the proposed approaches will scale with swarms of increasing size. We feel that the techniques introduced in this paper allow for a fully scalable algorithm that also can provide sufficient accuracy.

In a later research effort, we are planning to use evolutionary computing tools to identify swarm control strategies that are especially well suited to specific missions, and that afford a high degree of robustness and flexibility. It is our experience that when controlling a real, complex system, the space of possible implementations becomes so vast that an exhaustive search is impossible. We have developed a methodology that leverages evolutionary computing techniques, such as Genetic Algorithms and Genetic Programming, to narrow in on particularly promising areas of the solution space.

References

1. T. Balch, L. E. Parker (2002). *Robot Teams: From Diversity to Polymorphism*. A. K. Peters.
2. E. Bonabeau, C. Meyer (2001). Swarm intelligence: A whole new way to think about business. *Harvard Business Review*. (May): 107–114.
3. E. Bonabeau, M. Dorigo, G. Theraulaz (1999). *Swarm Intelligence: From Natural to Artificial Systems*. New York: Oxford University Press.
4. Y. U. Cao, A. S. Fukunaga and A. B. Kahng (1997). Cooperative mobile robotics: Antecedents and directions. *Autonomous Robots*, **4**, 1–23.
5. M. Dorigo, E. Şahin, Eds. Swarm robotics – special issue editorial. *Autonomous Robots* 17 (2004) 111–113.
6. D.W. Gage (1992). Sensor Abstractions to Support Many-Robot Systems. *Proceedings of SPIE Mobile Robots VII*, Boston MA, vol. 1831, pp 235–246.

7. D.W. Gage (2000). Minimum-resource distributed navigation and mapping. *SPIE Mobile Robots XV*, Boston, MA. Vol. 4195.
8. P. Gaudiano, B. Shargel, E. Bonabeau, B. Clough (2003). Swarm Intelligence: a New C2 Paradigm with an Application to Control of Swarms of UAVs. *8th International Command and Control Research and Technology Symposium.*
9. B.P. Gerkey, R.T. Vaughan, K. Støy, A. Howard, G.S. Sukhtame, M.J. Matarić (2001). Most Valuable Player: A Robot Device Server for Distributed Control. In *Proc. of the IEEE/RSJ Intl. Conf. on Intelligent Robots and Systems (IROS)*, 1226–1231, Wailea, Hawaii.
10. T. Hayes (2002). How Many Robots? Group Size and Efficiency in Collective Search Tasks. In *Proc. of the 6th Int. Symp. on Distributed Autonomous Robotic Systems DARS-02*, (June) Fukuoka, Japan, pp. 289-298.
11. A. Howard, M.J. Matarić, G.S. Sukhatme (2002). Localization for Mobile Robot Teams Using Maximum Likelihood Estimation. *Proceedings of the IEEE/RSJ International Conference on Intelligent Robots and Systems*, 434–459.
12. A. Howard, M. Matarić, G. S. Sukhatme (2002). An Incremental Self-Deployment Algorithm for Mobile Sensor Networks. *Autonomous Robots Special Issue on Intelligent Embedded Systems*, **13(2)**, 113–126.
13. M. J. B. Krieger and J.-B. Billeter (2000). The call of duty: Self organized task allocation in a population of up to twelve mobile robots. *Robotics and Autonomous Systems*, **30**, 65–84.
14. R. Kurazume, S. Hirose (2000a). An experimental study of a cooperative positioning system. *Autonomous Robots*, **8(1)**, 43–52.
15. R. Kurazume, S. Hirose (2000b). Development of a cleaning robot system with cooperative positioning system. *Autonomous Robots*, **9(3)**, 237–246.
16. A. Martinoli (1999). Swarm Intelligence in Autonomous Collective Robotics: From Tools to the Analysis and Synthesis of Distributed Collective Strategies, *Ph.D. Thesis Nr. 2069*, DI-EPFL, Lausanne, Switzerland.
17. M. Matarić (1996). Reinforcement learning in the multi-robot domain. *Autonomous Robots*, **4**, 73–83.
18. M. Matarić (2001). Learning in Behavior-Based, Multi-Robot Systems: Policies, Models and other Agents. *Cognitive Systems Research*, **2**, 81–93.
19. I. Rekleitis, G. Dudek, E. Milios (2001). Multi-robot collaboration for robust exploration. *Annals of Mathematics and Artificial Intelligence*, **31(1-4)**:7–40.
20. I.M. Rekleitis, G. Dudek, and E. Milios (2002). Multi-robot cooperative localization: A study of trade-offs between efficiency and accuracy. *Proceedings of the IEEE/RSJ International Conference on Intelligent Robots and Systems*, Lausanne, Switzerland.
21. Swarmbot web site: "http://www.irobot.com/rd/p07_Swarm.asp".
22. S. Thrun (2001). A probabilistic online mapping algorithm for teams of mobile robots. *International Journal of Robotics Research*, **20(5)**:335–363.

The I-SWARM Project:
Intelligent Small World Autonomous Robots
for Micro-manipulation

Jörg Seyfried, Marc Szymanski, Natalie Bender,
Ramon Estaña, Michael Thiel, and Heinz Wörn

Institute for Process Control and Robotics (IPR),
Universität Karlsruhe, D-76128 Karlsruhe, Germany
{seyfried,szymanski,nbender,estana,thiel,woern}@ira.uka.de
http://www.i-swarm.org

Abstract. This paper presents the visions and initial results of the I-SWARM project funded by the European Commission. The goal of the project is to build the first very large-scale artificial swarm (VLSAS) with a swarm size of up to 1,000 micro-robots with a planned size of $2 \times 2 \times 1 \text{ mm}^3$. First, the motivation for such a swarm is described and then first considerations and issues arising from the robots' size resembling "artificial ants" and the MST approach taken to realize that size are given. The paper will conclude with a list of possible scenarios inspired by biology for such a robot swarm.

1 Vision

In classical micro-robotics, highly integrated and specialized robots have been developed in the past years, which are able to perform micro manipulations controlled by a central high-level control system [1–5]. On the other hand, technology is still far away from the first "artificial ant" which would integrate all capabilities of these simple, yet highly efficient swarm building insects.

This has been the motivation of other research fields focusing on studying such swarm behavior [6] and transferring it to simulation or physical robot agents [7]. Realizations of small robot groups of 10 to 20 robots are capable to mimic some aspects of social insects, however, the employed robots are usually huge compared to their natural counterparts, and very limited in terms of perception, manipulation and co-operation capabilities.

The vision of the I-SWARM project is to take a leap forward in robotics research by combining expertise in micro-robotics, in distributed and adaptive systems as well as in self-organizing biological swarm systems. The project aims at technological advances to facilitate the mass-production of micro-robots, which can then be employed as a "real" swarm consisting of up to 1,000 robot clients. These clients will all be equipped with limited, pre-rational on-board intelligence. The swarm will consist of a huge number of heterogeneous robots, differing in

E. Şahin and W.M. Spears (Eds.): Swarm Robotic WS 2004, LNCS 3342, pp. 70–83, 2005.

Fig. 1. The I-SWARM: a vision.

the type of sensors, manipulators and computational power. Such a robot swarm can then be employed for a variety of applications, including micro assembly, biological, medical or cleaning tasks.

To realize the project's vision, the consortium has a large expertise in microrobot technologies. Topics like polymer actuators, collective perception, using (instead of fighting) micro scaling effects, artificial and collective intelligence will be addressed.

The primary goal of the integrated project I-SWARM is the realization of a "real" micro-robot swarm, *i.e.* a thousand micro manufactured autonomous robots will be designed for the collective execution of different tasks in the small world. This will be achieved:

- by the realization of collective intelligence of these robots
    - in terms of cooperation and
    - collective perception
    - using knowledge and methods of pre-rational intelligence, machine learning, swarm theory and classical multi-agent systems.
- by the development of advanced micro-robots hardware
    - being extremely small (planned size of a single robot: $2 \times 2 \times 1$ mm^3.)
    - by integrating novel actuators, miniaturized powering and miniaturized wireless communication
    - with ICs for on-board intelligence and
    - integrating sensors and tools for the manipulation in the small world.

The fundamental vision behind a swarm of micro-robots is the realization of capabilities that are not given by either a single micro-robot, or with a small group of micro-robots. The expected self-organization effects in the robot swarm should be similar to that seen within other ecological systems like ant states, bee colonies and other insect aggregations. The well-known potential benefits of a self-organized system include greater flexibility and adaptability of the system to the environment, robustness to failures, *etc.* Additionally, their collective behavior opens up new application fields, that cannot be solved with today's tools. A suitable sophisticated positioning system will be developed, possibly based on the ones used by insects and incorporating tactile sensors and a small but effective vision system, that will enable the individual agents to communicate between themselves and thus enable and promote the desired swarm effects.

Considering the natural world, it is apparent that insects have been a very successful species during evolution largely due to their ability to organize into large co-operative communities and swarms [8, 9].

A major goal of the project is to transform knowledge gained by observations of eusocial insect behavior, from observations of communicating insect aggregations and research already performed on swarm intelligence of robots and to apply this to a swarm of micro-robots. The micro-robots to be developed within the project will be capable of performing real micro manipulations similar to (some of) the capabilities of insects. In this paper, some of the work carried out within the project will be described, including:

1. Hardware design of a heterogeneous robot swarm: The realization of a large number of robot clients (up to 1,000 or more) will present a major technical challenge and will require new and novel approaches in terms of manufacture and miniaturization. New techniques for the co-design of the miniaturized hardware and its embedded software 'intelligence' will need to be developed.
    (a) In designing the robot hardware, locomotion principles such as insect-like walking will be examined. Research into enhancing this will lead to novel, low-power micro-robot walking mechanisms.
    (b) The knowledge gained by experiments on the "Laws of the small World" will significantly deepen our understanding of microphysics as applied to micro handling.
    (c) The development of pre-rational intelligence modules will help to create a swarm intelligence distributed over the whole system, thus making it less prone to failures and improving its capability to adapt to new situations.
2. More importantly, systems and methodologies will be developed which will enable the swarm's behavior for solving given tasks to be modelled and thus predicted. This will require the development of knowledge not only about the internal systemic behavior of a large number of heterogeneous agents. A major contribution will also be a simulation system which takes into account the hardware capabilities and restrictions of the swarm robots' hardware, *e.g.* sensory capabilities, uncertainties, *etc.* The result of this work will enable the building of customized swarms which will act in a predetermined way.

As a prerequisite of the co-design of the robot hard- and software, swarm scenarios have been identified and classified according to their requirements. A rough categorization of swarm could be the following:

- grouping
- pattern forming or making a queue
- object collection, surface cleaning
- collective perception
- collective transport
- collective sorting and building
- collective maintenance of global homeostasis

There are many applications which can be derived from these scenarios:

- Assembly tasks in the micro world such as assembling of gears, micro pumps and other micro systems,
- Self assembly/self recycling,
- Cleaning surfaces in a very short time,
- Mechanical self configuration,
- Testing and characterization of micro-parts,
- Future medical applications (e.g. examine and medicate the human body inside and outside),
- Energy harvesting and distribution within the swarm.

We believe that the availability of a (possibly commercially available) low-cost, mass fabricated swarm micro robot will have a great impact in the fields of education, science and possibly also entertainment.

2   The Micro Robotic Approach

The experience from previous micro-robotic projects shows that we are clearly at the limit of micro-robot development with a modular approach. If we want to develop smaller robots, the design has to change drastically and an integrated approach should be chosen. The selected concepts must allow further miniaturization in the future in order to really reach the micro-scale. The micro-agents' size and force must be in proportion to the size and fragility of the manipulated objects, such as, for instance DNA or living cells. As a large number of micro-agents will have to be realized, batch processes using micro system technology (or MEMS[1]) will be compulsory.

Within this project, robotic agents realized with techniques from micro system technology (MST) and employing insect as well as other motion principles will be investigated. This will allow making the link between two research fields, which do not have much interaction so far. On the one hand, there is a large number of micro-locomotion systems, walkers, conveyors or motors, which have been realized with MST. On the other hand, there is micro-robotics, where certain intelligence is present on autonomous platforms, which are assembled from discrete elements.

---

[1] Micro-Electro-Mechanical System.

Actuators based on piezo-optic, thermal or other solid-state effects with the possibility for a direct external energy supply will allow for agents without an energy buffer for locomotion, thus further decreasing the size. The projected size of a robot is $2 \times 2 \times 1 \text{ mm}^3$ and velocities of up to 1 mm/s. There will be different kinds of micro-agents, each designed for a specific task and each with an integrated nano-tool: optical sensor (1 or a few pixels), needle (e.g. functionalized AFM like probe) etc. As for the robot itself, a modular approach for the tools is excluded due to the limitations in size.

To create a breakthrough in micro-robot actuation, we are pursuing a bio-inspired approach: in several insects the mechanical structure for locomotion is based on shells and muscles in contrast to e.g. bones and muscles in larger animals. A shell structure where bending hinges are used as joints is e.g. one way to "mimic" the biological world with artificial structures since most of the micro system techniques allow for planar shell fabrication. Agile limbs and antennas can be made when a suitable "muscle" (actuator) material is integrated with the shell structure. So far most integrated micro-robots have been based on silicon technology. To mimic the biological world, the materials for the backbone of the insect robot could instead be polymeric. Fortunately, there are several micro system technologies for polymeric materials available and the lacking fabrication steps for the actuators will be successively developed. While several of the injection moulding techniques would give large volumes at low prices the most straightforward way of building small microsystems is to use flexible printed circuit boards (FPCB). These boards are extensively used in miniature systems as consumer electronics and high-tech components. The FPCB gives flexibility, electrical connects, three-dimensionality and high-quality material properties. The more expensive FPCB use a polyimide base material that gives high performance and some extraordinary properties. The processing technology will allow for well-defined structures (the shells etc. in the insect robot) and well-controlled grooves for the bending hinges. The stiffness can easily be controlled by structural definition (ridges etc.) or by metal reinforcement since the main application of the FPCB is as a printed circuit board with metal conductors in top of the carrier.

The actuator development for the integrated robots is performed in several steps. The first evaluation is made with a functional but not optimized muscle material. One example is a thermo-mechanical material that is well compatible with the FPCB processing technology: a photo-patternable polyimide. There are also other interesting actuators that will be considered for the swarm robots. The high power consumption is however the main problem for autonomous operation. One of the more interesting actuator groups are electro-active polymers [10], e.g. piezoelectric polymer materials with two main advantages. Firstly, the power consumption should be possible to decrease with two orders of magnitude allowing for long operation times or uninterrupted operation with a continuous power supply. Secondly, the movement stability should be much improved since the actuation is controlled by electric voltage instead of temperature. Particularly the possibility to stop at a given joint angle without any power consumption is important in many of the planned applications. The development of electro-active polymers is rather fast and it can be suspected that some new alternatives will be possible to evaluate soon. At present, modified PVDF types of piezoelectric actuators appear to be the best choice. These materials have a strain and stiffness close to the thermo-mechanical polyimide while the energy consumption per cycle should be two orders of magnitude less. The main challenges with introducing this material in a polymeric micro system are the high electric fields, the electrode materials and the processing techniques.

In the final phase of this project, micro system technologies such as bulk micro machining, piezoelectric thin or thick films, polymer film technologies *etc.* will be employed in the creation of the small mobile micro-robot agents combining features from both the autonomous micro-robots and the MST-based systems.

The functions of the agents will be reduced to locomotion, integrated tool (one per agent) permitting basic manipulation, possibility to attach and release other agents, a limited capability to store information on the state of the agent as well as the possibility to transfer basic information from agent to agent and eventually between agent and a supervisory system / robot.

3   Methodology and Initial Results

Since the project has just started[2], at the time of preparing this paper, no results beyond first hardware tests and initial simulations on the impact of the very limited robot capabilities are yet available. However, the nature of the project has led to very interesting and challenging design issues which will be described in the following along with our approach on how to tackle them.

The fundamental difference in this project as compared to other (swarm) robotics endeavors is that we have not proposed a fixed scenario the final robot swarm is to perform. The proposition, as sketched in Section 1 was rather to realize a swarm consisting of mm-sized robots which should subsequently be programmed and deployed on various scenarios.

This situation is very uncommon in classical engineering, since it implies a co-design of the problem along with the solution, Fig. 2. Since the Consortium comprises partners involved in the design and fabrication of robot hardware and partners involved in software, we initially faced a deadlock situation: Hardware partners requested the required capabilities of the hardware from the software partners, who in turn wanted to know the constraints which will be imposed by the hardware given the stringent limitations in space.

In other words, this project tries not only to explore the space of solutions for swarm robotics as in classical engineering, but also the space of possible problems at the same time. To overcome this deadlock situation, we have started to collect all available data on constraints imposed by physics, available technologies and interactions of subsystems. The resulting analysis is presented in the next two sections. A preliminary list of possible swarm scenarios inspired by biological swarms will conclude this Chapter.

---

[2] Project start was in January 2004.

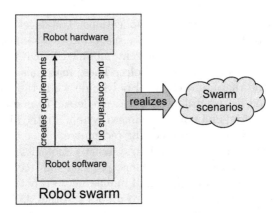

Fig. 2. Unconventional engineering problem in co-design.

3.1   Hardware Constraints

The Consortium is currently investigating principles and techniques for all robot subsystems. Here, the subsystems most crucial for the resulting swarm scenarios will be discussed.

Energy Supply: Speaking of autonomous[3], highly miniaturized robots, the first limitation to be considered is the amount of available on-board energy. If one takes a pessimistic approach, the energy will be limited to $150\,\mu$W. One can then further estimate an energy breakdown onto the robots' subsystems: 70% will be consumed by each robot's actuation system, 20% by its hardware circuitry and the rest is available for other functions.

While examining these figures in more detail, it becomes clear that the amount of energy available on the robots is crucial while being a function of the robot's size. For some solutions, it depends only on its surface, for others on the available volume. The list of possible energy sources for an autonomous swarm micro robot is:

- **Batteries**
    - **Non-rechargeable:** commercial types deliver $1\,$J/mm^3, package sizes are around $30\,$mm^3 which renders them useless for our case.
    - **Rechargeable:** thick-film batteries deliver $1\,$J/mm^3, too, and could be used at $0.2\,$W for about 5,000 seconds (1.4 hours, sufficient for most conceivable scenarios even with very slow robots).
- **Capacitors:** super caps could be operated at $0.2\,$mW for 1,000 seconds (16 minutes), package sizes are around $65\,$mm^3.
- **Inductive Energy Transfer:** on-board coils of $2\,$mm ø could supply $1\,$mW.
- **Micro Fuel Cells:** size [11, 12] are today still too large for on-board operation and refuelling with methanol will be a major problem given the robots', besides the production of waste water.

---

[3] In terms of power supply, and to a large extent of control.

– **Micro Solar Cells:** could deliver between $0.14\,\mathrm{mW/mm^2}$ to $0.35\,\mathrm{mW/mm^2}$ with a light source equivalent to daylight.

The conceivable power supply systems can therefore be classified into continuous and recharging, while the continuous scenario is the more desirable one.

Sensor System: The sensor subsystem of the robots could consist of a tactile sensor principle using a feeler-like design. Principles currently under investigation are piezo- or polymer strips which can operate either passively, or in active modes, by vibration or bringing them to resonance which opens up possibilities to sense the robot's surroundings (approximately one robot's length in distance) or even communicate through this sensor system, too; see Fig. 3. Other principles which will be evaluated are capacitance measurements detecting changes in the dielectric in the robot's surroundings or optical principles.

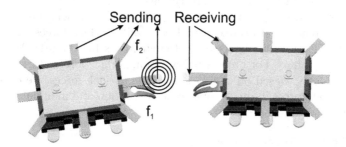

Fig. 3. Communication with a tactile sensor system.

Communication System: The principles which could be employed for robot-to-robot and robot-to-host communication are the following:

– **Classical RF:** commercial solutions like DECT, Bluetooth, WLAN and even ZigBee are not applicable due to the size constraints.
– **Infra-red:** available transceivers have dimensions of 30-40 $\mathrm{mm^3}$. Further problems will be discussed in the next paragraph.
– **Ultra-sound:** sound waves propagating in free air have a very low power efficiency. One alternative would be the transmission of sound through the floor.
– **Inductive:** could be achieved through micro-coils for transmission distances below 2 cm.

Considering these observations, robot-to-host communication will have to be performed using a hierarchical approach: propagating gathered data to (a few) higher-level robots with more advanced communication and sensing abilities which will then send the data to a host.

For optical sensor or communication principles, the restrictions of the available energy are the most striking: standard infrared light diodes require between 50 and 150 μW. This would mean that optical communication and actuation are mutually exclusive (or impossible at all in the worst case, since no power for the circuitry and other functions would be available when light is being emitted).

Since the radiation characteristics of standard diodes produce their maximum output upwards, robot-to-robot communication by optical means will require extra integration work to emit light in the robots' plane. Additional problems arise from technological restrictions[4]: processes which could be used to fabricate the robots' hybrid D/A circuitry rise compatibility issues with processes necessary to structure light emitting diodes. One possible solution (as employed in the Smart-Dust project) would be the use of an external light source and robot-mounted micro-mirrors (or shutters) which can be actuated to avoid the necessity of on-board light generation.

Summary: As a result of this first design phase, a document has been created which lists all necessary robot subsystems along with their characteristics regarding size, die-area, power consumption and compatibility with different manufacturing processes.

An additional task within the project deals with micro scaling effects. These effects occur when scaling an object, *e.g.* a cube with side length a to 1 mm and below: the gravitational decreases with a^3, while surface forces (adhesion due to humidity, electrostatic forces or molecular forces like Van-der-Waals forces) decrease only with a^2. For objects below 1 mm, surface forces start to dominate the volume forces. Based on simulation results of such forces, we expect to be able to use such forces in micro robotics for actuation and manipulation instead of avoiding them.

3.2   Software Considerations

To work towards possible swarm scenarios not only from the hardware side (which could result in a highly miniaturized robot which has too limited capabilities for even the most basic emergence effects to occur), we are also approaching possible scenarios from the simulation and robot design side.

For this, we have derived a morphological table of possible swarm scenarios as outlined in the next section (3.3) and added the requirements on the robot hardware to each scenario. To complement this analysis, we have also started simulations to assess the impact of the availability and performance of different robot subsystems (*i.e.* sensors, locomotion system *etc.*).

The considerations on the hardware and software side are now being iterated in order to gain a deeper understanding of the restrictions which have to be considered. Additionally, this process also yields new scenarios which have not been thought of before. One example is a non-continuous power supply scenario (*i.e.* the robots have rechargeable energy supplies on board), where robots are "rewarded" for achieving a task by energy. This could for example be a collection task where robots which deliver a workpiece will be "refuelled", while robots performing this task badly will eventually "die" due to a lack of energy.

3.3   Scenarios

In the following paragraphs, initial ideas inspired by biological counterparts [16] are presented. This description is still quite vanilla, since we are currently eval-

---

[4] Since the robot size will limit the electronics to basically a single chip.

uating the suitability and feasibility of the scenarios for a robotic swarm. Some initial hints on the realization are given below, but for each scenario, there are many ways to imitate the concepts that biological swarms use (for example, virtual pheromone [17]: this can be simulated by a projected light gradient [18], or by robot-to-robot communication, or other sensor principles).

Scenario 1: Aggregation: This scenario represents a simple aggregation of the robots in a self-organized manner. This behavior is inspired by slime molds or by cockroaches. The robots have the goal of positioning themselves into a larger group.

Scenario 2: Aggregation Controlled by an Environmental Template: In this scenario, the robots have to aggregate in the arena, too. In contrast to Scenario 1, an environmental template influences this aggregation. The environmental template could be a light source which has another color than the one used for a "virtual pheromone". The goal of this scenario is that the robots must aggregate as near as possible to the center of this template. This phenomenon can be found in nature by slime molds and cockroaches, too.

Scenario 3: Collective Building of Piles: The "Collective Building of Piles" scenario is one of the most researched scenarios in the AI community. The goal of the robots is to collect pucks, which are initially randomly distributed over the whole arena, and build up one ore more piles. This scenario is a good base for studying more advanced scenarios like the following one.

Scenario 4: Collective Sorting: This scenario is a more advanced version of the latter one. It involves a controlled environment with different regions within the arena. Those regions could be distinguished by the robots, for instance through different light intensities or colors, which are projected with a high-resolution beamer from the top of arena. Additionally, there are several sorts of pucks which differ in a feature that is recognizable by the robot. The goal of the robot is to bring a puck to the region of the arena which corresponds with the type of the puck. This behavior should lead to a guided sorting of the pucks within special regions. Ants use such mechanisms to sort their brood according to the ambient soil temperature and humidity. Depending on the robots' capabilities, the projected gradient could also be replaced by (local) broadcasts depending on the robots' communication capabilities.

At the first glance this scenario seems quite easy, but distinguishing between different objects is a very difficult task for micro-scale robots.

Scenario 5: Royal Chamber: The "Royal Chamber" scenario goes back to investigations on the ant species *Leptothorax albipennis* that build a wall around their queen. The distance of this wall is affected by a pheromone that is excreted by the queen. As in nature, the robots should collect building-material (pucks) and dispose it around an imaginary queen. The queen's pheromone is represented by a potential field that can be, as in the latter scenario, projected on the arena.

The robots should deposit the pucks at a given potential to form the royal chamber. If the potential field changes – the queen grows – the robots should reconfigure the built wall.

Scenario 6: A Court Around a "Robot Queen": In this scenario, we have two types of robots: the "queen robot" which is bigger in size and moves slowly in the arena, and the "worker robots". The "queen robot" emits a "virtual pheromone" that affects the random walk of the workers. They are directed uphill the pheromone gradient until they reach the queen. Then the worker robots join the court of the queen. By the time they are exposed to the pheromone, their reaction threshold increases. This effect will cause the robots to leave the court, at least when the queen is moving. The goals of this scenario are to have a maximum filled court of the queen and at the same time distribute the non-court robots uniformly in the arena.

This scenario is inspired by the honeybee queen court. In the case of the honeybee queen, the formation of the court as well as the joining frequency per bee seems to be affected by the moving speed and turning frequency of the queen. The moving activity of the honeybee queen is often associated with her egg laying, which then results in different egg laying patterns.

Scenario 7: Collective Foraging Using Bucket Brigades: In this scenario, the robots collectively forage a food from a known place and untread to the known nest. In this scenario we have only 3 distinct groups of robots: the "big", the "median" and the "small" robots which differ by their size and their speed. Every time a bigger robot has contact with a loaded smaller robot, the smaller, but faster robots drop the object and turn again towards to the food source. The bigger and slower robot lifts the object, turns and transports it towards to the nest. This behavior is inspired by ants. The common goal of the swarm behavior is to collectively maximize the number of transported objects per time unit.

Scenario 8: Collective Foraging for Objects Using Pheromone Trails: A group of robots in this scenario collectively chooses the optimal source by assessing the distance from the "nest" to the source. A "virtual pheromone" deposited on the best source by the robots can be detected by other foraging robots. Then several robots go to this source. A goal of this scenario is to collect an objects from several food sources by minimizing the time spent outside of the nest.

Scenario 9: Foraging with Distinction of the Source Quality: As in the last scenario, the robots should forage by building a "virtual" pheromone trail. In this case, however, they distinguish between the food sources and deposit more pheromone for a better source. This scenario builds also on the "Collective Sorting" scenario. The robots must recognize the different food sources and evaluate them. There are two possibilities for evaluating the food sources. The easiest one is that they know the value of the source after they identified it. The other one, and the harder one, would be that the robots are rewarded by an intelligent arena after delivering the food.

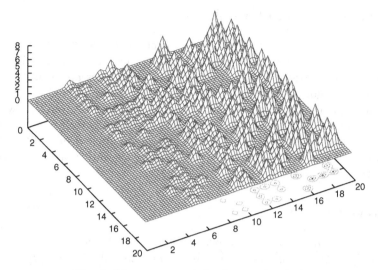

Fig. 4. Pheromone map for the nursing task.

Scenario 10: Dynamic Task Allocation: This scenario should model the process of brood nursing in social insects. There are two kinds of robots and two kinds of "virtual" pheromones. The two pheromones represent two different kinds of larvae. If a larva was not fed for a given time it starts secreting pheromone. This pheromone is spatially very strictly bounded, see Figure 4. Each kind of robot is more attracted to one kind of "virtual" pheromone. If a robot stays at the peak of a pheromone, the pheromone level there will decrease – the robot is feeding the larvae.

The goal is to keep the brood on an equal pheromone level even if the number of robots of the one kind is decreased (deactivated). The other robots should then take over their part. This should lead to a dynamic task allocation within the swarm.

3.4 Conclusions

The list of scenarios in the last section is currently far from being complete. It will also certainly comprise of scenarios which are plainly impossible for robots of the planned size (and even for much bigger ones). However, it currently serves us as a starting point for the assessment of a minimal robot configuration which is necessary for the I-Swarm to be of any scientific interest. Based on this list, a morphological table of possible swarm scenarios has been created in a spreadsheet which serves as a means of exploring the parameter space of all possible robot subsystem configurations and the impact on the possible scenarios.

One of the possible results of this initial design phase could clearly be that the planned size of $2 \times 2 \times 1$ mm^3 is not feasible since it will make the possible swarm scenarios too simple to be of any use. However, the design decisions taken could be re-used for later projects when more advanced micro techniques are available.

4   Discussion and Outlook

This paper presented a new challenging project, that will push the swarm and micro robotics to a new frontier. Currently, the project is in the starting phase. As described in Sections 1 and 2, several new techniques are being evaluated regarding new algorithms in swarm intelligence, collective perception and MST. As outlined in Section 3, a novel approach to building not only a swarm of robots, but also exploring the space of possible swarm scenarios as a function of the robots' capabilities has been taken. Being able to implement and test swarm algorithms with a VLSAS will lead to a new understanding of eusocial insects and swarm robotics.

Acknowledgment

This work is supported by the European Union within the IST "Beyond Robotics" Proactive Initiative – 6th Framework Programme: 2003-2007 (I-SWARM project, Project Number: 507006).

References

1. Seyfried, J.; Fatikow, S.; Fahlbusch, S.; Buerkle, A.; Schmoeckel, F.: Manipulating in the Micro World: Mobile Micro Robots and their Applications Int. Symposium on Robotics (ISR), Montreal, Canada, May 14–17, 2000
2. A. Almansa-Martin: "Micro and nanorobotics – present and future". In Proc. of the 35th International Symposium on Robotics, Paris, March 23–26 2004
3. Martel, Sylvain et al.: "Three-Legged Wireless Miniature Robots for Mass-Scale Operations at the Sub-Atomic Scale", Proc. 2001 IEEE Int. Conf. Robotics & Automation, ICRA 2001, Seoul, Korea, May 21–26, 2001, pp. 3423–3428
4. K. S. J. Pister, J. M. Kahn and B. E. Boser, "Smart Dust: Wireless Networks of Millimeter-Scale Sensor Nodes", Highlight Article in 1999 Electronics Research Laboratory Research Summary
5. S. Hollar, A. Flynn, C. Bellew, K.S.J. Pister, "Solar Powered 10 mg Silicon Robot," MEMS 2003, Kyoto, Japan, January 19–23, 2003
6. Eric Bonabeau, Marco Dorigo, Guy Theraulaz. Swarm Intelligence: From Natural to Artificial Systems. Oxford University Press 1999.
7. C. R. Kube, H. Zhang, "Collective Robotics: From Social Insects to Robots". Adaptive Behaviour, 1993, Vol. 2, No. 2, pp. 189–218.
8. Self-Organization in biological systems. S. Camazine, J.-L.Deneubourg, N.R. Franks, J. Sneyd, G. Theraulaz, E. Bonabeau. Princeton University Press (2001).
9. A.E. Hirsh, D.M. Gordon. Distributed problem solving in social insects. Annals of Mathematics and Artificial Intelligence 31, pp. 199–221 (2001).
10. Y. Bar-Cohen (Book Editor and author/co-author of 5 chapters), "Electroactive Polymer (EAP) Actuators as Artificial Muscles – Reality, Potential and Challenges", ISBN 0-8194-4054-X, SPIE Press, Vol. PM98, (March 2001), 671 pages.
11. Ieropoulos, I., Greenman, J., Melhuish, C. (2003): "Imitating Metabolism: Energy Autonomy in Biologically Inspired Robotics", in Proceedings of the AISB 03, Second International Symposium on Imitation in Animals and Artifacts, SSAISB, Aberystwyth, Wales, pp. 191–4.

12. Chris Melhuish, John Greenman, Kevin Bartholomew, Ioannis Ieropoulos and Ian Horsfield. "Towards Robot Energetic Autonomy using Microbial Fuel Cells", (in press) J. Electrochimica Acta (special edition).
13. Woern, H.; Seyfried, J.; Fahlbusch, St.; Buerkle, A.; Schmoeckel, F.: Flexible Micro-robots for Micro Assembly Tasks International Symposium on Micromechatronics and Human Science (HMS 2000), Nagoya, Japan, October 22–25, 2000
14. Woern, Heinz; Schmoeckel, Ferdinand; Buerkle, Axel; Samitier, Josep; Puig-Vidal, Manel; Johansson, Stefan; Simu, Urban; Meyer, Jörg-Uwe; Biehl, Margit From decimeter- to centimeter-sized mobile microrobots – the development of the MINI-MAN system SPIE's Int. Symp. on Intelligent Systems and Advanced Manufacturing, Conference on Microrobotics and Microassembly Boston, MA, USA, October 28–November 2, 2001
15. Buerkle, Axel; Schmoeckel, Ferdinand; Kiefer, Matthias; Amavasai, Bala P.; Caparrelli, Fabio; Selvan, Arul N.; Travis, Jon R.: Vision-based closed-loop control of mobile microrobots for micro handling tasks SPIE's Int. Symp. on Intelligent Systems and Advanced Manufacturing, Conference on Microrobotics and Microassembly Boston, MA, USA, October 28–November 2, 2001, pp. pp. 187–198
16. Schmickl, Thomas: Scenarios for the robot swarm. Internal Report of I-Swarm Project. May 2004. University of Graz, Austria, IZG.
17. Payton, D.; Daily, M.; Estowski, R. et al.: "Pheromone Robotics" in Autonomous Robots vol. 11, pp. 319–324, 2001
18. Kazama, T; Sugawara, K; Watanabe, T.: "Collecting Behavior of Interacting Robots with Virtual Phero-mone" in Proc. of the 7th International Symposium on Distributed Autonomous Robotic Systems (DARS 2004), June 23–25, Toulouse, France, pp. 331–340

An Overview of Physicomimetics

William M. Spears, Diana F. Spears, Rodney Heil,
Wesley Kerr, and Suranga Hettiarachchi

Computer Science Department,
University of Wyoming, Laramie, WY, 82070, USA
wspears@cs.uwyo.edu
http://www.cs.uwyo.edu/~wspears

Abstract. This paper provides an overview of our framework, called *physicomimetics*, for the distributed control of swarms of robots. We focus on robotic behaviors that are similar to those shown by solids, liquids, and gases. Solid formations are useful for distributed sensing tasks, while liquids are for obstacle avoidance tasks. Gases are handy for coverage tasks, such as surveillance and sweeping. Theoretical analyses are provided that allow us to reliably control these behaviors. Finally, our implementation on seven robots is summarized.

1 Vision

The focus of our research is to design and build rapidly deployable, scalable, adaptive, cost-effective, and robust swarms of autonomous distributed robots. Our objective is to provide a scientific, yet practical, approach to the design and analysis of swarm systems.

The team robots could vary widely in type, as well as size, e.g., from nanobots to micro-air vehicles (MAVs) and micro-satellites. A robot's sensors perceive the world, including other robots, and a robot's effectors make changes to that robot and/or the world, including other robots. It is assumed that robots can only sense and affect nearby robots; thus, a key challenge has been to design "local" control rules. Not only do we want the desired global behavior to emerge from the local interaction between robots (self-organization), but we also require fault-tolerance, that is, the global behavior degrades very gradually if individual robots are damaged. Self-repair is also desirable, in the event of damage. Self-organization, fault-tolerance, and self-repair are precisely those principles exhibited by natural physical systems. Thus, many answers to the problems of distributed control can be found in the natural laws of physics.

This paper provides an overview of our framework for distributed control, called "physicomimetics" or "artificial physics" (AP). We use the term "artificial" (or virtual) because although we are motivated by natural physical forces, we are not restricted to them [1]. Although the forces are virtual, robots *act* as if they were real. Thus the robot's sensors must see enough to allow it to compute the force to which it is reacting. The robot's effectors must allow it to respond to this perceived force.

E. Şahin and W.M. Spears (Eds.): Swarm Robotic WS 2004, LNCS 3342, pp. 84–97, 2005.

There are two potential advantages to this approach. First, in the real physical world, collections of small entities yield surprisingly complex behavior from very simple interactions between the entities. Thus there is a precedent for believing that complex control is achievable through simple local interactions. This is required for very small robots, since their sensors and effectors will necessarily be primitive. Second, since the approach is largely independent of the size and number of robots, the results scale well to larger robots and larger sets of robots.

2   The Physicomimetics Framework

The basic AP framework is elegantly simple. Virtual physics forces drive a multi-robot system to a desired configuration or state. The desired configuration (state) is one that minimizes overall system potential energy. In essence the system acts as a molecular dynamics ($F = ma$) simulation.

At an abstract level, AP treats robots as physical particles. This enables the framework to be embodied in robots ranging in size from nanobots to satellites. Particles exist in two or three dimensions and are point-masses. Each particle i has position x and velocity v. We use a discrete-time approximation to the continuous behavior of the system, with time-step Δt. At each time step, the position of each particle undergoes a perturbation Δx. The perturbation depends on the current velocity, i.e., $\Delta x = v \Delta t$. The velocity of each particle at each time step also changes by Δv. The change in velocity is controlled by the force on the particle, i.e., $\Delta v = F \Delta t / m$, where m is the mass of that particle and F is the force on that particle. A frictional force is included, for self-stabilization. This is modeled as a *viscous friction* term, i.e., the product of a viscosity coefficient and the robot's velocity (independently modeled in the same fashion by Howard et al. [2]). We have also included a parameter F_{max}, which restricts the maximum force felt by a particle. This provides a necessary restriction on the acceleration a robot can achieve. Also, a parameter V_{max} restricts the velocity of the particles, which is very important for modeling real robots.

Given a set of initial conditions and some desired global behavior, it is necessary to define what sensors, effectors, and local force laws are required for the desired behavior to emerge. This is explored, in the next section, for a variety of simulated static and dynamic multi-robot configurations. Our implementation with robots is discussed in Section 3.2.

3   Physicomimetic Results

Our research has focused on robotic behaviors that are similar to those shown by solids, liquids, and gases. Solid crystalline formations are useful for distributed sensing tasks, to create a virtual antenna or synthetic aperture radar. For such tasks it is important to maintain connectivity and a lattice geometry. Liquids are for obstacle avoidance tasks, since fluids easily maneuver around obstacles while retaining connectivity. Solid and liquid behaviors are formed using a similar force law, that has attractive and repulsive components. The transition between solids and liquids can be performed via a change in only one parameter, which balances the attractive and repulsive components [3].

Finally, gases are handy for coverage tasks, such as surveillance and sweeping maneuvers. For these tasks it is imperative that coverage can be maintained, even in the face of individual robot failures. Gas-like behaviors are created using purely repulsive forces.

3.1   Simulation Results

Solids: Our initial application required that a swarm of MAVs self-organize into a hexagonal lattice, creating a distributed sensing grid with spacing R between MAVs [4]. Potential applications include sensing grids for the mapping or tracing of chemical/biological plumes [5] or the creation of virtual antennas to improve the resolution of radar images [1]. To map this into a force law, each robot repels other robots that are closer than R, while attracting robots that are further than R in distance. Thus each robot has a circular "potential well" around itself at radius R – and neighboring robots will be separated by distance R. The intersection of these potential wells is a form of constructive interference that creates "nodes" of low potential energy where the robots are likely to reside. A simple compass construction illustrates that this intersection of circles of radius R will form a hexagonal lattice where the robot separation is R. Note that potential energy (PE) is never actually computed by the robots. Robots compute local force vectors. PE is only computed for visualization or mathematical analysis.

With this in mind, we defined a force law $F = Gm_im_j/r^p$, where $F \leq F_{max}$ is the magnitude of the force between two particles i and j, and r is the distance between the two particles. The variable p is a user-defined power, which ranges from -5.0 to 5.0. Unless stated otherwise, we assume $p = 2.0$ and $F_{max} = 1$ in this paper. Also, $m_i = 1.0$ for all particles (although the framework does not require this). The "gravitational constant" G is set at initialization. The force is repulsive if $r < R$ and attractive if $r > R$. Each particle has one sensor that can detect the distance and bearing to nearby particles. The one effector enables movement with velocity $v \leq V_{max}$. To ensure that the force laws are local, we allow particles to sense only their nearest neighbors. Hence, particles have a visual range of only $1.5R$.

A simple generalization of this force law will also create square lattices. If robots are arbitrarily labeled with one of two colors, then square lattices are formed if robots that have unlike colors have a separation of R, while robots that have like colors have separation $\sqrt{2}R$. Furthermore, transformations between square and hexagonal lattices (and vice versa) are easily accomplished. Figure 1 illustrates formations with 50 robots. The initial deployment configuration (left) is assumed to be a tight cluster of robots. The robots move outwards into a square formation (middle). Then they transform to a hexagonal formation (right). Self-repair in the face of agent failure is also straightforward [6].

The total PE of the initial deployment configuration is an excellent indicator of the quality of the final formation. High PE predicts high quality formations.

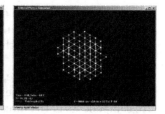

Fig. 1. The initial deployment configuration (left) is assumed to be a fairly tight cluster of robots. The robots move outwards into a square formation (middle). Then they transform to a hexagonal formation (right).

This energy is dependent on the value of G, and it can be proven that the optimal value of G for hexagonal lattices is [7]:

$$G_{opt}{}^{\triangle} = F_{max} R^p [2 - 1.5^{1-p}]^{p/(1-p)} \tag{1}$$

The value of G_{opt} does not depend on the number of particles, which is a nice result. However, for square lattices:

$$G_{opt}{}^{\square} = F_{max} R^p \left[\frac{\sqrt{2}(N-1)[2 - 1.3^{1-p}] + N[2 - 1.7^{1-p}]}{\sqrt{2}(N-1) + N} \right]^{p/(1-p)} \tag{2}$$

Note that in this case G_{opt} depends on the number of particles N. It occurs because there are two classes (colors) of robots. However, the dependency on N is not large and goes to zero as N increases.

Our current research is focused on the movement of formations through obstacle fields towards some goal. Larger obstacles are created from multiple, point-sized obstacles; this enables flexible creation of obstacles of arbitrary size and shape. As a generalization to our standard paradigm, goals are attractive, whereas obstacles are repulsive (similar to potential field approaches, e.g., [8]).

Figure 2 illustrates how a square formation moves through an obstacle field via a sequence of rotations and counter-rotations of the whole collective. This

Fig. 2. A solid formation moves through an obstacle field towards a goal (upper left part of the field). The rotations and counter-rotations of the whole collective are an emergent property.

behavior emerges from the interaction of forces and is not a programmed response. If this cannot be accomplished, the formation may not be able to make further progress towards the goal.

Liquids: As stated above, the difference in behavior between solid formations and liquid formations depends on the balance between the attractive and repulsive components of the forces. In fact, the parameter G once again plays a crucial role. Below a certain value of $G \equiv G_t$, liquid behavior occurs. Above that value, solid behavior occurs. The switch between the two behaviors acts very much like a phase transition. Using a standard *balance of forces* argument we can show that the phase transition for hexagonal lattices occurs at [3]:

$$G_t{}^{\triangle} = \frac{F_{max} R^p}{2\sqrt{3}} \tag{3}$$

The phase transition law for square lattices is:

$$G_t{}^{\square} = \frac{F_{max} R^p}{2\sqrt{2}+2} \tag{4}$$

Neither law depends on the number of robots N, and the difference in the denominators reflects the difference in hexagonal and square geometries. There are several uses for these equations. Not only can we predict the value of G_t at which the phase transition will occur, but we can also use G_t to help design our system. For example, a value of $G \approx 0.9 G_t$ yields the best liquid formation, while a value of $G \approx 1.8 G_t \approx G_{opt}$ yields the best solid formations.

As mentioned before, liquids are especially interesting for their ability to flow through obstacle fields, while retaining their connectivity. Figure 3 illustrates how a "square" liquid formation moves through the same obstacle field as before. In comparison with the solid formation shown above, far more deformation occurs as the liquid moves through the obstacles. However, the movement is quicker, because the liquid does not have to maintain the rigid geometry of the solid. Despite this, connectivity is maintained. One can easily imagine a situation where a formation lowers G to move around obstacles, and then raises G to "re-solidify" the formations after the obstacles have been avoided.

Fig. 3. A liquid formation moves through the same obstacle field towards the goal. Far more deformation occurs, but connectivity is maintained.

Gases: The primary motivation for gas behavior is regional coverage, e.g., for surveillance and sweeping. For stealth it is important for individual robots to have an element of randomness, while the emergent behavior of the collective is still predictable. Furthermore, any approach must be robust in the face of robot failures or the addition of new robots. The AP algorithm for surveillance is simple and elegant – agents repel each other, and are also repelled by perimeter and obstacle boundaries, providing uniform coverage of the region. If robots are added/destroyed, they still search the enclosed area, but with more/less virtual "pressure" [6]. An interesting phase transition for this system depends on the value of G. When G is high, particles fill the corridor uniformly, providing excellent on-the-spot coverage. When G is low, particles move toward the corners of the corridor, providing excellent line-of-sight coverage. Depending on whether the physical robots are better at motion or sensing, the G parameter can be tuned appropriately.

Currently we are investigating the more difficult task of "sweeping" a region, while avoiding obstacles. This task consists of starting a swarm of robots at one end of a corridor-like region, and allowing them to travel to the opposite end, providing maximum coverage of the region in minimal time. A goal force causes the robots to traverse the corridor length. As they move, robots must not only avoid obstacles, but they must also sweep in behind the obstacles to minimize holes in the coverage. One obvious tradeoff is the speed at which the robots move down the corridor. If they move quickly, they traverse the corridor in minimal time, but may move too quickly to sweep in behind obstacles. On the other hand, excellent sweeping ability behind obstacles can significantly slow the swarm. What is required is a Pareto optimal solution that balances sweeping ability with traversal speed $v_{traversal}$.

To address this task we modified our standard AP algorithm to employ a more realistic gas model that has Brownian motion and expansion properties [9]. The collective swarm behavior appears as Brownian motion on a small scale, and as a directed bulk movement of the swarm when viewed from a macroscopic perspective. The expansion properties provide across-corridor coverage and the ability to sweep in behind obstacles. An analogy would be the release of a gas from the ceiling of the room that has an atomic weight slightly higher than the normal atmosphere. This gas drifts downward, moving around obstacles, and expanding back to cover the areas under the obstacles.

As mentioned above, speed of movement down the length of the corridor is governed by $v_{traversal}$. However, the expansion properties (across the corridor width) are governed by a temperature parameter T, which determines the *expected* kinetic theory speed [9]:

$$\langle v_{kt} \rangle = \frac{1}{4} \sqrt{\frac{8\pi kT}{m}} \tag{5}$$

where k is Boltzmann's constant. Note that $\langle v_{kt} \rangle$ is an emergent property of the system – each robot can continually change its velocity, based on "virtual" robot/robot, robot/obstacle, and robot/corridor collisions. The net effect is to

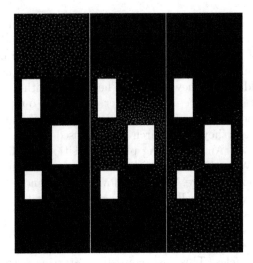

Fig. 4. These three figures depict a sweep of a swarm of robots from the top of a corridor to the bottom.

provide a stochastic component to each robot, while maintaining predictable collective behavior. The resultant velocity of each robot depends on both $v_{traversal}$ and $\langle v_{kt} \rangle$. In other words, although the speed of the swarm is predictable, the individual robot velocities are *not*. This is especially valuable for stealthy surveillance.

Figure 4 illustrates the compromise between traversal speed and the quality of the sweep, providing effective coverage in reasonable time, with the exception of small gaps behind the obstacles. Numerous experiments with different corridors confirm this effectiveness in simulation [10].

3.2   Results with Robots

The current focus of this project is the physical embodiment of AP on a team of robots.

For our experiments, we built seven robots. The "head" of each robot is a sensor platform used to detect other robots in the vicinity. For distance information we use Sharp GP2D12 IR sensors. The head is mounted horizontally on a servo motor. With 180° of servo motion, and two Sharp sensors mounted on opposite sides, the head provides a simple "vision" system with a 360° view. After a 360° scan, object detection is performed. A first derivative filter detects object boundaries, even under conditions of partial occlusion. Width filters are used to ignore narrow and wide objects. This algorithm detects nearby robots, producing a "robot" list that gives the bearing/distance of neighboring robots.

Once sensing and object detection are complete, the AP algorithm computes the virtual force felt by that robot. In response, the robot turns and moves to some position. This "cycle" of sensing, computation and motion continues until we shut down the robots or they run out of power. Figure 5 shows the AP code.

```
void ap() {
    int theta, index = 0;
    float r, F, fx, fy, sum_fx = 0.0, sum_fy = 0.0;
    float vx, vy, delta_vx, delta_vy, delta_x, delta_y;
    vx = vy = 0.0; // Full friction.
    // Row i of robots[][] is for the ith robot located.
    // Column 0/1 has the bearing/range to that robot.
    while ((robots[index][0] != -1)) { // For all neighboring robots do:
        theta = robots[index][0];         // get the robot bearing
        r = robots[index][1];             // and distance.
        if (r > 1.5 * R) F = 0.0; // If robot too far, ignore it.
        else {
            F = G / (r * r);     // Force law, with p = 2.
            if (F > F_MAX) F = F_MAX;
            if (r < R) F = -F; // Has effect of negating force vector.
        }
        fx = F * cos(theta);    // Compute x component of force.
        fy = F * sin(theta);    // Compute y component of force.
        sum_fx += fx;           // Sum x components of force.
        sum_fy += fy;           // Sum y components of force.
        index++;
    }
    delta_vx = delta_T*sum_fx; // Change in x component of velocity.
    delta_vy = delta_T*sum_fy; // Change in y component of velocity.
    vx = vx + delta_vx;        // New x component of velocity.
    vy = vy + delta_vy;        // New y component of velocity.
    delta_x = delta_T*vx;      // Change in x component of position.
    delta_y = delta_T*vy;      // Change in y component of position.
    // Distance to move.
    distance = (int)sqrt(delta_x*delta_x + delta_y*delta_y);
    // Bearing of movement.
    turn = (int)(atan2(delta_y, delta_x));
    // Turn robot in minimal direction.
    if (delta_x < 0.0) turn += 180; }
```

Fig. 5. The main AP code, which takes as input a robot neighbor list (with distance and bearing information) and outputs a vector of motion.

It takes a robot neighbor list as input, and outputs the vector of motion in terms of a turn and distance to move.

To evaluate performance we ran two experiments. The objective of the first experiment was to form a hexagon. The desired distance R between robots was 23 inches. Using the theory, we chose a G of 270 ($p = 2$ and $F_{max} = 1$). The beginning configuration was random. The results were very consistent, producing a good quality hexagon ten times in a row and taking approximately seven cycles on average. A cycle takes about 25 seconds to perform, almost all of which is devoted to the scan of the environment. The AP algorithm itself is extremely fast. A new localization technology that we are developing will be much faster and

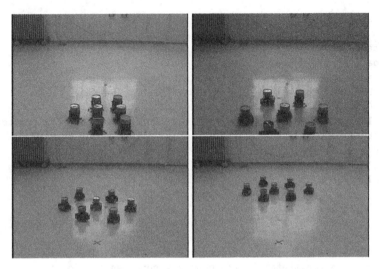

Fig. 6. Seven robots self-organize into a hexagonal formation, which then successfully moves towards a light source (a window, not the reflection of the window). Pictures taken at the initial conditions, at two minutes, fifteen minutes, and thirty minutes.

will replace the current scan technique. For all runs the robots were separated by 20.5 to 26 inches in the final formation, which is only slightly more error than the sensor error.

The objective of the second experiment was to form a hexagon and then move in formation to a goal. For this experiment, we placed four photo-diode light sensors on each robot, one per side. These produced an additional force vector, moving the robots towards a light source (a window). The magnitude of the goal force must be less than $\sqrt{3}G/R^p$ for cohesion of the formation to be maintained [11]. The results, shown in Figure 6, were consistent over ten runs, achieving an accuracy comparable to the formation experiment above. The robots moved about one foot in 13 cycles of the AP algorithm.

In conclusion, the ability to set system parameters from theory greatly enhances our ability to generate correct robotic swarm behavior.

4   Discussion and Outlook

This paper has summarized our framework for distributed control of swarms of robots in sensor networks, based on laws of artificial physics (AP). The motivation for this approach is that natural laws of physics satisfy the requirements of distributed control, namely, self-organization, fault-tolerance, and self-repair. The results have been quite encouraging. We illustrated how AP can self-organize hexagonal and square lattices. Results showing fault-tolerance and self-repair are in [1]. We have also summarized simulation results with dynamic multi-agent behaviors such as obstacle avoidance, surveillance, and sweeping. This paper also outlines several physics-based analyses of AP, focusing on potential energy, force balance equations, and kinetic theory. These analyses provide a predictive technique for setting parameters in the robotic systems. Finally, we have shown AP on a team of seven mobile robots.

We consider AP to be one level of a more complex control architecture. The lowest level controls the movement of the robots. AP is at the next higher level, providing "way points" for the robots, as well as providing simple repair mechanisms. Our goal is to put as much behavior as possible into this level, in order to provide the ability to generate laws governing important parameters. However, levels above AP are needed to solve more complex tasks requiring planning, learning, and global information [12].

5   Future Work

Currently, we are improving our mechanism for robot localization. This work is an extension of Navarro-Serment et. al. [13], using a combination of RF with acoustic pulses to perform trilateration. This will distinguish robots from obstacles in a straightforward fashion, and will be much faster than our current "scan" technique.

We also plan to address the topic of optimality, if needed. It is well understood that *potential field* (PF) approaches can yield sub-optimal solutions. Since AP is similar to PF, similar problems arise with AP. Our experience thus far indicates that this is not a crucial concern, especially for the tasks that we have examined. However, if optimality is required we can apply new results from control theory to design force laws that guarantee optimality [14, 15]. Although oscillations of the formations do not occur, excess movement of the robots can occur due the fact that the force law $F = Gm_im_j/r^p$ is not zero at the desired separation distance R. Current work using an alternative force law based on the Lennard-Jones potential, where the magnitude of the force is negligible at the desired separation, greatly minimizes this motion.

From a theoretical standpoint, we plan to formally analyze other important aspects of AP systems. This analysis will be more dynamic (e.g., kinetic theory) than the analysis presented here. We also intend to expand the repertoire of formations, both static and dynamic. For example, initial progress has been made on developing static and dynamic linear formations. Many other formations are possible within the AP framework. Using evolutionary algorithms to create desired force laws is one intriguing possibility that we are currently investigating. We summarize one preliminary experiment here.

5.1   Evolving Force Laws for Surveillance

This task consists of an environment with areas of forest and non-forest. The goal is for a swarm of MAVs to locate tanks on the ground. Tanks are hidden from the MAVs if they are in the forest. Each MAV has a target sensor with a small field of view for locating the tanks (with probability of detection P_d), and a foliage sensor with a larger field of view for detecting forest below it. The environment is shown in Figure 7 with three MAVs. The smallest circle represents the target sensor. The next largest circle represents the foliage field of view. Each MAV acts as if it were contained in a "bubble" that has a certain radius (depicted as the outer circle). If the bubbles of two MAVs are separated from each other, the MAVs are attracted to one another. If the bubbles overlap, they are repelled. The optimum MAV separation occurs when the bubbles touch.

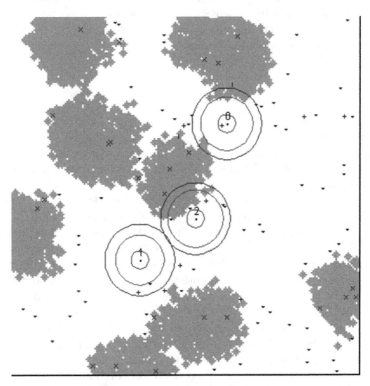

Fig. 7. The surveillance environment, showing areas of forest, three MAVs, and 100 tanks. The triangle represents a tank that has not yet been seen but is visible, the + represents a tank that has been seen and is visible, the × represents a hidden tank that has not been seen, and the | represents a tank that is currently hidden but has been previously seen.

A genetic algorithm is used to find the optimum bubble radius, as well as the G, p, and F_{max} parameters of the force law. We generated one environment with 100 tanks, 25% forest coverage, 20 MAVs, and $P_d = 1$. The GA fitness function was the percentage of tanks seen within 3000 time steps. In this "training" phase the GA was used to evolve a force law, that when used by all MAVs, created perfect coverage (all tanks were seen).

Testing consisted of generating other environments and performing ablation studies. First, nine other environments were created with the same parameter settings. The MAVs had no difficulty finding all tanks. Next, the percentage of foliage was systematically changed from 0% to 90% in increments of 10%. In all cases the MAVs found all tanks. Finally, two ablation studies were performed. First, the number of MAVs was reduced from 20, to 15, to 10, and then to 5. The results were quite robust; performance only suffered when the number of agents was reduced to 5. Second, we also lowered the probability of detection P_d from 1.0, to 0.75, to 0.5, and then to 0.25. Again, the results were quite robust, showing negligible performance drops (see Figure 8).

In summary, the results are extremely promising. Using only one training environment, the GA evolved a force law that showed surprising generality over changes in the environment, the number of MAVs, and the quality of the target detection sensor.

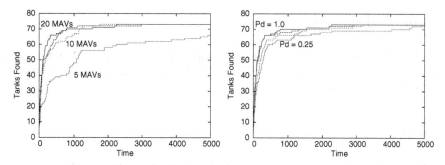

Fig. 8. The number of tanks found as the number of MAVs is reduced (left graph). The number of tanks found as the probability of detection (P_d) of the target sensor is reduced (right graph). The number of visible tanks is 73.

6 Related Work

Most of the swarm literature can be subdivided into *swarm intelligence, behavior-based, rule-based, control-theoretic* and *physics-based* techniques. Swarm intelligence techniques are ethologically motivated and have had excellent success with foraging, task allocation, and division of labor problems [16]. In Beni et. al. [17, 18], a swarm distribution is determined via a system of linear equations describing difference equations with periodic boundary conditions. Behavior-based approaches [19–22] are also very popular. They derive vector information in a fashion similar to AP. Furthermore, particular behaviors such as "aggregation" and "dispersion" are similar to the attractive and repulsive forces in AP. Both behavior-based and rule-based (e.g., [23]) systems have proved quite successful in demonstrating a variety of behaviors in a heuristic manner. Behavior-based and rule-based techniques do not make use of potential fields or forces. Instead, they deal directly with velocity vectors and heuristics for changing those vectors (although the term "potential field" is often used in the behavior-based literature, it generally refers to a field that differs from the strict Newtonian physics definition). Control-theoretic approaches have also been applied effectively [14]. Our approach does not make the assumption of having leaders and followers [24].

One of the earliest physics-based techniques is the potential fields (PF) approach (e.g., [8]). Most of the PF literature deals with a small number of robots (typically just one) that navigate through a field of obstacles to get to a target location. The environment, rather than the agents, exert forces. Obstacles exert repulsive forces, while goals exert attractive forces. Recently, Howard et al. [2] and Vail and Veloso [25] extended PF to include inter-agent repulsive forces – for the purpose of achieving coverage. Although this work was developed independently of AP, it affirms the feasibility of a physics force-based approach. The *social potential fields* [26] framework by Reif and Wang is highly related to AP, in that they rely on a force-law simulation similar to our own. We plan to merge their approach with ours.

Acknowledgments

The surveillance task mentioned in this paper is supported by DARPA grant #DODARMY41700. Thanks to Vaibhav Mutha for an early version of the obstacle avoidance code.

References

1. Spears, W., Gordon, D.: Using artificial physics to control agents. In: IEEE International Conference on Information, Intelligence, and Systems, Washington, DC (1999) 281–288
2. Howard, A., Matarić, M., Sukhatme, G.: Mobile sensor network deployment using potential fields: A distributed, scalable solution to the area coverage problem. In: Sixth International Symposium on Distributed Autonomous Robotics Systems, Fukuoka, Japan, ACM (2002) 299–308
3. Gordon-Spears, D., Spears, W.: Analysis of a phase transition in a physics-based multiagent system. In Hinchey, M., Rash, J., Truszkowski, W., Rouff, C., Gordon-Spears, D., eds.: Lecture Notes in Computer Science. Volume 2699., Greenbelt, MD, Springer-Verlag (2003) 193–207
4. Kellogg, J., Bovais, C., Foch, R., McFarlane, H., Sullivan, C., Dahlburg, J., Gardner, J., Ramamurti, R., Gordon-Spears, D., Hartley, R., Kamgar-Parsi, B., Pipitone, F., Spears, W., Sciambi, A., Srull, D.: The NRL micro tactical expendable (MITE) air vehicle. The Aeronautical Journal **106** (2002) 431–441
5. Zarzhitsky, D., Spears, D., Thayer, D., Spears, W.: Agent-based chemical plume tracing using fluid dynamics. In Hinchey, M., Rash, J., Truszkowski, W., Rouff, C., eds.: Formal Approaches to Agent-Based Systems, Greenbelt, MD, Springer-Verlag (2005)
6. Spears, W., Spears, D., Hamann, J., Heil, R.: Distributed, physics-based control of swarms of vehicles. Autonomous Robots **17** (2004)
7. Spears, W., Spears, D.: A formal analysis of potential energy in a multiagent system. In Hinchey, M., Rash, J., Truszkowski, W., Rouff, C., eds.: Formal Approaches to Agent-Based Systems, Greenbelt, MD, Springer-Verlag (2005)
8. Khatib, O.: Real-time obstacle avoidance for manipulators and mobile robots. International Journal of Robotics Research **5** (1986) 90–98

9. Kerr, W., Spears, D., Spears, W., Thayer, D.: Two formal fluids models for multiagent sweeping and obstacle avoidance. In Hinchey, M., Rash, J., Truszkowski, W., Rouff, C., eds.: Formal Approaches to Agent-Based Systems, Greenbelt, MD, Springer-Verlag (2005)

10. Kerr, W., Spears, D., Spears, W., Thayer, D.: Swarm coverage through a partially obstructed corridor. (in preparation)

11. Spears, W., Heil, R., Spears, D., Zarzhitsky, D.: Physicomimetics for mobile robot formations. In: International Conference on Autonomous Agents and Multi Agent Systems. (2004)

12. Gordon, D., Spears, W., Sokolsky, O., Lee, I.: Distributed spatial control, global monitoring and steering of mobile physical agents. In: IEEE International Conference on Information, Intelligence, and Systems, Washington, DC (1999) 681–688

13. L. Navarro-Serment, L., Paredis, C., Khosla, P.: A beacon system for the localization of distributed robotic teams. In: International Conference on Field and Service Robots, Pittsburgh, PA (1999) 232–237

14. Fax, J., Murray, R.: Information flow and cooperative control of vehicle formations. In: IFAC World Congress, Barcelona, Spain (2002)

15. Olfati-Saber, R., Murray, R.: Distributed cooperative control of multiple vehicle formations using structural potential functions. In: IFAC World Congress, Barcelona, Spain (2002)

16. Bonabeau, E., Dorigo, M., Theraulaz, G.: Swarm Intelligence: From Natural to Artificial Systems. Oxford University Press, Santa Fe Institute Studies in the Sciences of Complexity, Oxford, NY (1999)

17. Beni., G., Hackwood, S.: Stationary waves in cyclic swarms. Intelligent Control (1992) 234–242

18. Beni, G., Wang, J.: Swarm intelligence. In: Proceedings of the Seventh Annual Meeting of the Robotics Society of Japan, Tokyo, Japan (1989) 425–428

19. Balch, T., Arkin, R.: Behavior-based formation control for multi-robot teams. In: IEEE Transactions on Robotics and Automata. Volume 14. (1998) 1–15

20. Balch, T., Hybinette, M.: Social potentials for scalable multirobot formations. In: IEEE Transactions on Robotics and Automata. (2000)

21. Matarić, M.: Designing and understanding adaptive group behavior. Technical report, CS Dept, Brandeis Univ. (1995)

22. Payton, D., Daily, M., Hoff, B., Howard, M., Lee, C.: Pheromone robotics. In: SPIE Symposium on Intelligence Systems and Manufacturing, Boston, MA (2000)

23. Wu, A., Schultz, A., Agah, A.: Evolving control for distributed micro air vehicles. In: IEEE Conference on Computational Intelligence in Robotics and Automation, Belgium (1999) 174–179

24. Desai, J., Ostrowski, J., Kumar, V.: Modeling and control of formations of nonholonomic mobile robots. IEEE Transactions on Robotics and Automation **17** (2001) 905–908

25. Vail, D., Veloso, M.: Multi-robot dynamic role assignment and coordination through shared potential fields. In Schultz, A., Parker, L., Schneider, F., eds.: Multi-Robot Systems, Hingham, MA, Kluwer (2003) 87–98

26. Reif, J., Wang, H.: Social potential fields: A distributed behavioral control for autonomous robots. In: Robotics and Autonomous Systems. Volume 27 (3). (1999) 171–194

Lattice Formation
in Mobile Autonomous Sensor Arrays

Eric Martinson[1] and David Payton[2]

[1] Georgia Institute of Technology, Atlanta GA 30332, USA
[2] HRL Laboratories, LLC 3011 Malibu Canyon Rd, Malibu CA 90265, USA

Abstract. The purpose of this work is to enable an array of mobile sensors to autonomously arrange themselves into a regularly spaced lattice formation such that they may collectively be used as an effective phased-array sensor. Existing approaches to this problem encounter issues with local minima which allow the formation of lattice patterns that are locally regular but have discontinuities or defects that would be undesirable in a narrow-band beamforming application. By exploiting a common reference orientation, such as might be obtained from a magnetic compass, we have been able to create control laws that operate on orthogonal axes and thereby minimize the occurrence of local minima. The result is that we can now form lattice patterns with greater uniformity over extended distances, with significantly less energy or movement per robot. Despite the need for a shared directional reference, our methods are also robust to significant error in the reference readings.

1 Introduction

Distributed sensor arrays have featured prominently in recent years. With the decreasing sensor prices, and the availability of inexpensive wireless networking hardware, many envision massively parallel sensor arrays distributed over large areas, but a significant impediment to this vision is how to distribute the sensors. Some researchers have proposed simply dropping them from airplanes, or other airborne vehicles, letting the sensors lay wherever they land [1]. Still others have placed the sensors on robot platforms and used control strategies to optimize coverage area by a team of mobile robots [2]. Either strategy results in an irregular sensor distribution. However, if the incoming signal properties are known, then a regular, or narrow band, sensor configuration may improve the array's global performance. In this work, we propose a control strategy for constructing such a regular array using a team of mobile robots with only local information.

A regular pattern, also called regular planar tiling in graphics, is a pattern constructed of only one type of regular polygon. Only triangles, squares and hexagons can be used to construct a regular pattern. For our sensor array, we focused on square and/or rectangular arrays. This is because receivers aligned in space can be used to accurately reconstruct wavelengths related to the physical spacing. If a user can specify the properties of the incoming signal, then a dynamic array could configure itself to better recover the signal.

E. Şahin and W.M. Spears (Eds.): Swarm Robotic WS 2004, LNCS 3342, pp. 98–111, 2005.
© Springer-Verlag Berlin Heidelberg 2005

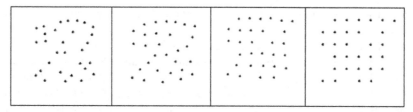

Fig. 1. Starting from a random initial position (left) a regularly spaced square array is formed (right).

A square array can be decomposed into two perpendicular sets of equally spaced lines. Similarly, the problem of moving initially randomly spaced robots into a regular pattern can be broken into two parts, or behaviors. Start by specifying the desired orientation of one set of lines (the primary axis). Then a group of mobile robots can use the detected positions of their neighbors and an onboard compass to autonomously construct a formation consisting of a set of parallel lines in the direction of the primary axis. Let us call this a primary axis line force. To form a rectangular array, a secondary axis line force is applied in the perpendicular direction. Figure 1 demonstrates a rectangular array being created from an initially random configuration.

When combining forces in reactive systems, most local minima occur due to two or more behaviors having sometimes opposing goals. In the array formation problem, this type of local minima can be resolved by projecting each line force behavior only into a single perpendicular dimension. Thus, behaviors operating in perpendicular dimensions have no direct interaction with each other. Platt et. al. [3] called this casting control laws into each other's null-spaces, and demonstrated that by doing so, the conflicts between different objectives can be minimized. By minimizing such conflicts in the array-formation problem, we demonstrate how arrays can be formed faster and with less energy.

2   Related Work

Several works in recent years have looked at the problem of pattern formation using a group of mobile robots. Balch and Hybinette [4] demonstrated how some patterns do not require much information to maintain. Robots can hold a symmetric formation such as a diamond, line, or squares by generating an attraction force to the nearest recognized location within the formation. Fredslund and Mataric [5] extended this work by not only maintaining but constructing formations from initially random positions, using small numbers of robots. With unique recognizable ID tags on each robot, they can arrange themselves into concave formations about a leader.

Suzuki and Yamashita [6] looked at using groups of robots starting in initially random positions, and forming specific large formations. The types of formations constructed vary, as their exact shapes and positions are specified by an external user. Robots first use movement to align their X-Y coordinate systems then they can move to fill in vacant positions in the geometric design. Flocchini et. al. [7]

extended the algorithm to use a compass instead of manually aligning coordinate systems.

Spears and Spears [8] at the University of Wyoming constructed arrays of robots, from a behavioral perspective, specifically using a local artificial gravity force to build regular formations with consistent internal structure. Robots are either repulsed or attracted to their neighbors by a gravity force $F=G/R^2$, where the force is negative if $R < threshold$. The threshold variable is the desired spacing between robots. If all robots try to put themselves evenly between all neighbors, they would form a triangular lattice. The work also was extended to square lattices. Robots were allowed to choose virtual spins that could be recognized by their neighbors. Opposite spins applied different forces on each other than similar spins, forming a square lattice with similar spins along the diagonals.

The Artificial Physics method produces a large number of local minima, especially those of two robots vying for the same position. One reason is that robots only use purely local information when calculating forces, discarding the effects of robots greater than 1.5*R away from the robot. A second reason is that that the sum of the forces applied by surrounding robots on a robot in the middle of the array, serve to lock a robot in position, making it unable to move away from a bad configuration. At least two solutions were proposed. The first was to add noise to robots in a bad location, which helps remove global errors from the array but leaves a number of local minima. A further solution was suggested that gives each robot a unique ID and then allow the robots to perform a sorting application, but this requires a pre-specified position for each robot in the array.

3   Algorithm

Like the artificial physics model, this work uses simple locally applied behaviors to construct regular square lattices. Our methods are based on the idea of creating an ordered set of separable controllers such that subordinate controllers operate in the null-space of their superior controllers. The key to following the null-space criterion is to create a separation of control laws such that a subordinate controller cannot produce any action that moves against the objective functions of its superior controllers. We were able to accomplish this by establishing controllers that operate on orthogonal axes. Specifically, a primary control law operates so as to establish parallel lines of robots with an appropriate spacing between lines. Then, a secondary controller operates to establish proper spacing along each line. We found that this secondary controller can actually be the same line-forming controller as the primary controller, since its actions are limited to an axis orthogonal to the primary controller.

In addition to the array formation behaviors, an avoid obstacles behavior is utilized to avoid contact between robots or with environmental obstacles.

3.1   Line Force Behavior

The basic concept behind the line-force behavior is that each robot places an imaginary array of parallel lines over itself, oriented along the direction of a

Fig. 2. Array lines are centered about the target robot (solid). Other robots generate forces on the target robot relative to their distance from the array lines.

user-specified axis as shown in Figure 2. An onboard compass maintains the direction of the array axis relative to the robot's local reference frame. Force vectors are then generated for each detected robot based on its distance to the nearest line of the imaginary array. Notice that the resulting forces in this figure are all perpendicular to the specified axis. The sum of these force vectors is then determined, ignoring the moment about the center, yielding a net force vector perpendicular to the specified axis. Below are the series of steps taken to compute the line force.

1. Generate a list of all other team members and classify which line each neighboring robot should be located on. I.e. if they are on the same line as the target robot (the robot running the line force behavior), then they are on line 0. If on an immediately adjacent line, then they are on line 1.
   - β = desired spacing between parallel lines [meters]
   - α = current heading minus desired alignment [radians]
   - V_i = vector towards the ith robot $[V_i^\theta, V_i^\rho]$
   - $d\theta_i = V_i^\theta - \alpha$

$$whichline = round(\frac{V_i^\rho \sin(d\theta_i)}{\beta})$$

2. If the detected robot is too close to the target, generate a repelling vector from that robot, and otherwise generate an attractive vector toward that robot.

$$dist_i = |\frac{whichline_i * \beta}{\sin(d\theta_i)}|$$

3. Sum the resulting vectors.

$$vector\_output = \sum(\frac{V_i^\rho - dist_i}{dist_i}, V_i^\theta)$$

4. Return only the component of $vector\_output$ perpendicular to α.

The Line-Force behavior still suffers from local minima when multiple robots are vying for the same position on the lines. This can result either in contention between two robots, or the formation of new lines with incorrect spacing. Both happen more frequently when robots are initialized closer together. The solution is to increase the strength of the avoid obstacles force used in the controller, which separates the robots out to approximately the desired spacing.

3.2   Hypothesis Generation

A significant variant to the basic line-force method has been developed by assuming that array lines may not be centered on the target robot, but instead that neighboring robots might already form a suitable set of lines and the target robot must move onto the nearest of those lines. Instead of building vectors that would place neighboring robots on the line running through the target, we first identify the "best" array that fits the local neighbors, and then drive the target robot toward that array. The trick now is determining the target robot's offset to that "best" array.

The hypothesis generation (HypGen) method solves this problem by treating each neighbor as a member of a hypothetical set of lines, or hypothesis. Moving the target robot into formation is just a vector to the nearest parallel line in the hypothesis. Since every vector is in the same direction (with positive/negative magnitudes), each hypothesis can actually be represented as a single real magnitude. To choose the "best" hypothesis, we treat each magnitude as the center of a Gaussian distribution with unit standard deviation. If we were to sum the Gaussians, then the point with the highest sum should point to the average magnitude between the hypotheses. Instead, we want the robot to choose just one hypothesis and move. To do that, we first score each hypothesis by summing up all of the Gaussians at that magnitude and choose the hypothesis with the highest score. This will be the hypothesis we use for getting the robot into the desired formation.

The second step in Hypothesis-Generation is to generate a force from the target robot to the nearest hypothetical line. The final step is to generate an adjustment force that indicates how the selected hypothesis should be adjusted to better fit with the remaining robots. This second force is computed using the standard line-force algorithm described in the previous section. The two forces are then summed together as the output of the HypGen behavior. This drives the target robot toward the adjusted line. When all robots perform this behavior, they line up along the axis determined by the compass.

1. Generate a hypothesis for every detected neighboring robot. A hypothesis is represented by a magnitude along the line perpendicular to the hypothetical lines.
   - H_i = hypothesis, given V_i

$$l_i = round(\frac{V_i^\rho \sin(d\theta_i)}{\beta})$$
$$H_i = V_i^\rho \sin(d\theta_i) - l_i * \beta$$

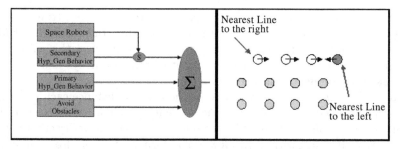

Fig. 3. (left) Behavioral controller for robots using the HypGen behaviors. (right) A type of local minima which can occur when using HypGen.

2. Score each hypothesis. Let η_i be a normal distribution centered at H_i with $\sigma = 1$. Then $\eta_i(x)$ is normal distribution η_i sampled at x.

$$score_i = \sum_{k-1}^{n} \eta_k(H_i)$$

3. Choose the hypothesis with highest score (H_S)
4. Generate a vector towards the chosen hypothesis (V_H)
5. Run the normal lineForce algorithm, adjusting $whichline_i$ as follows, adding the result of the normal LineForce behavior to V_H

$$whichline_i = round(\frac{V_i^\rho \sin(d\theta_i) - H_S}{\beta})$$

For the best performance in constructing a regular array, an additional force is needed to first separate the robots along the secondary axis. Unlike the Line-Force behavior, the force is needed only along the secondary axis and is not used all of the time. The controller for this design can be seen in Figure 3(left). A simple threshold on the magnitude of the space robots force determines when the secondary HypGen behavior is suppressed.

4   Comparative Performance

In this section, we compare a number of array construction algorithms, including our own and the artificial physics method. All of the methods tested assumed a set of 30 robots, with a sensor range of 1.75 times the desired spacing between the robots. For initial placement, 100 different starting positions were created randomly. Tests were run in simulation, allowing 5000 time-steps for each starting position using the Team-Bots simulation environment. Results were then averaged over all starting positions.

4.1   Performance Metrics

Two performance metrics were used to evaluate the most important aspects of robotic array construction: resulting global formation error, and average energy consumption. The global formation error was determined by fitting a perfect grid to the positions of the robots in the last time step, then using Least Mean Squares to determine the error in the grid. We normalized this measure by averaging least mean squares error for a set of random arrays and expressing errors as a percentage of this average.

Energy consumption was evaluated as the average distance each robot traveled over the fixed time period of the simulation. This metric is critical for performance, because movement by the sensor robots equates directly to energy consumption. If an algorithm with low global formation error also requires a lot of movement, then it is not economically feasible to implement on real robots.

4.2   Methods Tested

To evaluate the effectiveness of the Line-Force and Hypothesis-Generation algorithms, we compared them to a variety of other array formation methods. This includes a simple dispersion model using an avoidance behavior, a behavior based implementation of the artificial physics model [8], and a basic spring model for array formation. For the spring model in this test, virtual springs are attached to the 4 neighboring robots that are closest to the locations that would be found in an ideal square lattice.

Because none of these alternative methods incorporate any concept of steering the array, we assumed that orienting the array to the user's specifications would have to be done after the array construction was completed. Furthermore, we evaluated the performance without re-orienting the array so as not to introduce any additional error.

None of the methods tested could remove all local minima from the resulting array. For this reason, we also include some additional strategies for removing them. The simplest is to introduce a weak noise behavior to the summation. A better solution is to add a noise vector whose magnitude is dependent upon the ratio of the magnitude of component force vectors and the sum of those vectors at each local node. Nodes where this ratio is high are usually at the center of a defect. Causing these nodes to include more random movement typically helps remove the defect. We call this strategy "local annealing."

The Hypothesis-Generation behaviors also result in a particular type of local minima, seen in Figure 3(right). Robots on the same line are in contention for the same spot in the array, skewing the entire line. Out of 100 tests, the Hypothesis-Generation behavior with no noise resulted in 24 out of place lines. A fix for this solution was to use a variant on the spin idea introduced in the Artificial Physics method. After 1000 time-steps, robots probabilistically change their spin state if robots on the same line are of different spins or if robots on neighboring lines are the same spin. This causes most robots on the same line to have the same spin state and robots on alternating lines to have opposite spin states. Depending on the spin state, a weak vector forward or backward along the primary axis is added to the summation controller. If no error exists, then the force is weak enough that the robots do not move. However, if an error in the array does exist, then this technique adds noise in the vicinity of the error and the line corrects itself.

4.3   Results

The Line-Force behaviors produced a similar amount of formation error as the Artificial Physics method, with as much as 104 times less distance moved by each robot (see Figure 4). In practice, a simple threshold could be used to reduce the amount of movement using artificial physics, but it might also increase the average formation error. In comparison, the line-force method required only 3 times as much movement on average as the basic dispersion method. Furthermore, by adding a small noise vector to the Line-Force controller we could reduce the formation error to 7% of random, better than springs with local annealing, which had the lowest formation error of any non-LineFormation based method.

Hypothesis-Generation methods showed the greatest ability to reduce formation error. Although the basic HypGen behavior required 10 times as much

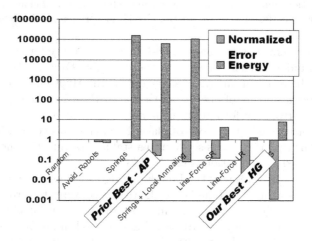

Fig. 4. Comparative performance between different methods. The prior best method by Spears and Gordon, is displayed in the center, while our best, Hypothesis Generation, is on the far right. The line formation methods in general required orders of magnitude less energy to form arrays with similar or less formation error.

Method	Formation Error (% of Random)	Energy (Distance Moved)
Random	100	-
Avoidance Force(Dispersion)	79	0.76
Springs	77	1.6x105
Springs with Local Annealing	9	1.1x105
Artificial Physics	18	6.3x104
Artificial Physics with Noise	15	6.1x104
Line-Force	19	2.6
Line-Force with Noise	7	31.61
Line-Force with Extended Range	6	1.3
Hypothesis-Generation	3	24.53

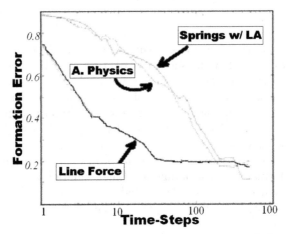

Fig. 5. Formation Error in the array over time. The LineForce behavior converges to a stable array much faster than either the physics or springs based methods.

movement on average as the basic Line-Force, the average formation error was only 3% of random, much better than the best Line-Force controller. Furthermore, all of the errors in arrays constructed by the HypGen controller were of the same type, a shifting of one line of the array. By using the spin-flip method to repair this error, the formation error nearly goes to zero. Out of 100 tests, only one robot in one test was out of place. Removing this type of local minima early on means that the robots settle into a stable array quickly and the average distance required for formation is cut by 1/3.

Figure 5 demonstrates why the Line-Force algorithm uses so much less movement to form the array. The Line-Force algorithms converge toward the minimum much faster than either the springs method, or the artificial physics method. While the alternative methods are working out local minima through a lot of local movement, the line-force methods move quickly into formation in the beginning and stop.

5   Sensor Noise

The Line-Force and Hypothesis Generation algorithms both depend on the reliability of two sensors for success. The first sensor is a compass, which allows each robot to align with a user-specified axis. The second sensor is a relative localization sensor, for finding other robots in the domain. The validity of any error results depends heavily on the sensitivity of these algorithms to noise in this sensor data. The following set of tests was designed to explore the robustness of the algorithms with that purpose in mind.

All of the tests in this section were performed with 30 simulated robots using just the Line-Force algorithm. The robots had 2.75 unit sensor range, where 1 unit is the desired spacing between robots in formation. Unless otherwise stated, each sample point is the mean result over 10 different initial configurations. Finally, all graphs were smoothed with an averaging filter of window size 3.

5.1   Compass Error

Two types of noise in the compass measurements were explored: gaussian noise in the readings, and delayed measurements due to time lag. Although most noise in robot-mounted compass readings are due to environmental effects, such as the robot itself, or large pieces of nearby metal, these types of errors are systematic and can often be corrected or filtered. Our modeling noise as gaussian lets us explore how the system reacts to unpredictable compass noise. Furthermore, a common solution for environmental noise is to add large window filters which add significant time-delay to the system; a second type of noise that we explore.

The change in formation error vs compass error is seen in Figure 6(top). In both charts, the formation error actually improves with small amounts of noise, as a little randomness helps the system work out remaining local minima. In the case of gaussian noise, the system actually improves up to a standard deviation of 0.1 radians. With time lag, this distributed system is very resilient. It handles up to 6 time-steps of time lag before performance significantly degrades.

5.2   Localization Error

Accurate tracking of neighboring robots is a tough problem, and the resulting error is highly dependent on the sensors used. To explore the relative localization problem, we split the problem into two aspects: distance and angle. Figure 6 shows the change in formation error for each of these parts. Given that

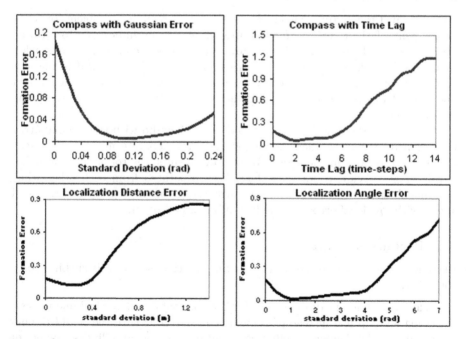

Fig. 6. [Top]Formation Error vs. Compass error, assuming gaussian noise(left) and time lag(right). [Bottom]Formation Error vs Localization Error.

the desired radius between robots was 2 meters, the distributed system could handle a standard deviation of roughly 0.4 meters in distance error before the formation error dramatically increased. This being 20% of the desired distance between robots, it demonstrates the general robustness of the distributed system as robots use each other for proper alignment. With angular error, the system could handle up to 4 radians in standard deviation before seeing the same performance degradation.

All of these tests assume ideal performance from the other sensor, and except for time lag, also assume error centered around the true value. While the magnitude of the tolerance observed in simulation is not likely to be the same in the real implementation, these tests indicate that the system can handle reasonable amounts of error in its sensors. Furthermore, these tests provide guidelines for a real implementation by illustrating how strongly different forms of error alter array performance.

6   Beyond Square Arrays

In this section we focus on how to extend the basic Line-Force algorithm to other types of arrays. We build arrays in the presence of environmental obstacles, construct more general rectangular arrays, and vary the intersecting angle between forces to build skewed arrays.

6.1   Environmental Obstacles

Obstacles in the environment are going to always remain a problem for array deployment. If there are too many obstacles, it will be impossible to form an array with any degree of regularity. However, if there are only a few obstacles, then the robots should be able to construct a regular array without deformations around the obstacle. Figure 7 (left) is an example of the robots using the straight line force algorithm with an avoid obstacles behavior to build an array around the obstacles.

Although the robots start close together, as they did with the original array formation tests, the obstacles force the robots to separate more as they seek acceptable positions in the array. For the best results, the robots need a higher sensor range to view robots that have been separated from each other while avoiding obstacles. With a low sensor range, the robots may create several small arrays with low local error, but high error across all robots.

6.2   Rectangular Arrays

Rectangular arrays can be created by making two changes to the basic Line-Force controller:

- Select two different desired radii (β) for horizontal and vertical line forces.
- Using an elliptical instead of circular repulsion zone with the Avoid Robots primitive. We defined an elliptical repulsion zone as an elliptical sphere of influence passed into the $avoid - static - obstacle$ primitive, defined in [9].

Depending on the angle α at which each detected robot was located relative to the primary axis, an elliptical sphere of influence was defined as:

$$sphere\_of\_influence = \sqrt{\left(\frac{S_x^2}{\cos^2(\alpha)} + \frac{S_y^2}{sin^2(\alpha)}\right)}$$

Where S_x is the maximum sphere of influence along the primary axis, and S_y is the maximum sphere of influence along the secondary axis. For the infinite repulsion zone, we maintained a spherical distance about the center of the robot.

Figure 7(Right) demonstrates a rectangular array with some skew.

6.3 Skewed Arrays

Skewed arrays are created by altering the angle at which the vertical and horizontal line forces operate. Instead of using two orthogonal line forces, one line force still operates along the desired compass angle, while the second operates along a direction greater or less than 90°. For small delta, the two lines will still form regular planar arrays. Figure 7(Right) demonstrates a skewed rectangular array where the lines intersect at 75°.

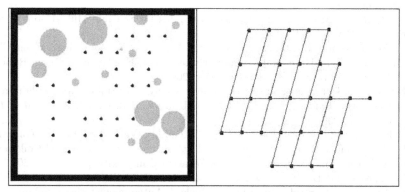

Fig. 7. (Left)The robots form a regular grid around the obstacles in the environment. (Right) Changing the distances between line forces creates rectangular arrays. Changing the angle of intersection creates a skew in the array. The lines are superimposed on the array to demonstrate the skew.

7   Conclusion

In this paper a distributed algorithm for the formation of regular spaced square arrays was developed and compared against alternative approaches. It was demonstrated that our technique using orthogonal line formation forces required orders of magnitude less movement to form arrays with similar formation error.

Furthermore, using the Hypothesis Generation methods, we could reduce the formation error to 0.1% of random, with a small increase in average movement.

We further demonstrated that the line force methods are robust in the presence of sensor noise. Testing multiple types of compass and relative formation error, we demonstrated ranges of sensor noise over which the formation error remains low. This will help in a hardware implementation when it becomes necessary to select particular sensors that meet the requirements for the algorithm.

Finally, we demonstrated that the line force methods are extendable to arrays other than regular square arrays. Arrays can be formed in the presence of, and around, environmental obstacles. Line forces can also be used to build rectangular arrays by varying the distances between vertical vs. horizontal forces, and skewed arrays by varying the angle at which the forces intersect. In general, line forces provide a useful set of methods for constructing a variety of arrays with a minimum of local minima.

References

1. P. Gorman, "The Defense of Fombler's Ford", part of the DARPA Command Post of the Future
2. L. Parker and B. Kannan and X. Fu and Y. Tang, "Heterogeneous Mobile Sensor Net Deployment Using Robot Herding and Line-of-Sight Formations," IROS, 2003
3. R. Platt and A. Fagg and R. Grupen, "Nullspace Composition of Control Lays for Grasping," IROS, 2002
4. T. Balch and M. Hybinette, "Social Potentials for Scalable Multi-Robot Formations," ICRA, p. 73–80, 2000
5. J. Fredslund and M. Mataric, "A General Algorithm for Robot Formations Using Local Sensing and Minimal Communication," in IEEE Transactions on Robotics and Automation, vol. 18, number 5, Oct. 2002
6. I. Suzuki and M. Yamashita, "Distributed Anonymous Mobile Robots: Formation of Geometric Patterns," in SIAM Journal on Computing, vol. 28, number 4, p. 1347–1363, 1999
7. P. Flocchini and G. Prencipe and N. Santora and P. Widmayer, "Pattern Formation by Autonomous Robots Without Chirality," in proc. of International Colloquium on Structural Information and Communication Complexity, p. 147–162, 2001
8. W. Spears and D. Spears and J. Hamann and R. Heil (in press). "Distributed, Physics-Based Control of Swarms of Vehicles," Autonomous Robots, Volume 17(2–3), August 2004.
9. R.C. Arkin. **Behavior-Based Robotics**. The MIT Press. Cambridge, MA. 1998

Appendix: Artificial Physics Implementation

Our implementation of the Artificial Physics model was created to fit into the same robot controller as the Line-Force methods. The AP behavior outputs a force vector which is weighted and summed with the vector from an avoid obstacle behavior. The steps to create the force vector are outlined below.

1. Generate a list of all other team members, and divide them into categories: same spin, or opposite spin.
2. For all detected robots (V_i) of an opposite spin from the target robot, calculate the force vector (A_i) exerted on the target. The angle remains the same for all robots ($A_i^\theta = V_i^\theta$). Sum the resulting the forces.

$$A_i^\rho = \begin{cases} \frac{G}{\left(V_i^\rho\right)^2}, & if\ V_i^\rho \geq \beta \\ \frac{-G}{\left(V_i^\rho\right)^2}, & V_i^\rho < \beta \end{cases}$$

$$F_{opposite} = \sum_{i=1} A_i$$

G is a gravitational constant set at initialization.

3. For all detected robots (V_i) with the same spin as the target robot, calculate the magnitude of the force vector (B_i) exerted on the target. The angle remains the same for all robots ($B_i^\theta = V_i^\theta$). Sum the resulting forces.

$$B_i^\rho = \begin{cases} \frac{2*G}{\left(V_i^\rho\right)^2}, & if\ \frac{V_i^\rho}{\sqrt{2}} \geq \beta \\ \frac{-2*G}{\left(V_i^\rho\right)^2}, & \frac{V_i^\rho}{\sqrt{2}} < \beta \end{cases}$$

$$F_{same} = \sum_{i=1} B_i$$

4. Sum the two vector forces ($F_{output} = F_{same} + F_{opposite}$).
5. Switch spins with some small probabability (1%) if any robots of the same spin have $V_i^\rho < \beta$.

It is worth noting that in our implementation, we interpreted the 'force' vector as a velocity command whereas in the standard Artificial Physics method, this vector is treated as an acceleration command.

Swarming Behavior
Using Probabilistic Roadmap Techniques

O. Burçhan Bayazıt[1], Jyh-Ming Lien[2], and Nancy M. Amato[2]

[1] Washington University, St. Louis, MO 63130, USA
bayazit@wustl.edu
[2] Texas A&M University, College Station, TX 77843, USA
{neilien,amato}@cs.tamu.edu

Abstract. While techniques exist for simulating swarming behaviors, these methods usually provide only simplistic navigation and planning capabilities. In this review, we explore the benefits of integrating roadmap-based path planning methods with flocking techniques to achieve different behaviors. We show how group behaviors such as exploring can be facilitated by using dynamic roadmaps (e.g., modifying edge weights) as an implicit means of communication between flock members. Extending ideas from cognitive modeling, we embed behavior rules in individual flock members and in the roadmap. These behavior rules enable the flock members to modify their actions based on their current location and state. We propose new techniques for several distinct group behaviors: homing, exploring (covering and goal searching), passing through narrow areas and shepherding. We present results that show that our methods provide significant improvement over methods that utilize purely local knowledge and moreover, that we achieve performance approaching that which could be obtained by an ideal method that has complete global knowledge. Animations of these behaviors can be viewed on our webpages.

1 Vision

Coordinating the movement of a swarm of robots plays an important role in robotics. Although techniques to achieve coordinated movements have attracted the attention of many researchers, most research has focused on techniques for modeling individual behaviors of flock members inspired by Reynolds' *boids* [1]. Boids exhibit so-called *emergent behavior* in which characters only react to immediate events. Although, they can be coupled with simple methods for guiding global flock movement [2], existing methods have difficulty if complex navigation is required, such as in cities, through crowded rooms, or over rough terrain. In contrast, path planning algorithms developed in the robotics community are capable of navigation in complex environments [3]. In particular we note the *roadmap*-based methods which construct, usually during preprocessing, a network of representative feasible paths in the environment. While roadmap methods can efficiently support complex navigation, they have generally not been customized to support coordinated group behavior.

E. Şahin and W.M. Spears (Eds.): Swarm Robotic WS 2004, LNCS 3342, pp. 112–125, 2005.
© Springer-Verlag Berlin Heidelberg 2005

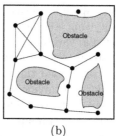

(a)   (b)

Fig. 1. Roadmaps in navigation: (a) global navigation information can assist coordinated group behaviors, such as flocking or mine sweeping (shown here), in complex environments, (b) a PRM roadmap (C-space).

In this review, we present the benefits of integrating flocking techniques with roadmap-based path planning methods to achieve different swarming behaviors. The details of our approach including the related work can be found in [4–7]. We find that the global navigation information provided by the roadmaps can also be exploited to support more sophisticated group behaviors than possible using traditional (local) flocking methods. In particular, we consider several different behaviors: homing, goal searching, covering, passing through narrow passages and shepherding. Our new techniques can be applied to an entire flock, to individual flock members, or to an external agent that may influence the flock (e.g., a sheep dog).

2   The Swarm Robotic Environment/Methodology

In this section, we briefly describe probabilistic roadmap techniques and then discuss how these techniques can be used for swarming behaviors.

2.1   Probabilistic Roadmap Methods and Flocking Systems

Given a description of the environment and a movable object (the 'robot'), the motion planning problem is to find a feasible path that takes the movable object from a given start to a given goal configuration [3]. Since there is strong evidence that any complete planner (one that is guaranteed to find a solution, or determine that none exists) requires time exponential in the number of degrees of freedom (DOF) of the movable object [3], attention has focused on randomized or probabilistic methods.

As mentioned in Section 1, our approach utilizes a roadmap encoding representative feasible paths in the environment. While noting that our techniques could use any roadmap, our current implementation is based on the probabilistic roadmap (PRM) approach to motion planning [8]. Briefly, PRMs work by sampling points 'randomly' from the robot's configuration space (C-space), and retaining those that satisfy certain feasibility requirements (e.g., they must correspond to collision-free configurations of the movable object). Then, these points are connected to form a graph, or roadmap, using some simple planning method to connect 'nearby' points. During query processing, the start and goal are connected to the roadmap and a path connecting their connection points is extracted from the roadmap using standard graph search techniques (see Figure 1(b)).

We use a particular variant of the PRM called the Medial-Axis PRM, or MAPRM [9]. In MAPRM, instead of generating the nodes uniformly at random in C-space, they are generated on or near the medial-axis of C-Space. MAPRM is particularly well suited to flocking behavior since roadmap nodes tend to maximize clearance from obstacles. Note that although the initial roadmap is found for the static environment, the roadmap, or a path extracted from it, can be modified according to dynamic changes in the environment, e.g., a new roadmap could be built from scratch [10], the existing roadmap can be modified [11–13], or a path containing collisions (an approximate path) can be modified to fit the new requirements [14].

Basic flocking systems [1] model simple group behavior by providing individual members with simple rules that implement separation (to avoid collision with nearby neighbors), alignment (to move in the same direction as its neighbors) and coherence (to stay close to neighbors) maneuvers based on the positions and velocities of the flockmates inside the sensing range. Constraints are satisfied by generating forces for each rule and applying an integrated force to change the state of the flock member, e.g., the flock member's velocity vector updated by finding the acceleration resulted from the integrated force using the Newtonian equation $F = ma$. Our implementation of this is based on particle systems [15]. In the presence of obstacles, force is also generated to push the flock member away. This basic system can be seen in Figure 2. More complicated behavior is usually simulated by adding other forces.

2.2   Roadmap-Based Group Behavior

In this section, we show how roadmap-based techniques can be used to achieve different behaviors. We consider several behaviors: *homing, exploring (covering and goal searching), traversing narrow passages* and *shepherding*. The first two behaviors influence *where* the flock goes – reaching a pre-defined goal (homing), attempting to cover (visit) all reachable areas of the environment (covering) or search for a goal whose location is not known. The narrow passage behavior influences *how* the flock members position themselves relative to each other when they move through the passage. In the shepherding, an external agent controls the movement of the flock.

Homing Behavior. Homing behavior is usually simulated by adding an attractive force toward the goal [16]. However, this method may easily be trapped in a local minimum even in a simple environment. A method commonly used in computer games requiring motion of a group of objects is a grid-based A^* search [17]. In this approach, the environment is discretized to small grid cells and the search for the flock's path is based on expanding toward the most promising neighbor of already visited positions. Although A^* search finds shortest paths and it is usually fairly fast, it does have some drawbacks. Of particular note here

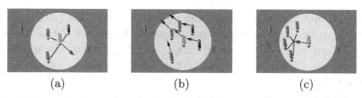

Fig. 2. Individual member behavior for flocks. (a) Separation: avoid crowding neighbors. (b) Alignment: match velocity of neighbors. (c) Cohesion: stay close to neighbors. The arrow represents steering direction.

Fig. 3. Covering an environment. (a) A roadmap is built. (b–c) Robots move to the roadmap and increase the weights as they move along the edges. At an intersection the robots select their destination by a probability function based on the edge weights (edges with small weights are preferred).

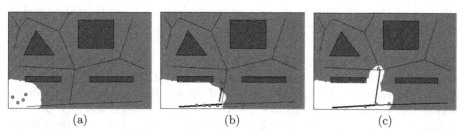

Fig. 4. Ten flock members are searching for an unknown goal. (a) The flock faces a branch point. (b) Since both edges have the same weight, the flock splits into two groups. (c) After dead ends are encountered in the lower left and upper right, edge weights leading to them are decreased. (d) As some members find the goal, edge weights leading to it are increased. (e) The remaining members reach the goal.

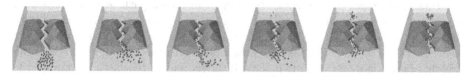

Fig. 5. Passing through a narrow passage using the FOLLOW THE LEADER behavior (Algorithm 2.4).

is the necessity of finding a completely new path for each new goal which reduces efficiency and increases the computation time for complex environments.

In contrast, roadmap-based path planning methods work on a global scale and once the roadmap is generated, finding new paths is fast and efficient. Once a path is found, individual flock members follow the path. The path is partitioned into a set of subpaths (identified by subgoals) based on the individual flock member's sensor range. Each member keeps track of subgoals and as soon as a subgoal comes within sensory range the next subgoal becomes the steering direction for the global goal.

With other interacting forces from neighboring flock members and obstacles, steering toward the subgoal has the lowest priority, so individual members still move together while moving toward the subgoal. Since the subgoals are usually away from the obstacles, due to global roadmap, this approach results in a flocking toward the goal and avoids getting trapped in local minima. The homing behavior is shown in Algorithm 2.1.

Covering the Environment. In this behavior we want some member of our flock to have covered every location in the environment. We assume we start with a roadmap covering all relevant portions of the environment and the roadmap has adaptive edge weights. In this approach, each individual member uses the roadmap to wander around. Specifically, the flock members follow roadmap edges and there are no predefined paths. The goal is to have some flock member visit every edge and vertex of the roadmap (see Figure 3). The edge weights represent how relevant the edge is to the current task, in this case exploring the environment. Initially, edges all have weight one. As the flock members traverse a roadmap edge they increase its weight. This is similar to ant pheromones which increase as more ants follow the same path. Since our goal is to cover the environment, the individual flock members are biased toward relatively uncovered areas of the roadmap. This is achieved by having them select roadmap edges with smaller weights with some higher probability at the intersections (roadmap nodes). This algorithm is shown in Algorithm 2.2.

Goal Searching. Our goal searching behavior is similar to *ant colony optimization (ACO)*. Although the individual flock members know the environment, they don't know the location of the goal. If an individual reaches a location where the goal is within sensor range, all other members try to reach the goal. Like the previous case, we implemented this behavior using adaptive roadmap edge weights. The weight of an edge shows how promising a path segment is. Again, the member chooses an edge to leave a roadmap node with some probability based on the edge's weight. As an individual traverses a path in the roadmap, it remembers the route it has taken. Then, when it reaches a goal, it increases the weight of the edges on the route it took. If the individual reaches a roadmap node without any outgoing connections (i.e., with only one edge) or a node already contained in the current path (i.e., a cycle), the weight of the edges it followed will be decreased. This approach is summarized in Algorithm 2.3 and illustrated in Figure 4.

Narrow Passage Behavior. Sometimes the flock's behavior depends on the surrounding environment. For example, different group formations may be used in relatively open areas than are used when passing through narrow regions. One

Algorithm 2.1 Homing

1: **if** (goal is in view range) **then**
2:    set goal as target.
3: **else if** (target is in view range) **then**
4:    set next subgoal as the target.
5: **end if**
6: steer toward the target.

Algorithm 2.3 Goal Searching

1: **for** (each flock member) **do**
2:    **if** (goal found) **then**
3:       increase edge weights on path to goal
4:    **else if** (dead end found) **then**
5:       pop stack until a new branch is found
6:       decrease weight of edge corr. to popped node
7:    **else**
8:       select a neighboring node of the current node
9:       push this node onto the stack
10:   **end if**
11: **end for**

Algorithm 2.5 Shepherding (for dog)

1: Find a path on roadmap
2: **while** (goal not reached) **do**
3:    Select the next node on the path as subgoal
4:    **while** (subgoal not reached) **do**
5:       Move to rear of flock on the far side of subgoal
6:       **if** (flock separates) **then**
7:          Move the subgroup that is farthest from subgoal toward other subgroups
8:       **end if**
9:    **end while**
10: **end while**

Algorithm 2.2 Covering the Env.

1: **for** (each flock member) **do**
2:    **while** (not all nodes visited) **do**
3:       **if** (not in the roadmap) **then**
4:          move to closest roadmap node
5:       **end if**
6:       **if** (current node has no outgoing edge) **then**
7:          pop stack until a new branch is found
8:       **else**
9:          probabilistically pick a lower-weight edge
10:         increase edge weight
11:         push this node onto the stack
12:      **end if**
13:   **end while**
14: **end for**

Algorithm 2.4 Narrow Passage

1: **while** (not all flock members in gathering area) **do**
2:    set individual members' goal to gathering area
3: **end while**
4: set leader to NIL
5: **while** (there are flock members outside passage) **do**
6:    select the closest unselected member as Current
7:    **if** (Leader is NIL) **then**
8:       set Leader to Current and set Leader's goal to next step in the path
9:    **else**
10:      set Current's goal to Previous
11:   **end if**
12:   set Previous to Current
13:   increase neighbor avoidance threshold
14: **end while**

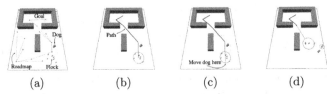

| (a) | (b) | (c) | (d) |

Fig. 6. Shepherding: sheep are represented by large circles and the dog by a small dark circle. (a) Roadmap, (b) path selected by dog, (c) dog's steering location, (d) flock is separated.

nice property of roadmaps is that, the roadmap nodes can be the representatives of different regions of the environment. Hence, different rules or navigation strategies can be assigned to different nodes and if a flock member reaches a node, it follows the rules associated with that node.

We employ different rules to pass through a narrow passage. A naive way to achieve narrow passage traversal by the flock is to use the homing behavior and to select two nodes as goals, first a node in front of the entrance to the passage and then a node outside the exit from the passage. One drawback of this approach is that flock members may bunch up and conflict with each other as they try to move through the passage.

A *follow-the-leader* strategy may avoid the congestion problems of the naive strategy (see Figure 5). In this strategy, we first assemble the flock in front of the narrow passage, and then select the closest agent to the narrow passage entrance as the leader. Then, the remaining flock members are arranged into a queue that follows the leader. Their position in the queue depends on their distance to the entrance of the narrow corridor. They can be kept from crowding each other by selecting appropriate values for the repulsive force from other flock members.

Note that different behaviors can be achieved by using a different criterion to select the next flock member in line 6 of Algorithm 2.4. For example, instead of selecting the next closest flock member to the narrow passage, one might select the farthest, which would create a 'milling around' effect at the entrance to the passage.

Shepherding Behavior. In the previous sections we have observed two distinct class of flocking behaviors. In the first case, the flock members were moving toward a goal together, i.e., as a flock. The motion was planned for the flock. In the second case, the flock members were exploring and planning their motions individually. In a sense, the flock had control of the motion in the first case and individual flock members had control in the second case. In our third scenario, neither the flock nor the individuals have control of the motion. Instead, an outside agent guides or shepherds them. In the simulation shown in Figure 6(a), the external agent is a dog whose objective is to move the flock of sheep toward the goal. The only motion control for the flock is to move away from the dog. A similar implementation has been done in [18] where a robot was programmed to move geese toward a goal position. We would like to implement a similar algorithm where a subgoal will be a roadmap node found in the path. Until the subgoal is reached, the robot will move toward that goal and then will choose the next roadmap node on the path as the next subgoal (see Figure 6(b)).

To move the flock toward the goal, the dog steers the flock from behind (Figure 6(c)). If any subgroup separates from the flock, it is the dog's job to move the subgroup back to the flock (Figure 6(d)). Our approach is presented in Algorithm 2.5. We present an improved shepherding algorithm in [7].

3 Results

In this section we evaluate our roadmap-based techniques for the homing, exploring, and shepherding behaviors that were described in Section 2. Movies illustrating the experiments as well as the behaviors in three-dimensional space with rigid or deformable objects can be found on our webpage (http://www.cse.wustl.edu/~bayazit).

Our experiments are designed to compare our roadmap-based techniques with more traditional approaches for simulating flocking behavior and to study the improvements possible by incorporating global information about the environment as encoded in a roadmap.

To study the efficiency of our covering and goal searching techniques, we also compare our roadmap-based techniques with 'ideal' variants which have complete knowledge of the environment and the current status of the search. For example, in the goal searching behavior, the location of the goal is known at all times in the ideal variant. A more through evaluation of our approach can be found in [4–7] where we presented additional results for narrow passage and shepherding.

All of our experiments were run on a Linux system with Athlon 1.33 processor and 256MB memory.

3.1 Homing Behavior

For the homing behavior, our roadmap-based technique is compared with a basic flocking behavior using a potential field [16] and a grid-based A^* search behavior.

The environment is a square with sides measuring 420 meters (see Figure 7). It contains a total of 301 randomly placed obstacles (six types of obstacles are used). At any given time there is one goal, and when all flock members reach it, a new goal is randomly generated; this process continues until eight goals have been generated and reached. The experiment involves 40 flock members, which are initially placed according to a Gaussian distribution around the center of the square environment. The simulation is updated every 100 ms.

For the flocking behavior using a potential field, flock members are attracted towards the current goal. For the grid-based A^* behavior, a bitmap of the environment of 914×914 cells is constructed; the length of a side of each square cell is equal to the diameter of a flock member. Cells are classified as free cells and collision cells. Path to the current goal is found in this bitmap using A^* search. For the roadmap-based behavior, the roadmap is built using the MAPRMmethod (Section 2.1) to generate 400 roadmap nodes and we attempt to connect each

Fig. 7. Environment for homing experiments.

node to its 4 nearest neighbors. Path to the current goal is found using this roadmap.

Table 1 shows that, without global information, only a few flock members reach the last goal and most are trapped in local minima. On the other hand, when global navigation information is utilized, either with the grid-based A^* method or our roadmap-based method, all flock members reach the goal.

In Table 2 we show the time spent searching for paths, the number of local minima encountered along all paths, and the total time spent escaping from local minima. This offers some insight into the methods studied, as can be seen more clearly in Figure 8. Although the flock takes a shorter path with the grid-based A^* search than with the roadmap-based method (Figure 8(a)), the flock reaches the final goal faster with the roadmap-based method (Figure 8(b)). As A^* search

Table 1. Homing behavior. This table shows how many of the 40 flock members reach the last goal (8th) within 30 seconds using the basic flocking behavior, the grid-based A^* behavior, and the roadmap-based behavior.

Homing behavior: Basic v.s. Roadmap

METHOD	#flockmates reaching the goal
Basic	10
grid-based A^*	40
roadmap-based	40

Table 2. Homing behavior. This table shows the time for initialization, the average time to find a path, and the total time spent by all flockmates escaping local minima if they stuck in a place due to quickly changing forces.

Homing behavior: Roadmap v.s. grid-based A^*

BEHAVIOR METHOD	init time	find path time	local minima #	local minima escape (s)
roadmap-based	0.88	0.652	255	22.99
grid-based A^*	6.02	5.757	2005	1035.43

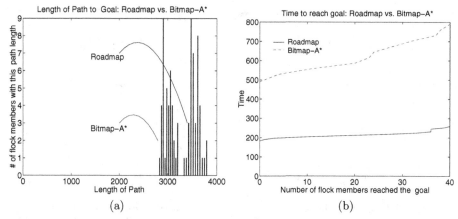

Fig. 8. Homing behavior: (a) The number of flock members reaching goals with respect to the length of the paths they took. (b) The number of flock members reaching goals over time. Although the grid-based A^* behavior finds shorter paths, the flock spends less time to reach the goals with the roadmap-based behavior.

is known to be fast and to find shortest paths, this example illustrates that our roadmap-based method indeed is a competitor for grid-based A^* methods – while the paths found are a bit longer, they are found faster.

3.2   Covering the Environment

Space covering is tested on the environment shown in Figure 9, which requires flock members to pass through narrow passages to access undiscovered areas. In this experiment, we compare basic flocking behavior, roadmap-based behavior, and an ideal variant of the roadmap-based behavior that has dynamic knowledge of the undiscovered regions.

The environment (80 × 100) is populated with 16 obstacles (6 types of obstacles) and in total 24% of the environment is occupied by obstacles. 50 flock members are simulated and states are updated every 100ms. A bitmap is built to record discovered/undiscovered information. A bitmap cell is discovered when it is inside the sensory range of any flock member. We set the radius of the sensory circle as 5m. For the roadmap, 120 nodes are sampled and connections are attempted to each node's 4 nearest neighbors.

The roadmap-based covering behavior is described in Section 2.2.

The basic behavior uses only local information, and is essentially a random walk through the environment. It shows that the lack of global knowledge results in some areas never being discovered, especially those nearly surrounded by obstacles.

The behavior with perfect knowledge of the undiscovered locations uses the roadmap to find paths from a flockmate's current position to the closest unexplored spot. Although such knowledge would not be available in this covering application, this variant gives us an idea of how fast an environment can be covered in the best case.

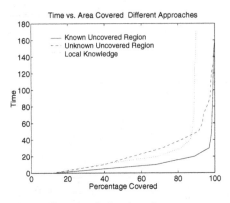

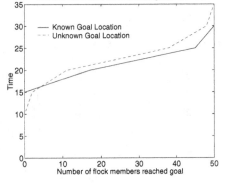

Fig. 9. Covering behavior: the percentage of the environment covered in terms of time (seconds).

Fig. 10. Goal searching behavior: the number of flock members reaching the goal area in terms of time (seconds).

As seen in Figure 9, the perfect behavior rapidly covered almost 91% of the environment in the first 30 seconds. The roadmap-based behavior, using indirect communication (adaptive edge weights) takes about three times as long (90 seconds), to reach a similar coverage point of 91.6%. Nevertheless, like the perfect behavior, the roadmap-based behavior found most reachable areas. In contrast, the basic flocking behavior had difficulty covering more than 80% of the environment. However, it is interesting to note that the basic flocking behavior found more undiscovered areas than the roadmap-based approach in the first 40 seconds; this is due to the basic behavior which tends to bounce around and discover 'easy' areas very quickly.

3.3   Searching for a Goal

In this experiment, the roadmap-based behavior is compared with a simple flocking behavior that has only local information about the environment and no knowledge of the goal position, and with an ideal variant of the roadmap-based behavior that has *a priori* knowledge of the position of the goal. The environment is the same as that used in the covering experiment.

We are interested in how many flock members reach the goal and how fast they get there. As previously mentioned, the behavior with complete knowledge is used to establish a best case (lowerbound) for the simulation efficiency, and the basic behavior using only local information is used to illustrate the importance of global knowledge. The results of some experiments are shown in Figure 10. The flocks using the basic behavior do not discover any goals within 35 seconds, and in particular, none of the flock members discover the narrow passage out of the confined region in which they start. Overall, the roadmap-based behavior is competitive with the ideal roadmap-based behavior – only taking 5 seconds longer than the method in which the position of the goal is known *a priori*. In addition, it is surprising to note that two of the flock members in the roadmap-based method reach the goal earlier than any of their flockmates in the ideal roadmap-based behavior. While we expect the roadmap-based method to continue to perform well in more complex environments, we expect its efficiency relative to the ideal method to decline somewhat.

4   Discussion and Outlook

In this paper, we have shown that complex group behaviors can be generated if some global information of the environment is available. The global knowledge used is a roadmap of the environment. The information it contains, such as topological information and adaptive edge weights, enables the flock to achieve behaviors that cannot be modeled with local information alone. Moreover, since in many cases global knowledge involves high communication costs between individuals, indirect communication though dynamic updates of the roadmap's edge weights provides a less expensive means of obtaining global information.

Our simulation results for the types of behaviors studied show that the performance of the roadmap-based behavior is very close to an ideal behavior that has complete knowledge. Our future work will focus on shepherding with multiple external agents and searching for moving goals, as in pursuit/evasion games. We are also working on exploration strategies if the environment is not known a priori.

5   Related Work

Reynolds' influential flocking simulation [1] showed that flocking is a dramatic example of emergent behavior in which global behavior arises from the interaction of simple local rules. Each individual member of the flock (boid), has a simple rule set stating that it should move with its neighbors. This concept has been used successfully by researchers both in computer graphics and robotics. Tu and Terzopoulos [19] used flocking behaviors with intention generators to simulate a school of fish. They also demonstrated shepherding behavior in which a T-Rex herds raptors out of its territory.

A number of related methods for achieving group behaviors have been proposed. Nishimura and Ikegami [20] used flocking dynamics to investigate collective strategies in a "prey-predator" game model. Ward et al. [21] studied an evolving sensory controller for producing schooling behavior based on "boids". Brogan and Hodgins [22] investigated group behavior with significant dynamics, such as human-like bicycle riders. Sun et al. [23] achieve swarm behaviors based on a biological immune system. Balch and Hybinette [24] propose a behavior-based solution to the robot formation-keeping problem. Fukuda et al. [25] describe group behavior for a Micro Autonomous Robotics System. Mataric [26] classifies a basic set of group behaviors which can be used to create more complex behaviors including flocking and herding. Saiwaki et al. [27] use a chaos model to simulate a moving crowd. An interesting approach by Vaughan et al. [18] used a robotic external agent to steer a flock of real geese.

Although there is little research on path planning for flocks, many methods have been proposed for planning for multiple robots. These methods can be characterized as centralized or decoupled. Centralized methods consider all robots as one entity, while decoupled methods first find a path for each robot independently and then resolve conflicts. In work from Li et al. [28], each group of crowds is guided by a leader and the paths of the leaders are generated using a decoupled approach.

The observation of the behavior of ant colonies has inspired the ant colony optimization (ACO) meta-heuristic for discrete optimization. Dorigo et al. [29] exploit this ant-like behavior to optimize solutions for several NP-Complete problems. In our work, the flock's ability to explore comes from using an ACO-like approach to adaptively adjust roadmap edge weights.

References

1. Reynolds, C.W.: Flocks, herds, and schools: A distributed behavioral model. In: Computer Graphics. (1987) 25–34
2. Reynolds, C.W.: Steering behaviors for autonomous characters. In: Game Developers Conference. (1999)
3. Latombe, J.C.: Robot Motion Planning. Kluwer Academic Publishers, Boston (1991)
4. Bayazit, O.B., Lien, J.M., Amato, N.M.: Better flocking behaviors using rule-based roadmaps. In: Proc. Int. Workshop on Algorithmic Foundations of Robotics (WAFR). (2002)
5. Bayazit, O.B., Lien, J.M., Amato, N.M.: Better group behaviors in complex environments using global roadmaps. In: Artif. Life. (2002)
6. Bayazit, O.B., Lien, J.M., Amato, N.M.: Roadmap-based flocking for complex environments. In: Proc. Pacific Graphics. (2002) 104–113
7. Lien, J.M., Bayazit, O.B., Sowell, R.T., S. Rodrigues, L., Amato, N.M.: Shepherding behaviors. In: Proc. IEEE Int. Conf. Robot. Autom. (ICRA). (2004) 4159–4164
8. Kavraki, L., Svestka, P., Latombe, J.C., Overmars, M.: Probabilistic roadmaps for path planning in high-dimensional configuration spaces. IEEE Trans. Robot. Automat. **12** (1996) 566–580
9. Amato, N.M., Bayazit, O.B., Dale, L.K., Jones, C.V., Vallejo, D.: OBPRM: An obstacle-based PRM for 3D workspaces. In: Robotics: The Algorithmic Perspective, Natick, MA, A.K. Peters (1998) 155–168 Proceedings of the Third Workshop on the Algorithmic Foundations of Robotics (WAFR), Houston, TX, 1998.
10. Hsu, D., Kindel, R., Latombe, J.C., Rock, S.: Randomized Kinodynamic Motion Planning with Moving Obstacles. In: Proc. Int. Workshop on Algorithmic Foundations of Robotics (WAFR). (2000) SA1–SA18
11. Bohlin, R., Kavraki, L.E.: Path planning using Lazy PRM. In: Proc. IEEE Int. Conf. Robot. Autom. (ICRA). (2000) 521–528
12. Nielsen, C.L., Kavraki, L.E.: A two level fuzzy prm for manipulation planning. IEEE/RSJ International Conference on Intelligent Robotics and Systems (2000)
13. Song, G., Miller, S.L., Amato, N.M.: Customizing PRM roadmaps at query time. In: Proc. IEEE Int. Conf. Robot. Autom. (ICRA). (2001) 1500–1505
14. Bayazit, O.B., Song, G., Amato, N.M.: Enhancing randomized motion planners: Exploring with haptic hints. Autonomous Robots, Special Issue on Personal Robotics **10** (2001) 163–174 Preliminary version appeared in *ICRA 2000*, pp. 529–536.

15. Witkin, A., Baraff, D.: Physically Based Modeling: Principles and Practice. SIG-GRAPH'97 Course Notes #19, SIGGRAPH-ACM publication (1997)
16. Khatib, O.: Real–time obstacle avoidance for manipulators and mobile robots. Int. J. Robot. Res. **5** (1986) 90–98
17. Russell, S., Norvig, P.: Artificial Intelligence: A Modern Approach. 1th edn. Prentice Hall (1994)
18. Vaughan, R.T., Sumpter, N., Henderson, J., Frost, A., Cameron, S.: Experiments in automatic flock control. J. Robot. and Autonom. Sys. **31** (2000) 109–117
19. Tu, X., Terzopoulos, D.: Artificial fishes: Physics, locomotion, perception, behavior. In: Computer Graphics. (1994) 24–29
20. Nishimura, S., Ikegami, T.: Emergence of collective strategies in prey-predator game model. Artif. Life **3** (1997) 243–260
21. Ward, C., Gobet, F., Kendall, G.: Evolving collective behavior in an artificial ecology. Artif. Life **7** (2001) 191–209
22. Brogan, D.C., Hodgins, J.K.: Group behaviors for systems with significant dynamics. In: Autonomous Robots. (1997) 137–153
23. Sun, S.J., Sim, D.W.L.K.B.: Artificial immune-based swarm behaviors of distributed autonomous robotic systems. In: Proc. IEEE Int. Conf. Robot. Autom. (ICRA). (2001) 3993–3998
24. Balch, T., Hybinette, M.: Social potentials for scalable multirobot formations. In: Proc. IEEE Int. Conf. Robot. Autom. (ICRA). (2000) 73–80
25. Fukuda, T., Mizoguchi, H., Sekiyama, K., Arai, F.: Group behavior control for MARS (micro autonomous robotic system). In: Proc. IEEE Int. Conf. Robot. Autom. (ICRA). (1999) 1550–1555
26. Mataric, M.J.: Interaction and Intelligent Behavior. PhD thesis, MIT EECS (1994)
27. Saiwaki, N., Komatsu, T., Yoshida, T., Nishida, S.: Automatic generation of moving crowd using chaos model. In: IEEE Int. Conference on System, Man and Cybernetics. (1997) 3715–3721
28. Li, T.Y., Jeng, Y.J., Chang, S.I.: Simulating virtual human crowds with a leader-follower model. In: Proceedings of 2001 Computer Animation Conference. (2001)
29. Dorigo, M., Caro, G.D., Gambardella, L.M.: Ant algorithms for discrete optimization. In: Artificial Life. Volume 5. (1999) 137–172

Towards Dependable Swarms
and a New Discipline of Swarm Engineering

Alan F.T. Winfield, Christopher J. Harper, and Julien Nembrini

Intelligent Autonomous Systems Laboratory,
UWE Bristol, Coldharbour Lane, Bristol BS16 1QY, UK
Alan.Winfield@uwe.ac.uk
http://www.ias.uwe.ac.uk/

Abstract. This review paper sets out to explore the question of how future complex engineered systems based upon the swarm intelligence paradigm could be assured for dependability. The paper introduces the new concept of 'swarm engineering': a fusion of dependable systems engineering and swarm intelligence. The paper reviews the disciplines and processes conventionally employed to assure the dependability of conventional complex (and safety critical) systems in the light of swarm intelligence research and in so doing tries to map processes of analysis, design and test for safety-critical systems against relevant research in swarm intelligence. A case study of a swarm robotic system is used to illustrate this mapping. The paper concludes that while some of the tools needed to assure a swarm for dependability exist, many do not, and hence much work needs to be done before dependable swarms become a reality.

1 Vision

From an engineering standpoint the design of complex distributed systems based upon swarm intelligence is compellingly attractive but problematical. A distinguishing characteristic of distributed systems based upon swarm intelligence is that they have no hierarchical command and control structure, and hence no common mode failure point or vulnerability. Typically, individual agents make decisions autonomously, based upon local sensing and communications [5, 6]. Systems with these characteristics could, potentially, exhibit very high levels of robustness, in the sense of tolerance to failure of individual agents; much higher levels of robustness than in complex distributed systems based on traditional design approaches. However, that robustness comes at a price. Complex systems with swarm intelligence might be very difficult to control or mediate if they started to exhibit unexpected behaviours. Such systems would therefore need to be designed and validated for a high level of assurance that they exhibit intended behaviours and *equally importantly* do not exhibit unintended behaviours. It seems reasonable to assert that future engineered systems based on the swarm intelligence paradigm would need to be subject to processes of design, analysis and test no less demanding that those we expect for current complex systems.

E. Şahin and W.M. Spears (Eds.): Swarm Robotic WS 2004, LNCS 3342, pp. 126–142, 2005.

Some might argue that a 'dependable swarm' is an oxymoron; that the swarm intelligence paradigm is intrinsically unsuitable for application in engineered systems that require a high level of integrity. The idea that overall desired swarm behaviours are not explicitly coded anywhere in the system, but are instead an emergent consequence of the interaction of individual agents with each other and their environment, might appear to be especially problematical from a dependability perspective. This paper suggests that this is not so: that systems which employ emergence should, in principle, be no more difficult to validate than conventional complex systems and, indeed, that some characteristics of swarm intelligence are highly desirable from a dependability perspective.

The aim of this paper is to explore the question of how future engineered systems based on the swarm intelligence paradigm might be designed, analysed and tested for dependability. The paper attempts to do this by the juxtaposition of two hitherto disconnected disciplines: dependable systems engineering and the design of multi-agent systems based on the swarm intelligence paradigm (which we shall term 'swarm engineering'). This is a big question, a complete answer to which is well beyond the scope of this paper. The paper instead tries to set out the important questions for the ongoing study of dependable swarms.

In order to illustrate the questions raised by this paper an example of a robotic swarm is presented as a case study. The case study is incomplete, since the tools and disciplines needed to fully validate the system in question do not exist: that is of course the point of this paper. The case study does, however, help us to think about the rather abstract issues of dependable systems engineering with reference to a robotic swarm that could see real-world application within the near future. This paper proceeds as follows. Section 2 introduces the case study that will be used throughout the rest of the paper. Section 3 is a review of current best practice in the field of dependable systems engineering. While outlining and referencing the processes and methodologies of analysis, design and test, this section will reflect on what these might mean in practice, for swarm engineering, with reference to the case study. Section 4 then concludes with a discussion and outlook, setting out a roadmap of the work that needs to be done before real-world swarm engineering can become a reality.

2   Case Study: Swarm Containment

As a case study let us consider a swarm robotics approach to physical containment or encapsulation, as illustrated in figure 1.

Potential applications for such an approach might include a swarm of marine robots that find and then contain oil pollution or *in-vivo* nano-bots that seek and isolate harmful cells in the blood stream (a kind of artificial phagocyte). The latter application is not so far-fetched when one considers the rate of progress in the engineering of genetic circuits, see Yokobayashi et al [27].

The emergent encapsulation behaviour of figure 1 is one of a number of emergent properties of a class of algorithms that we have developed, which make use of local wireless connectivity information alone to achieve swarm aggregation; see Nembrini et al. [18]. Wireless connectivity (what Støy termed *situated com-*

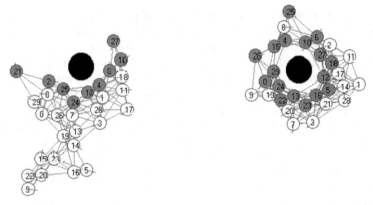

Fig. 1. Emergent encapsulation; (left) encapsulation in progress and (right) encapsulation complete.

munication [24]) is linked to robot motion so that robots within the swarm are wirelessly 'glued' together. This approach has several advantages: firstly the robots need neither absolute or relative positional information; secondly the swarm is able to maintain its coherence (i.e. stay together) even in unbounded space, and thirdly, the connectivity needed for and generated by the algorithm means that the swarm naturally forms an ad-hoc communications network. Such a network would be a requirement in many swarm robotics applications. The algorithm requires that connectivity information is transmitted only a single hop. Each robot broadcasts its ID and the IDs of its immediate neighbours only, and since the maximum number of neighbours a real robot can have is physically constrained and the same for a swarm of 100 or 10,000 robots, the algorithm scales linearly for increasing swarm size. The algorithm thus meets the criteria for swarm robotics, articulated by Sahin [21] and Beni [3]. We have a highly *robust* and *scalable* swarm of homogeneous and relatively incapable robots with only local sensing and communication capabilities, in which the required swarm behaviours are truly emergent. Furthermore we observe *flexibility* to its environment in that our wireless connected swarm demonstrates emergent taxis towards a beacon (which, in this case, is the object to be contained), emergent obstacle avoidance and emergent beacon encapsulation.

Our algorithms for coherent swarming of wireless networked mobile robots have been tested extensively in simulation and, rather less extensively, using a fleet of physical laboratory robots. A group of these robots ('Linuxbots') are shown in figure 2. The real robot implementation does not, however, constitute a real-world application. It is instead an 'embodied' simulation, whose main purpose is to verify that algorithms tested in computer simulation will transfer to the real world of non-ideal and noisy sensors and actuators.

3   Dependable Swarm Engineering

Current best practice in assuring the dependability of complex systems requires that a set of processes and disciplines are transparently applied during system

Fig. 2. The Linuxbots, used for embodied simulations.

analysis, design and *test*, see Anderson et al [1]. This paper now considers the approaches that would typically need to be applied to safety-critical systems in the context of swarm engineering, under these three headings. Note that best practice requires that the processes of analysis, design and test are applied concurrently and iteratively, so the ordering of the following sections should not be taken to imply sequence.

3.1 Analysis

From a dependability perspective, analysis is concerned with trying to establish two properties of a system: 'liveness' and 'safety'. Liveness is defined as the property of exhibiting desirable behaviours (doing the right thing) and safety is defined as the property of not exhibiting undesirable behaviours (not doing the wrong thing). While these properties are clearly somewhat complementary proof of one does not imply proof of the other, by inversion. A system that is provably safe could, for example, do the wrong thing safely. Although it may appear counter-intuitive, the methods needed to verify these two properties are not the same.

Verification of Liveness. Verification of 'liveness' requires that we formally prove that a system exhibits desirable behaviours. Conventionally this requires analytical or mathematical modelling. In the safety systems community the use of testing alone to prove liveness is now deprecated on the grounds that systems are becoming too complex to allow anything like acceptably complete test coverage, or even to allow complete test specifications to be written. Simulation is similarly regarded as unacceptable as an analysis tool (an interesting observation given the widespread use of simulation within swarm intelligence research[1]). Simulation is nevertheless accepted as a useful tool in prototyping,

---

[1] For a valuable discussion of the role of simulation in embodied systems research see Ziemke [29].

to for instance refine the system specification and to understand the design or parameter space.

Complete verification of the liveness of a swarm system thus requires mathematical modelling at two levels: the individual agent, and the swarm as a whole.

Let Us First Consider the Individual Agent. Often, single artificial agents within swarms are designed using the behaviour-based control paradigm [7]. Behaviour-based control is appropriate given that such agents are typically reactive finite-state machines with relatively few states. We have developed an approach, based on a second order extension of Lyapunov stability theorems, proving both marginal and asymptotic stability [11]. The significance of second order stability is that position control in mobile agents can generally only be achieved through actuators that generate forces which govern acceleration; the second derivative of position. Of particular significance is that these new stability theorems provide an explicit mathematical representation of subsumption. Based on this observation Harper has developed a design methodology called 'Direct Lyapunov Design' which leads from analysis directly to a colony-style behaviour based controller which is provably stable (in the sense of Lyapunov), and exhibits the liveness property [12]. In a fixed-priority behaviour-based architecture such as the colony-style subsumption architecture [9], the transfer functions of behaviour modules must be *partial functions*, i.e. which do not generate outputs continuously, in order that lower priority behaviour modules will have a chance to drive the system. Direct Lyapunov Design allows the construction of behaviour modules as partial functions and hence their integration into a colony-style subsumption controller. This approach thus advantageously encompasses both analysis and design.

Case Study: Figure 3 shows the colony-style subsumption controller for a single robot in the coherent swarm described in section 2. For simplicity only the bottom three layers are shown; the beacon-taxis layer is omitted. Notice that the local neighbourhood connectivity information can be treated as, in effect, sensory input to the coherence layer. In fact, the coherence layer makes use of memory to store neighbourhood connectivity, but in modelling the controller as a subsumption architecture we can treat the memory as part of the connectiv-

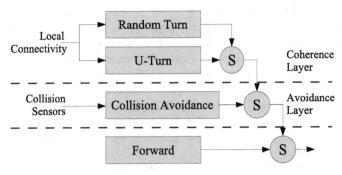

Fig. 3. Case study: single robot control architecture.

ity 'sensor'. The two behaviours in the coherence layer are 'U-turn', executed when the connectivity-sensor estimates that the robot is leaving the swarm; and 'Random turn', executed when the connectivity-sensor estimates that the robot has regained the swarm (for a description of how these estimates are made refer to [18]).

As a demonstration of the application of the second order stability theorems consider the analysis of the avoidance layer module. If we describe the state-space vector for the avoidance layer as $\underline{x}_A(t)$, and assume the existence of a candidate Lyapunov function[2] $V_A(\underline{x})$, then the value of that Lyapunov function along the state trajectories of the avoidance behaviour can be defined as function $W_A(t)$ where

$$W_A(t) \equiv V(\underline{x}_A(t)) \tag{1}$$

The principle of the method is based on the observation that the first order asymptotic stability theorem subsumes the second order theorem whenever the system motion is stable in the first order sense, i.e. whenever the motion is naturally convergent on the desired goal and $\dot{W}_A(t) < 0$. The second order asymptotic stability theorem can be used to design stable behaviour even if $\dot{W}_A(t) \geq 0$ within limits, as long as the second derivative $\ddot{W}_A(t)$ is negative and the motion is decelerating, i.e.

$$0 \leq \dot{W}_A(t) < \dot{W}_{max} \wedge \ddot{W}_A(t) < \ddot{W}_{max} < 0 \tag{2}$$

In order to achieve stable collision avoidance behaviour the transfer function of the collision avoidance behaviour module needs only to be defined for states where $\dot{W}_A(t) \geq 0$, generating outputs (actions) which ensure that $\ddot{W}_A(t) < 0$ and therefore it is a partial function over the state space of the collision avoidance behavioural domain. Since it is a partial function it can be included within a fixed-priority subsumption architecture. The same argument would apply to the coherence layer and the value of the Lyapunov function along the state trajectory for the coherence behaviour, $W_C(\underline{x})$. Thus, we are able to move toward verification of the liveness property for a single robot within our case study.

Now Consider the Mathematical Modelling of the Whole Swarm. There has been relatively little work in this direction, but one very promising approach is the probabilistic model developed by Martinoli et al. [19]. In this approach the interactions of agents with each other and their environment are modelled as a series of stochastic events, with probabilities determined by simple geometrical analysis. By modelling several series together, one for each agent, the overall behaviour of the swarm can be studied. The approach of Martinoli et al may be thought of as bottom up (or microscopic as they describe it). A top down (or macroscopic) approach has been developed by Lerman and Galystan [14]. Like Martinoli, Lerman and Galystan regard the behaviour of each agent as inherently probabilistic and Markovian, because their next state is a function only of

---

[2] Which could be as straightforward as the Euclidian distance between $\underline{x}(t)$ and the goal state $\underline{x}_g(t)$.

their current state. However, they develop an overall model of the system using the stochastic Master Equation (from stochastic dynamical systems), then derive rate (differential) equations from it, which describe how the average macroscopic system properties change over time. A review of modelling and analysis methods for swarm robotic systems is given in Lerman et al. [15].

Case Study: Analysis suggests that mathematical modelling of our swarm containment case will not yield to the method proposed by Martinoli, et al [19]. We are able to model the single robot controller as a state transition diagram (see figure 4), however, because our swarm operates in an unbounded space then geometrical analysis cannot be used to develop expressions for the state transition probabilities. In particular transitions between the forward state and the U-turn or Random-turn states in the coherence behaviour depend on local network topology. Similarly, we are unable to use the macroscopic approach of Lerman et al [14] because the individual agents in our case cannot be modelled as simple Markovian processes; they have memory and their next state may depend on the recent history of the local network topology.

Verification of Safety. To verify 'safety' we need to prove that a system does not exhibit undesirable behaviours. In order to attempt such a proof first requires that we identify and articulate all possible undesirable behaviours. This is called 'hazard analysis' and is problematical with conventional complex systems; and there is no reason to suppose that identifying the hazards in swarm engineered systems will be any different. Hazards analysis is problematical because there are no formal methods for identifying hazards. It simply has to be done by inspection (typically by 'extreme brainstorming' to try and list all possible hazards no matter how seemingly implausible or improbable).

Given a reasonably well understood operational environment there are two reasons for undesirable behaviours: random errors, or systematic (design) errors. Random errors are those due to hardware or component faults, and these are typically analysed usingtechniques such as Failure Mode and Effects Analysis

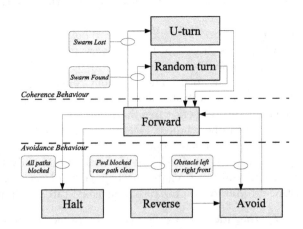

Fig. 4. Case study: single robot state transition diagram.

(FMEA). The likelihood that random errors cause undesirable behaviours can be reduced, in the first instance, by employing high reliability components. But systems that require high dependability will typically also need to be fault tolerant, through redundancy for example. This is an important point since swarm engineered systems should, in this respect, offer significant advantages over conventional complex systems. Two characteristics of swarms work in our favour here. Firstly, simple agents with relatively few rules lend themselves to FMEA, and their simplicity facilitates design for reliability. Secondly, swarms consist of multiple agents and hence, by definition, exhibit high levels of redundancy and tolerance to failure of individual agents. Indeed, swarms may go far beyond conventional notions of fault tolerance by exhibiting tolerance to individuals who actively thwart the overall desired swarm behaviour.

Systematic errors are those aspects of the design that could allow the system to exhibit undesirable behaviours. For swarm engineered systems analysis of systematic errors clearly needs to take place at two levels: in the individual agent and for the swarm as a whole. Analysis of systematic errors in the individual agent should be helped by the relative simplicity of the agents, but is not trivial. In general terms we would need to prove that an agent's state-space trajectory is always 'away from' the hazard states. Following the discussion of section 3.1 we conjecture that the 2nd order Lyapunov approach could be extended to cover the analysis of hazard states as well as goal states, thus offering the possibility of verifying liveness and safety with a single analysis, see Appendix A. Analysis of systematic errors for the swarm as a whole is much more problematical, particularly if the desired behaviours are emergent. Proof of safety for the overall swarm would appear to require that we prove that there are no undesired emergent behaviours. How to prove this to an acceptable level of confidence is by no means clear.

Case Study: A valuable measure of the 'coherence' of our swarm is network connectivity. Within the coherence layer of our single robot controller comparison of local network connectivity against a threshold determines the estimate of 'swarm lost' and hence triggers the U-turn behaviour. Adjusting this threshold value for the whole swarm controls the network connectivity, and hence area coverage; a low value of threshold generates a low density swarm with relatively few wireless connections between individual robots, whereas a high threshold value generates a dense and highly connected swarm. We have developed, from graph theory, upper and lower bounds on the area coverage of the swarm, for given threshold values and swarm sizes. While these bounds are rather loose, they nevertheless provide valuable confidence that the swarm will not exceed a given area coverage. Of course, the swarm exceeding a given area is only one possible 'hazard', so our upper bounds analysis provides proof of swarm safety for just this one identified hazard.

3.2 Design

The design of systems based on the swarm intelligence paradigm is challenging, not least because there are no principled design approaches for determining the behaviours required of the individual agents in order to give the desired emergent overall swarm behaviour. Indeed, some would argue that a principled approach to the design of emergence is impossible. This paper is however concerned with dependability, and there is no reason to suppose that emergent behaviours cannot form part of a dependable system.

Most complex systems are designed top-down from an overall functional design specification (FDS), by functional decomposition: breaking down the overall system into smaller and smaller components, then defining each of those components and the interfaces between them. What differentiates design for dependable, or safety critical, systems is that it will typically use a structured design methodology to provide a framework for capturing and documenting the design as it progresses, top down. The Yourdon structured design methodology, for instance, is based upon the dataflow paradigm. It starts at the top level by describing the overall system and its interfaces with its operational environment as a 'context diagram': this is level 0. The context diagram is then decomposed into level 1 'processes' and the dataflows between them, expressed in a data flow diagram (DFD). Each process in level 1 is then further decomposed into lower level DFDs, and so on, see Yourdon [28]. The structured design may well be applied within the discipline of a document driven approach [13], together with code inspection [10].

If we consider the applicability, and utility, of the Yourdon structured design methodology to swarm engineered systems it is clear that, at the top level, we can express the single swarm and its interfaces with the environment as a context diagram (level 0). Equally well, we could describe the internal processes of an individual agent with a data flow diagram (level 2). What is interesting, however, is how we might express the intermediate level 1 as a DFD. If we assume that single agents are (a) mobile, and (b) able to sense only their immediate neighbours [18, 25], then the level 1 DFD will reflect the instantaneous topography of the swarm. After the mobile agents have moved, the DFD must change to reflect the new swarm topography. This interestingly suggests an extension of the DFD which we could term the 'dynamic data flow diagram'.

Case Study: As discussed above we can express the design of our case study swarm robotic system graphically, as a hierarchy of data flow diagrams. Figure 5 shows the level 1 DFD but, in a departure from standard DFD notation, the data flows between level 1 processes - which happen to be robots - will change dynamically as the robots move. The DFD in figure 5 is thus a snapshot of the relationship between processes, rather than a static map. However, since every level 1 process (robot) and every dataflow between level 1 processes is identical then the DFD in figure 5 is simpler than it appears. The value of this approach is that we can make use of the full structured formalism of Yourdon to capture the design at both swarm and single robot level.

Figure 6 shows the DFD for a single level 1 process (robot), and its decomposition into level 2 processes. The 'behaviour-based control process' shown in figure 6 is described as a subsumption architecture in figure 3, and a state transition diagram in figure 4. When we add specifications for interfaces between

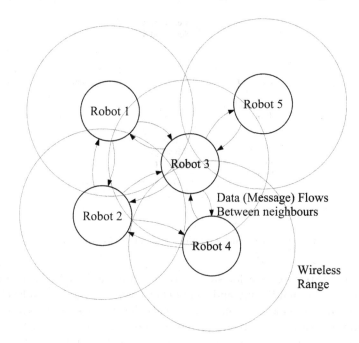

Fig. 5. Case study: swarm dynamic data flow diagram.

processes (dataflows) and data structures then we have a complete description of the design specification for the swarm and its robots. The Direct Lyapunov Design methodology [12] introduced in section 3.1 provides a design procedure for formally deriving implementations of individual robot behaviours, as 'motor schema', from the 2nd order Lyapunov stability analysis. The advantage of motor schema [2] is that they are simple piecewise mapping functions relating sensor inputs to actuator outputs which could be realised as gate arrays for very reliable controller hardware.

3.3 Test

Within the safety critical systems community there is general agreement that testing, whilst essential, can only provide a limited measure of confidence in the liveness and safety properties of a system [8]. There are two problems. Firstly, to write a complete test specification for a complex system is very difficult, and secondly to achieve 100% test coverage (which means exercising every possible execution path through control code or state machines under controlled conditions), whilst not technically impossible, is infeasibly time consuming for even moderately complex systems. Thus even the most safety critical systems in use today, such as aircraft flight management systems, will have been put through demanding but ultimately incomplete testing [16]. This is the reason that testing needs to go hand in hand with mathematical modelling, as discussed in 3.1 above.

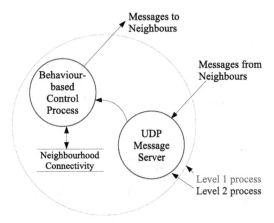

Fig. 6. Case study: single robot data flow diagram.

Typically, a test regime for safety critical systems is split into two parts: system level functional testing and component level testing. System level testing is primarily concerned with liveness, and treats the overall system as a black box, testing only for correct behaviour of the system as a complete entity against a system test specification. Component level testing breaks the system into its sub-systems and tests each one individually. Thus component level testing is the equivalent of system level white box testing.

At component level, sub-systems need to be tested functionally. This normally requires that test harnesses are created to enable components to be tested in isolation from the rest of the system. A test harness will set up input conditions for a component that might be extremely difficult to create by treating the system as an integrated whole. Test coverage can be measured directly in a process called dynamic analysis, which 'instruments' code such that each time it is executed a tally is kept of the number of times every possible execution path has been exercised. Dynamic analysis is an iterative (and cumulative) process in which ever more ingenious new tests are devised (typically by inspection of the code), in order to exercise those parts of the code revealed to have been not executed by the testing so far. The process continues until the target level of test coverage has been achieved. Needless to say dynamic analysis is a difficult and time consuming process. For completeness static analysis should also be mentioned since it often goes hand in hand with dynamic analysis. Static analysis measures code without actually executing it against coding standards including, typically, the McCabe complexity measure to assess the 'spaghetti-ness' of code [20].

If we now consider swarm engineered systems in the light of the discussion above, it is clear that system level testing needs to apply to the swarm as a whole, operating in its intended environment, and component level testing applies, in effect, to an individual agent. The fact that individual agents are often identical in swarm systems, and relatively simple in functional terms, suggests that component level testing should not be intractable. This view is, however, probably illusory, since the 'environment' for a single agent is the sum total of the other (presumably) neighbouring agents and the environment. Complete testing of a single agent would require that every possible configuration of neighbours and environment is specified, and repeatable tests devised (the neighbours plus environment becomes in effect the test harness). There has been little work in mobile robotics to quantitatively assess the effect of its environment on an individual robot, but see Schöner et al. [22]; Smithers [23]. The recent paper of Nehmzow and Walker [17] suggests methods based on dynamical systems theory, time series analysis and deterministic chaos theory.

The question of how to write a swarm test specification (STS) for the swarm as a whole might appear to be problematical given that the internal structure of the swarm is typically highly dynamic and chaotic. However, if we discipline ourselves to treating the swarm as a single entity then it should be possible to develop tests for the desired swarm behaviours. These will almost certainly be statistical, measuring for instance the frequency with which a given behaviour reaches a quantitative threshold condition of achievement within a given time frame, over repeated test runs. Thus, developing an STS for a swarm engineered system is likely to require careful attention to defining criteria for the achievement of swarm behaviours, including metrics for swarm properties such as mean swarm velocity, or mean area coverage.

Case Study: Providing the means to repeatably test a real robotic swarm could well, depending upon the size and form of the robots, present a significant engineering challenge. This requires, in the first instance, an instrumented test arena in which a representative operational environment can be created so that the performance of the swarm in achieving its desired behaviours can be observed and measured. This is itself not straightforward. Of course ultimately the swarm would also need to be tested in its real operational environment and that could be an even greater challenge, so let us confine ourselves here to thinking about the controlled test environment. Figure 7 shows two successive frames from a test run of our case study swarm. It must be stressed that these robots are not the real robots of a real-world application of our case study; the setup shown here is an embodied simulation aimed at providing proof-of-concept confirmation of the basic algorithms. Nevertheless, it will serve to illustrate the tools and techniques that will be required to test the real swarm.

Figure 7 shows a test of our embodied simulation in progress. Here we are trying to experimentally verify that the swarm maintains coherence, i.e. stays together. Note that the seven robots in figure 7 are grouped together by virtue of their wireless connectivity, not the physical bounds of the experimental arena; it follows that in our case the arena needs to be large enough with respect to the coherent swarm to provide it with an effectively unbounded space. The tests of figure 7 are concerned with, firstly, testing when, how and with what probability robots become detached from the swarm and, secondly, measuring the swarm area coverage. Area coverage is indicated by the bounded polygon of figure 7. The swarm test arena needs to provide the means to (a) motion capture test runs, (b) track and label individual robots and (c) process the captured test sequences

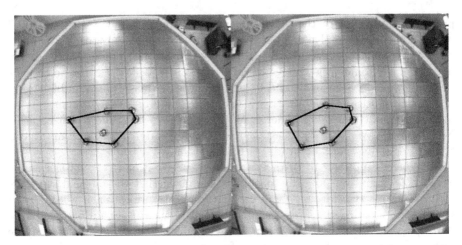

Fig. 7. Case study: two successive frames from a system level test run (captured by the overhead camera in the laboratory test arena).

to identify lost robot events and measure area coverage. The fact that our robots are equipped with wireless LAN [26] is a distinct advantage here, since it provides us with, firstly, the ability to be able to command the robots to a given starting position to initialise each test run and, secondly, the means to obtain continuous telemetry on each robot's internal state, connectivity, and odometry. Recording and time synchronising this data against the motion capture is important since it provides us with the information to be able to conduct deep analysis of the progress of test runs. In fact, a test script which automatically initialises each test run then, at the end of the run, halts the robots and re-initialises them for the next run, allows us to automate the whole of the swarm test sequence, from the STS to plots of swarm performance metrics.

If we now consider the problem of conducting component level tests, i.e. tests on a single robot, we can see that the experimental test environment described here provides us with the means to verify the correct operation of a single robot under a very wide range of 'environmental' conditions (recall that the test environment for a single robot is the sum total of its neighbouring robots plus the external (to the swarm) environment). By collecting data on internal state, connectivity and odometry for every robot, we can track the progress of a single robot through the swarm and - for a wide range of local conditions (proximity and connectivity) - confirm that the control action actually taken by the robot is the action that would be expected for those particular conditions. The dynamicity of the swarm provides us naturally with a very wide range of 'test' conditions for an individual robot, and by running a simple simulation of a single robot controller we can automate the process of verifying actual against expected control actions. Thus, in a sense, the single Robot Test Specification (RTS) does not need to be written (in that every possible test condition does not need to be written down), nor does it need to be manually executed. The system level test provides both the tests, and test environment, for the single robot.

4   Discussion and Outlook

This paper has proposed a framework for a new discipline of 'Swarm Engineering'. The paper has attempted a juxtaposition of dependable systems engineering with swarm intelligence and in so doing has tried to map processes of analysis, design and test for safety-critical systems against relevant work in swarm intelligence research. Perhaps not surprisingly, there is not a great deal of overlap between the two fields. To the authors' knowledge there has not been, to date, a single real-world application of swarm engineering with real physical agents. Thus no-one has yet had to face the challenge of assuring the dependability of such a system.

In respect of *analysis*, this paper has shown that promising mathematical modelling approaches are emerging for establishing the *liveness* property, for both the overall swarm and its constituent robots. These approaches are at present limited; for the overall swarm, to swarms in which individual robots can be treated as stochastic Markov processes; and for individual robots in which the controller can be modelled as a colony-style subsumption architecture. The more serious weakness, from a dependability perspective, is that no tools exist for establishing the *safety* property, that is to determine that a robotic swarm cannot exhibit undesirable behaviours. How to do this is by no means clear, although this paper has suggested two possible approaches: an extension of the Lyapunov stability approach for the individual robot, and a 'bounding' approach for the overall swarm.

From a *design* perspective, this paper has shown that the Yourdon structured design methodology might be usefully employed to describe the design of a robotic swarm; the approach has the merit of consistency when moving from the description of the overall swarm to its constituent robots. However, this approach is largely a description tool. Ideally, we require a formal, provable approach to the design of individuals within the swarm, and to the design of overall swarm behaviours. This paper has indicated one possible approach to the former with the technique we term Direct Lyapunov Design. Overall swarm design is problematical because there are at present no principled approaches to the design of emergent behaviours: finding the set of 'atomic' behaviours for the individuals in the swarm that will result in the overall desired emergent behaviour is at present more a process of discovery than design. This paper has, however, argued that this is not necessarily a problem for dependability providing that the emergent swarm behaviours can be assured for liveness and safety.

Finally, in respect of *test*, this paper has highlighted the need to establish robust measures for determining when and how desired swarm behaviours have been achieved, then define (statistical) tests for these measures. The paper has argued that testing, while certainly challenging, is feasible if an appropriate test environment can be created. A surprising conclusion of this paper is that an instrumented test environment for the whole swarm also provides an environment for rigorously testing the swarm at component (i.e. robot) level - for free.

To summarise, from a dependability perspective, future work is needed:

- to extend methods for the mathematical modelling of swarm robotic systems;
- to extend and strengthen formal approaches to provably stable single robot control;
- to start work on 'safety' analysis at both swarm and individual robot levels;
- to develop, if possible, a principled approach to the design of emergence;
- to extend the Direct Lyapunov Design approach to a wider class of behaviour-based controllers, and
- to develop methodologies and practices for the testing of swarm engineered systems.

It is clear that a great deal of work needs to be done before dependable robotic swarms can become an engineering reality.

Acknowledgments

The authors gratefully acknowledge discussions with Chris Melhuish during early preparation of this paper. We are also grateful to the referees for helpful and constructive criticism.

Appendix A

The work of Harper [12], shows that if we have a behaviour-based controller in which behaviours are implemented as motor schema, then we can prove that the Euclidian distance $\|x - x_g\|$ is a Lyapunov function for that schema and therefore that its behaviour is stable with respect to the goal states x_g. This represents a formal proof of 'liveness'.

Conjecture: that there is a Lyapunov function $V(x)$ defined as the ratio of the Euclidian distance of the goal states x_g and the hazard states x_h,

$$V(x) = \frac{\|x - x_g\|}{\|x - x_h\|} \tag{3}$$

and if the trajectory of $V(x)$ is negative, i.e. $\dot{V}(x) < 0$ then the agent will both seeks its goals and avoid its hazards at the same time. In other words the liveness and safety properties are stable over state space.

References

1. Anderson T, Avizienis A and Carter WC: Dependability: Basic Concepts and Terminology, Series: Dependable Computing and Fault-Tolerant Systems Volume 5, Laprie, J-C (ed), Springer-Verlag, New York (1992)
2. Arkin RC: Motor Schema based Navigation for a Mobile Robot, Proc. IEEE Conf. Robotics and Automation, Raleigh NC (1987) 264–271

3. Beni G: From swarm intelligence to swarm robotics, Proceedings of the SAB'04 Swarm Robotics Workshop, Santa Monica (2004)
4. Bennett P: Software Development for the Channel Tunnel: A Summary, Journal of High Integrity Systems, **1**(2) (1994) 213–220
5. Bonabeau E, Dorigo M, and Theraulaz G: Swarm Intelligence: from natural to artificial systems, Oxford University Press (1999)
6. Bonabeau E and Theraulaz G: Swarm Smarts, Scientific American, March (2000) 72-79
7. Brooks RA: Cambrian Intelligence: the Early History of the New AI, MIT Press (2000)
8. Butler RW and Finelli GB: The infeasibility of quantifying the reliability of life-critical real-time software, IEEE Trans. Software Engineering, **19**(1) (1993) 3–12
9. Connell JH: Minimalist mobile robotics: a colony-style architecture for an artificial creature, Academic Press Professional, San Diego (1990)
10. Fagan ME: Design and Code Inspections to Reduce Errors in Program Development, IBM Systems Journal, **15**(3) (1976)
11. Harper C and Winfield A: Direct Lyapunov Design – A Synthesis Procedure for Motor Schema Using a Second-Order Lyapunov Stability Theorem, Proc. IEEE/RSJ International Conference on Intelligent Robots and Systems, Lausanne, October (2002)
12. Harper C: A Rational Methodology for Designing Behaviour Based Systems for Safety Related Applications, PhD Thesis, University of the West of England, Bristol (2004)
13. Institution of Electrical Engineers: Guidelines for the documentation of computer software for real time and interactive systems, IEE London, 2nd Edition (1990)
14. Lerman K and Galstyan A: A General Methodology for Mathematical Analysis of Multi-Agent Systems, USC Information Sciences Technical Report ISI-TR-529, (2001)
15. Lerman K, Martinoli A and Galystan A: A Review of Modeling Methods for Swarm Robotic Systems, Proceedings of the SAB'04 Swarm Robotics Workshop, Santa Monica (2004)
16. Littlewood B and Thomas M: Reasons why Safety-Critical Avionics Software cannot be Adequately Validated, Proc. 1st UK Safety Systems Symposium, Springer-Verlag (1993)
17. Nehmzow U and Walker K: The Behaviour of a Robot is Chaotic, AISB Journal **1**(4) (2003) 373–388
18. Nembrini J, Winfield A and Melhuish C: Minimalist Coherent Swarming of Wireless Connected Autonomous Mobile Robots, Proc. Simulation of Artificial Behaviour '02, Edinburgh, August (2002)
19. Martinoli A, Ijspeert AJ and Gambardella LM: A Probabilistic model for understanding and comparing collective aggregation mechanisms, In Floreano D, Nicoud JD and Mondada F (eds), Proc. 5th European Conference on Advances in Artificial Life (ECAL-99), Vol 1674 of LNAI, Berlin (1999) 575–584
20. McCabe TA: A Cyclomatic Complexity Measure, IEEE Trans. on Software Engineering, **2**(4) (1976)
21. Şahin, E: Swarm Robotics: from sources of inspiration to domains of application, Proceedings of the SAB'04 Swarm Robotics Workshop, Santa Monica (2004)
22. Schöner G, Dose M and Engels C: Dynamics of behavior: theory and applications for autonomous robot architectures, Robotics and Autonomous Systems, **16** (1995)
23. Smithers T: On quantitative performance measures of robot architectures, Robotics and Autonomous Systems, **15** (1995) 107–133

24. Støy K: Using situated communication in distributed autonomous robotics, Proc. 7th Scandinavian Conference on Artificial Intelligence (2001)
25. Winfield AFT: Distributed sensing and data collection via broken ad hoc wireless connected networks of mobile robots, in Parker LE, Bekey G and Barhen J (eds) Distributed Autonomous Robotic Systems 4, Springer-Verlag (2000) 273–282
26. Winfield AFT and Holland OE: The application of wireless local area network technology to the control of mobile robots, Microprocessors and Microsystems, **23**(10) (2000) 597–607
27. Yokobayashi Y, Collins CH, Leadbetter JR, Arnold FH and Weiss R: Evolutionary Design of Genetic Circuits and Cell-Cell Communications, Advances in Complex Systems, **6**(1) (2003) 37–45
28. Yourdon E: Modern Structured Analysis, Prentice-Hall (1989)
29. Ziemke T: On the role of Robot Simulations in Embodied Computer Science, AISB Journal **1**(4) (2003) 389–399

A Review of Probabilistic Macroscopic Models for Swarm Robotic Systems

Kristina Lerman[1], Alcherio Martinoli[2], and Aram Galstyan[1]

[1] USC Information Sciences Institute,
Marina del Rey CA 90292, USA
lermand@isi.edu
http://www.isi.edu/~lerman/
[2] Swarm-Intelligent Systems Group, Nonlinear Systems Laboratory, EPFL,
CH-1015 Lausanne, Switzerland

Abstract. In this paper, we review methods used for macroscopic modeling and analyzing collective behavior of swarm robotic systems. Although the behavior of an individual robot in a swarm is often characterized by an important stochastic component, the collective behavior of swarms is statistically predictable and has often a simple probabilistic description. Indeed, we show that a class of mathematical models that describe the dynamics of collective behavior can be generated using the individual robot controller as modeling blueprint. We illustrate the macroscopic modelling methods with the help of a few sample results gathered in distributed manipulation experiments (collaborative stick pulling, foraging, aggregation). We compare the models' predictions to results of probabilistic numeric and sensor-based simulations as well as experiments with real robots. Depending on the assumptions, the metric used, and the complexity of the models, we show that it is possible to achieve quantitatively correct predictions.

1 Vision

Swarm Robotics is an emerging area in collective robotics which uses a fully distributed control paradigm and relatively simple robots to achieve coordinated behavior at the group level. Swarm robotic systems are *self-organizing*, meaning that constructive *collective* (or macroscopic) behavior emerges from *individual* (or microscopic) decisions robots make. These decisions are based on purely local information that comes from other robots as well as the environment. Swarm Robotics takes its inspiration from examples of collective behavior exhibited by biological systems, such as social insects [3], and the swarming, flocking, herding, and shoaling phenomena in vertebrates. In all these systems, the abilities of the collective appear to transcend the abilities of the constituent individuals.

The main advantages of the application of the swarm approach to the control of a group of robots are: (i) scalability: the control architecture can be kept exactly the same from a few units to thousands of units; (ii) flexibility: units can be dynamically added or removed, they can be given the ability to reallocate

E. Şahin and W.M. Spears (Eds.): Swarm Robotic WS 2004, LNCS 3342, pp. 143–152, 2005.

and redistribute themselves in a self-organized way; (iii) robustness: the resulting collective system is robust not only through unit redundancy but also through unit simplicity and an appropriate balance between exploitative and exploratory behavior.

The main difficulty in designing swarm robotic systems with desirable self-organized behavior is understanding the effect individual robot characteristics have on the collective behavior. In the past, few analysis tools have been available to researchers. Experiments with physical robots are very costly and time consuming, and systematically studying group behavior is often impractical. Simulations, such as with embodied simulators [5, 13], attempt to realistically model the environment, the robots' imperfect sensing of and interactions with it. Though simulations are much faster and much more reliable than experiments, their results are not easily generalizable. Exhaustive scan of the design parameter space is often required to reach any conclusion. Moreover, simulations do not scale well with the system size – unless computation is performed in parallel, the greater the number of agents, the longer it takes to obtain results.

Macroscopic modeling and mathematical analysis offer an alternative to experiments and simulations. Using mathematical analysis we can quickly and efficiently study swarm robotic systems, predict their long term behavior, gain insight into system design: *e.g.*, how individual robot characteristics affect group behavior. Additionally, mathematical analysis may be used to select parameters that optimize group performance, prevent instabilities, *etc*. Finally, results of analysis can be used as feedback to guide performance-enhancing modifications of the robot controller.

In this paper we survey existing work on modeling collective behavior of robot swarms with macroscopic models. The robots themselves in these systems are simple, usually using reactive control: robots decide about future actions based solely on input from sensors (including communication with other robots) and the action they are currently executing. They do not rely on abstract representation, planning, or higher order reasoning functions. Such robots can be represented as stochastic Markov processes. An equation, known as the Rate Equation, describes the dynamics of their collective behavior. The Rate Equation formalism can be derived from theory of stochastic processes [8], although in practice, the equations are usually phenomenological and can be easily written down by considering details of the individual robot controller. The Rate Equation approach has been applied to study several distributed robot systems [14, 10, 7, 11, 1]. Below we review the elements of the mathematical formalism and illustrate with a few sample results from the robotics domain.

2   Methods for Modeling Swarm Robotic Systems

Models can generally be broken into two classes: *microscopic* and *macroscopic*. Microscopic descriptions treat the robot as the fundamental unit of the model. These models describe the robot's interactions with other robots and the environment. Solving or simulating a system composed of many such agents gives researchers an understanding of the global behavior of the system. Examples of such microscopic models are reported in [12, 6]; they have been used to study collective behavior of a swarm of robots engaged in object aggregation and collaborative pulling. Rather than compute the exact trajectories and sensory information of individual robots, the robot's interactions with other robots and the environment are modeled as a series of stochastic events, with probabilities determined by simple geometric considerations and systematic experiments with one or two real robots. Running several series of stochastic events in parallel, one for each robot, allows researchers to study the collective behavior of the swarm.

A macroscopic model, on the other hand, directly describes the collective behavior of the robotic swarm. It is computationally efficient because it uses fewer variables. Macroscopic models have been successfully applied to a wide variety of problems in physics, chemistry, biology and the social sciences. In these applications, the microscopic behavior of an individual (e.g., a Brownian particle in a volume of gas or an individual residing in US) is quite complex, often stochastic and only partially predictable, and certainly analytically intractable. Rather than account for the inherent variability of individuals, scientists model the behavior of some *average* quantity that represents the system they are studying (e.g., volume of gas or population of US). Such macroscopic descriptions often have a very simple form and are analytically tractable. It is important to remember that such models do not reproduce the results of a single experiment – rather, the behavior of some observable averaged over many experiments or observations. The two description levels are, of course, related: we can start from the Stochastic Master Equation that describes the evolution of a robot's probability density and get the Rate Equation, a macroscopic model, by averaging it [8]. In most cases, however, Rate Equations are phenomenological in nature, *i.e.*, not derived from first principles. Below we show how to formulate the Rate Equations describing dynamics of a homogeneous robot swarm by examining the details of individual robot controller.

The Rate Equation is not the only approach to modeling collective behavior. Anderson [2], for example, shows how geometric analysis can be used to predict distribution of individuals playing spatial participative games from the microscopic rules each individual is following.

2.1   Stochastic Approach to Modeling Robotic Swarms

The behavior of individual robots in a swarm has many complex influences, even in a controlled laboratory setting. Robots are influenced by external forces, many of which may not be anticipated, such as friction, battery power, sound or light signals, *etc.* Even if all the forces are known in advance, the robots are still subject to random events: fluctuations in the environment, as well as noise in the robot's sensors and actuators. A robot will interact with other robots whose exact trajectories are equally complex, making it impossible to know which robots will come in contact with one another. Finally, the designer can take advantage of the unpredictability and incorporate it directly into the robot's behavior: *e.g.*, the simplest effective policy for obstacle avoidance is for the robot to turn a

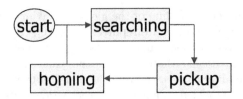

Fig. 1. Diagram of a robot controller for the simplified foraging scenario.

random angle and move forward. In summary, the behavior of robots in a swarm is so complex, it is best described probabilistically, as a stochastic process.

Consider Figure 1, it depicts a controller for a simplified foraging scenario. Each box represents a robot's state – the action it is executing. In the course of accomplishing the task, the robot will transition from searching to puck pick-up to homing. Transitions between states are triggered by external stimuli, such as encountering a puck. This robot can be described as a stochastic Markov process[1], and the diagram in Figure 1 is, therefore, the Finite State Automaton (FSA) of the controller.

The stochastic process approach allows us to mathematically study the behavior of robot swarms. Let $p(n,t)$ be the probability robot is in state n at time t. The Markov property allows us to write change in probability density as [8]

$$\Delta p(n,t) = p(n, t + \Delta t) - p(n,t)$$
$$= \sum_{n'} p(n, t + \Delta t | n', t) p(n', t) - \sum_{n'} p(n', t + \Delta t | n, t) p(n, t). \quad (1)$$

The conditional probabilities define the transition rates for a Markov process

$$W(n|n'; t) = \lim_{\Delta t \to 0} \frac{p(n, t + \Delta t | n', t)}{\Delta t}. \quad (2)$$

The quantity $p(n,t)$ also describes a macroscopic variable – the fraction of robots in state n, with Equation 1 describing how this variable changes in time. Averaging both sides of the equation over the number of robots (and assuming only individual transitions between states are allowed), we obtain in the continuous limit ($\lim_{\Delta t \to 0}$)

$$\frac{dN_n(t)}{dt} = \sum_{n'} W(n|n', t) N'_n(t) - \sum_{n'} W(n'|n, t) N_n(t), \quad (3)$$

where $N_n(t)$ is the *average* number of robots in state n at time t. This is the so-called Rate Equation. It is sometimes also written in a discrete form, as a finite difference equation that describes the behavior of $N(kT)$, k being an integer and T the discretization interval: $(N(t + T) - N(t))/T$. Equation 3 has the following interpretation: the number of robots in state n will increase in time

---

[1] A Markov process's future state depends only on its present state and none of the past states.

due to transitions *to* state n from other states, and it will decrease in time due to the transitions *from* state n to other states.

Rate Equations are deterministic. In stochastic systems, however, they describe the dynamics of average quantities. How closely the average quantities track the behavior of the actual dynamic variables depends on the magnitude of fluctuations. Usually the larger the system, the smaller are the (relative) fluctuations. In a small system, the experiment may be repeated many times to average out the effect of fluctuations. The agreement increases as the size of the system grows.

2.2   A Recipe for Model Construction

The Rate Equation is a useful tool for mathematical analysis of collective dynamics of robot swarms. To facilitate the analysis, we begin by drawing the macroscopic state diagram of the system. *The collective behavior of the swarm is captured by an FSA that is functionally identical to the individual robot FSA, except that each state of the automaton now represents the number of robots executing that action* [10, 7, 11]. Not every microscopic robot behavior need to become a macroscopic state. In order to keep the model tractable, it is often useful to coarse-grain it by considering several related actions or behaviors as a single state. For example, we may take the searching state of robots to consist of the actions *wander in the arena, detect objects* and *avoid obstacles*. When necessary, the searching state can be split into three states, one for each behavior; however, we are often interested in the *minimal* model that captures the important behavior of the system. Coarse-graining presents a way to construct such a minimal model.

The macroscopic automaton can be directly translated into the Rate Equations. Each state in the automaton becomes a dynamic variable $N_n(t)$, with its own Rate Equation. Every transition will be accounted for by a term in the equation: a positive term for the incident $(W(n|n')N_{n'})$ arrows and negative term for the outgoing $(W(n'|n)N_n)$ arrows.

Finding an appropriate mathematical form for the transition rates is the main challenge in studying real systems. The transition is triggered by some stimulus – be it another robot in a particular state, an object to be picked up, *etc.* In order to compute the transition rates, we assume, for simplicity, that robots and stimuli are uniformly distributed. The transition rates then have the following form: $W(n|n') \approx M$, where M is the environmental stimulus encountered (*e.g.*, number of sticks in the arena). The proportionality factor connects the model to experiments, and it depends on the rate at which a robot detects sticks. It can be roughly estimated from first principles ("scattering cross section" approach [10]), measured from simulations or experiments with one or two robots, or left as a model parameter. There will be cases where the uniformity assumption fails: *e.g.*, in overcrowded scenarios where robots, depending on their obstacle avoidance controller, tend to clump, forming "robotic clouds" [11]. If the transition rates cannot be calculated from first principles, it may be expedient to leave them as parameters of the model and obtain them by fitting the model to data.

3   Application to Swarm Robotic Experiments

The Rate Equation has been used to study a variety of distributed robot systems. Below we illustrate the approach with a few sample results from swarm robotic experiments, for which a body of experimental and simulations data exists.

3.1   Collaborative Stick Pulling

The stick-pulling experiments were carried out to study dynamics of collaboration in robots [6]. The robots' task was to locate sticks scattered around the arena and pull them out of their holes. A single robot cannot complete the task on its own: rather, when a robot finds a stick, it lifts it partially out of the hole and waits for a period specified by its *gripping time parameter* for a second robot to find it. If a second robot finds the first during this time interval, it will pull the stick out; otherwise, the first robot releases the stick and returns to the searching state.

Lerman *et al.* [10] studied a minimal continuous time model of the system. A minimal model includes only the salient details of the process it describes. They found that this model reproduced key experimental observations and qualitatively agreed with results of experiments and simulations (see Figure 2(a)). Martinoli & Easton [11] formulated a more detailed model based on finite difference equations that accounts for every state in the robot control diagram.

Figure 2 depicts the collaboration rate, the rate at which robots pull sticks out, as a function of the individual robot gripping time parameter for the minimal (a) and the detailed (b) models. Figure 2(b) also shows results of embodied and probabilistic numeric simulations for the same set of parameters. One can see quantitative agreement already with swarms as small as 8 robots. The minimal model shows the same qualitative behavior as the more detailed model.

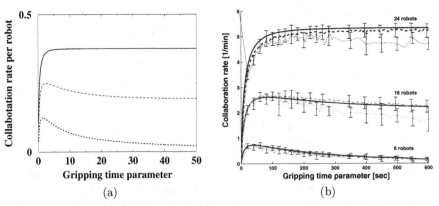

Fig. 2. Collaboration rate per robot vs gripping time parameter for different robot group sizes and 16 sticks. (a) Results of the minimal model for 8 (short dash), 16 (long dash) and 24 (solid line) robots. (b) Results for detailed model (solid lines), embodied simulations (dotted lines), the microscopic model (dashed lines).

3.2   Collective Object Collection

Mathematical models have been applied to study collective collection experiments (aggregation and foraging). In the aggregation experiments, the task was to gather small objects in a single cluster starting from a situation where they were all randomly scattered in an arena [12, 1]. Swarms of robots of different group size, or differing in the sensing and actuation capabilities, were used to aggregate different types of objects. These publications considered both microscopic and macroscopic models as well as a few metrics for measuring the evolution of aggregation (average cluster size, number of clusters, size of the biggest cluster). Figure 3(a) shows the results of macroscopic model's predictions compared to realistic embodied simulation for swarm sizes of one and five robots (see [1] for details). It is worth nothing that, although certain swarm sizes considered were extremely small, quantitative agreement between model and realistic simulation was achieved. The authors also report experiments using variable swarm sizes, by enabling robots to decide whether to continue aggregating the objects or rest. Also in this scenario, theoretical predictions were extremely faithful not only in predicting dynamics of aggregation but also the number of active workers over time.

In foraging experiments, Lerman and Galstyan studied the influence of physical interference on the swarm performance [7]. Interference is a critical issue in swarm robotics, in particular in foraging experiments where there is a spatial bottleneck at the predefined "home" region where the collected objects must be delivered. When two robots find themselves within sensing distance of one another, they will execute obstacle avoidance maneuvers. Because this behavior takes time, interference decreases robots' efficiency. Clearly, a single robot working alone is relatively more efficient, because it does not experience interference from other robots (the larger the swarm, the greater the degree of interference). However, parallel work helps speed up the foraging process and increases the system robustness in case of individual robot failures.

Figure 3(b) shows the total time required to complete the task for two different interference strengths, as measured by the avoiding time τ. For both cases task completion time is minimized for some swarm size and increases for larger swarms. The greater the effect of interference (larger τ), the smaller the optimal swarm size. Results show good quantitative agreement with embodied simulations with swarms of one to 20 robots.

4   Discussion

The macroscopic methods used to analyze collective behavior of robot swarms are based on viewing individual robots as stochastic Markov processes. In order to construct a description of the behavior of a swarm, we do not need to know the exact trajectories of every robot; instead, we derive a model that governs the dynamics of the aggregate, or average, swarm behavior.

A number of simplifying assumptions and specific conditions were used in the methods presented in this paper. While these are not strictly necessary for the

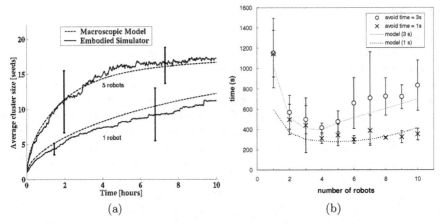

Fig. 3. (a) Evolution of the mean cluster size in an arena with 20 objects to gather and swarms of one and five robots. Macroscopic model (dashed lines) and embodied simulation (continuous lines) are compared. (b) Time it takes the swarm of robots to collect objects in the arena for two difference interference strengths. Symbols are results of embodied simulations, while lines give the model's predictions.

validity of the overall approach, they are important for producing mathematically tractable macroscopic models. First, we assume that robot's actions are largely independent of one another (dilute limit), and the transition rates can be represented by aggregate quantities that are spatially uniform and independent of individual robots or their trajectories. Second, up to date we considered exclusively nonspatial metrics for evaluating collective swarm performance. As long as detection areas do not overlap between the objects placed in the arena and the metric does not specifically address spatiality, these assumptions are correct. Third, we assumed that modeled robots have perfectly centered, uniform, and precise range of detection for each object they may encounter in the arena, in contrast to the individual, heterogeneously distributed, noisy sensors available to the real robots and in the embodied simulation. Fourth, modeled robots are characterized by a set of parameters, each of them representing the mean value of some real robot feature: mean speed, mean duration for performing a certain maneuver, and so on. We do not consider parameter distributions in our models. Fifth, further difficulties may arise due to behavioral granularity captured in the models. For instance, certain controllers can be approximated by a FSA, though certain routines (e.g., obstacle avoidance and interference) might rely on different control architectures. For instance, proximal control architectures such as neural networks are often used for such routines. They tightly couple actuators with sensors without passing through a distal representation as, for instance, is the case for behavior-based implementations. Parameters used to describe the states corresponding to such routines can still be measured in systematic tests with one or two real robots for achieving well calibrated models without using free parameters but this usually implies some inaccuracies. While for predicting high level metrics such as those considered in the distributed manipulation experiments mentioned above, this approximation is quite sufficient, for other metrics closer to the the robot movements (e.g., average number of robots in search or in obstacle avoidance) such inaccuracies might have a more relevant effect. As a consequence, it might be much more difficult to achieve quantitative agreement between models' predictions and experimental results without fitting the data. Finally, depending on the type of experiment performed and the metrics used, nonlinear mapping between microscopic and macroscopic representations might generate prediction discrepancies between the two type of models simply because average quantities in closed form at the macroscopic level cannot be calculated from the linear combination of the individual Markov chains constituting the microscopic model. As a general rule, discrepancies between the two modeling categories are usually more important with smaller swarm sizes. In such cases microscopic models are often more faithful than macroscopic ones.

5   Conclusion and Outlook

In this paper we have reviewed methods for macroscopically modeling and analyzing the behavior of robot swarms. Our analysis is based on the theory of distributed stochastic processes, which is applicable to robot swarms because the behavior of each robot is inherently probabilistic in nature and often not completely predictable, and its future state depends only on its present state. Despite the inherent unpredictability, the probabilistic description of the collective behavior is surprisingly simple. We showed that Rate Equations describe how the average collective system properties change in time. These equations can be easily written down from the details of the individual robot controller. We illustrated the formalism by reporting a few sample results from swarm robotics experiments presented in the past. Analysis yields important insights into the system, such as what are the important parameters that determine the behavior, how to optimize swarm performance, etc.

Much work remains to be done in extending stochastic mathematical models to new domains and overcoming limitations of the current models. For example, Lerman & Galstyan [9, 4] have moved beyond simple Markov processes to study distributed systems composed of adaptive robots that can change their behavior based on their estimates of the global state of the system. Another unexplored area is in modeling systems in which position has to be taken into account. Such systems include any that are based on diffusing pheromone fields. Another research direction is to move beyond the mean-field approximation and develop exact statistical formulations of problems. Such formulations will enable us to study directly stochastic effects, including the strength of fluctuations.

Acknowledgments

Martinoli is currently sponsored by a Swiss NSF Professorship contract Nr. PP002-68647/1. Lerman and Galstyan are supported in part by the Defense Advanced Research Projects Agency (DARPA) under contract F30602-00-2-0573.

References

1. Agassounon, W., Martinoli, A. and Easton, K. 2004 Macroscopic Modeling of Aggregation Experiments using Embodied Agents in Teams of Constant and Time-Varying Sizes. Special issue on Swarm Robotics, Dorigo, M. and Sahin, E. editors, *Autonomous Robots*, **17**(2-3):163–191.
2. Anderson, C. 2003. Linking Micro- to Macro-level Behavior in the Aggressor-Defender-Stalker Game, in *Workshop on the Mathematics and Algorithms of Social Insects (MASI-2003)*, December, 2003, Atlanta, GA.
3. Bonabeau, E., Dorigo M. and Theraulaz, G. 1999. *Swarm Intelligence: From Natural to Artificial Systems*. Oxford University Press, New York.
4. Galstyan, A. and Lerman, K. 2004. Analysis of a Stochastic Model of Adaptive Task Allocation in Robots, to appear in *Workshop on Engineering Self-Organizing Systems at AAMAS-2004*.
5. Gerkey, B. P., Vaughan, R. T., Stoy, K., Howard, A., Sukhatme G. S., Matarić, M. J. 2001. Most Valuable Player: A Robot Device Server for Distributed Control, in *Proc. of the IEEE/RSJ International Conference on Intelligent Robots and Systems (IROS 2001)*, Wailea, Hawaii, October 29–November 3, 2001.
6. Ijspeert, A. J., Martinoli, A., Billard, A. and Gambardella L. M. 2001. Collaboration through the Exploitation of Local Interactions in Autonomous Collective Robotics: The Stick Pulling Experiment. *Autonomous Robots* **11**(2):149–171.
7. Lerman, K. and Galstyan, A. 2002a. Mathematical model of foraging in a group of robots: Effect of interference. *Autonomous Robots*, **13**(2):127–141.
8. Lerman, K. and Galstyan, A. 2002b. Two paradigms for the design of artificial collectives. In *Proc. of the First Annual workshop on Collectives and Design of Complex Systems*, NASA-Ames, CA.
9. Lerman, K. and Galstyan, A. 2003. Macroscopic Analysis of Adaptive Task Allocation in Robots. pp. 1951–1956. In *Proc. of the Int. Conf. on Intelligent Robots and Systems (IROS-2003)*, Las Vegas, NV.
10. Lerman, K., Galstyan, A., Martinoli, A. and Ijspeert, A. 2001. A macroscopic analytical model of collaboration in distributed robotic systems. *Artificial Life Journal*, **7**(4):375–393.
11. Martinoli, A., Easton, K. and Agassounon, W. 2004. Modeling of Swarm Robotic Systems: A Case Study in Collaborative Distributed Manipulation. Special Issue on Experimental Robotics, Siciliano, B., editor, *Int. Journal of Robotics Research*, **23**(4):415–436.
12. Martinoli, A., Ijspeert, A. J., and Gambardella, L. M. 1999. A probabilistic model for understanding and comparing collective aggregation mechanisms. pp. 575–584. In D. Floreano, J.-D. Nicoud, and F. Mondada, editors, *LNAI:1674*, Springer, New York, NY.
13. Michel, O. 2004. Webots: Professional Mobile Robot Simulation. *Int. J. of Advanced Robotic Systems*, **1**(1):39–42.
14. Sugawara, K. and Sano, M. 1997. Cooperative acceleration of task performance: Foraging behavior of interacting multi-robots system. *Physica* **D100**:343–354.

Order by Disordered Action in Swarms

Gerardo Beni

Department of Electrical Engineering,
University of California Riverside, California 92521, USA
beni@ee.ucr.edu

Abstract. We consider swarms as systems with partial random synchronicity and look at the conditions for their convergence to a fixed point. The conditions turn out to be not much more stringent than for linear, one-step, stationary iterative schemes, either synchronous or sequential. The rate of convergence is also comparable. The main result is that swarms converge in cases when synchronous and/or sequential updating systems do not. The other significant result is that swarms can undergo a transition from non convergence to convergence as their degree of partial synchronicity diminishes, i.e., as they get more "disordered". The production of order by disordered action appears as a basic characteristic of swarms.

1 Introduction

1.1 The Problem

Swarm Intelligence [1–3] is a paradigm for designing "intelligent" systems as the result of cooperation among a relatively small number $(10^2 - 10^{<<23})$ of simple, (basically) identical, autonomous units, interacting without common clock, typically at short-range and without centralized control. Regardless of being or not considered to be "Swarm Intelligence", there are many paradigms for collective behavior with resemblance to biological systems [4–5]. They are methods imported from biology, physics and/or computer science, including: non linear dynamics, force fields, self-catalytic stochastic processes, diffusion-reaction equations, cellular automata, genetic algorithms, formation control, evolutionary algorithms, neural networks, etc. All these tools are generally characterized by: centralized control and a common clock. Note also that any model based on differential equations (unless explicitly solved asynchronously) is implicitly a synchronous system, with a centralized clock and a centralized mechanism for updating the units. In contrast, the swarm model is decentralized and not synchronous. Studies of asynchronous swarms stability are not very common. An exception is the work by Passino and coworkers [6–10]. The difference between the asynchronous swarm paradigm and synchronous methods has been pointed out, e.g., in the problem of morphogenesis [11]. The Turing (Diffusion-Reaction) model [12] implies synchronicity and central control, hence (unlike the Swarm model) it is physically not realistic for a scale of ˜100 cells.

E. Şahin and W.M. Spears (Eds.): Swarm Robotic WS 2004, LNCS 3342, pp. 153–171, 2005.

Although the swarm approach overcomes the unrealistic assumptions (synchronicity and central control) of other models, the basic design problem of how to make the collective system do a prescribed task, in most cases, remains unsolved. In this paper, it is shown why and how swarms can be applied to the "physical" solution of a very broad class of effects, namely most phenomena which can be modeled by linear systems of equations. This is the case, for example, of most systems described by difference equations. Hence, the design of swarms doing prescribed tasks becomes, at least in principle, more feasible.

2   Swarms as Physical Iterative Methods

2.1   The Swarm Model

In a swarm model, the units operate with no central control and no global clock. More precisely, they operate *partially* synchronously; they do not operate synchronously, but neither they operate strictly asynchronously, as, e.g., in sequential updating. In fact, for both synchronous and strictly asynchronous updating, central control is required. (Actually, a sort of strict asynchronicity could be obtained without central control, by letting the interval between updates of a single unit "go to infinity". But this is not a realistic option.) The units of a swarm generally run, partially synchronously, a distributed algorithm [13]. In many cases [14, 15], the algorithm consists in solving a system of linear difference equations – each unit updating autonomously its state based on a linear equation with values obtained from the neighboring units. Usually the units are identical but this is not a necessary restriction. A discussion of how various physical interpretations of one-dimensional swarms translate into systems of linear equations has been given in [16]. We generalize the definition of swarm of [16] to include a broader class of physical systems, and without restriction to one dimension. Without mathematical formalism we may define a *Swarm* as follows:

Definition 1. *A Swarm is an ordered set of N units described by the N components of a vector; any of the N units may update the vector, on its own time, using a function of the vector components.*

In many practical cases, the function is linear (*linear swarm*) and the updating is also linear (*strictly linear swarm*). Also, in most cases of interest, each unit of the swarm uses the same updating rule at the same average updating rate (*uniform swarms*). Non-uniformity may be with respect to the rule or the the average updating rate. Important in practice is also the case in which the swarm is uniform except for a few units which satisfy boundary conditions. The updating rule maybe deterministic or probabilistic (*stochastic swarms*). Also, of most practical interest are swarms that update each component from the components of the nearest neighbors or next-near neighbors only (*low -order swarms*). Some swarms have units that update other units (*governing swarms*) but many swarms are self-governing, i.e., each unit only updates itself. Finally, it is worth noting the case in which some function of the describing vector is conserved in the updating (*conservative swarms*).

The swarm is a physical entity but, if we regard it as a purely mathematical entity, then the swarm represents an iterative scheme; the partial random synchronicity of the swarm updating makes the mathematical iterative scheme non trivial. Much of the interesting properties and capabilities of swarms stem from the nature of this unusual iterative scheme. The Swarm of Definition 1 has very broad applicability, since non-linear problems are often reducible to a set of linear problems. Also, differential equations can be discretized to difference equations which are then solved from systems of linear equations. Thus, a physical system that represents linear systems can account for a very large class of phenomena, and can be used to design a very broad range of behavior. The difficulty is to get the swarm to produce the wanted solution, i.e., to make the swarm converge to the desired value of its describing vector, regardless of initial conditions and updating times of its units. Various partially synchronous updating rules have been explored for swarms. We briefly summarize them in the next subsection.

2.2   Updating Rules

First, we note the well known fact that the literature about iterative schemes for linear systems is very extensive (see, e.g., [17]). But the bulk of this effort is in finding new methods of numerical solutions, usually motivated by computational power. What it is sought are faster and more accurate numerical methods with the objective of getting a sufficiently approximate solution in the shortest time. The interest is in solving linear systems that approximate the equations for the evolution of a "physical" system. The point to note is that the evolution of the "physical" system is not modeled by the procedure of the linear system solution. In fact, the various methods of solutions of systems of linear equations have no physical meaning for the physical system they are applied to. The relation is not between the method of solution and the evolution of the physical system but only between the solution to the mathematical system and the final state of the physical system. The way the solution is reached is irrelevant to the physical interpretation of the results. On the other hand, the physical meaning of the mathematical method of solution is the essence of the swarm model since the swarm model describes the evolution of a system that solves autonomously its own system of equations.

For these reasons, the literature of methods of solutions of linear systems contains practically no method which reflects the actual operation of the physical system (unless the physical system is centrally controlled and synchronous). Clearly, methods based on direct solutions (e.g., Gaussian elimination and LD Decomposition) do not model the physical behavior of the system. Iterative methods are closer to physical swarms since they reach the solution via successive updating. On the other hand, the method of updating is dictated by the need of speed and not by the need to model the process. The classic iterative methods are either synchronous (e.g., Jacobi) or sequential (e.g., Gauss-Seidel). Many other more recent methods fall into one or other of these categories. Hybrid methods (partially synchronous and partially sequential also exist). The great majority of the methods in use are stationary, i.e. they repeat the same operation at each step. An exception is, e.g., the conjugate gradient method. But no method in current use relies on random repeated updates with randomly occurring partial synchronicity. There is no reason why such a process would speed up the reaching of the solution, hence it is of no computational interest. Interest in asynchronous schemes of solutions exists in the area of distributed computing. Asynchronous algorithms have been studied and important theorems about convergence have been proven [18]. But significant differences with the swarm behavior exist, as will be noted below.

A few basic types of updating rules have been proposed for swarms. A first type of rule [15–19], is non-linear but it is based on a linear relation between two neighboring units. A gradient type of swarm updating, has also been proposed [11]. A comparison between classic iterative methods and the Swarm iteration scheme (Sect.3) is given in Appendix. Comparisons between the latter scheme and other swarm-type updating [11, 15–19] are available from the author.

3   Swarm Iteration Scheme

3.1   Classic Iterative Methods

Consider first the classic stationary iterative methods: Jacobi, Gauss-Seidel, and related schemes [17]. The problem they solve is the system of linear equations $Au = b$, where A is a $N \times N$ non-singular matrix and b is a given N vector. Approximate solutions can be generated using a non-singular preconditioning matrix W and iterate according to:

$$u^{(n+1)} = u^{(n)} + W^{-1}(b - Au^{(n)}) \tag{3.1}$$

This procedure of starting with an initial guess $u^{(o)}$ and generating successive approximations using (3.1) has different names according to the choice of W. For W equal to D, where D is the diagonal of A, it is the *Jacobi* iteration; for W equal to the lower triangle of A, it is the *Gauss-Seidel* method; for W of the form $\omega^{-1} D (\omega$ is the so-called relaxation, or acceleration, parameter), it is the *Jacobi OverRelaxation (JOR)* method; for W of the form $\omega^{-1} D + L$ where L is the strict lower triangle of A, it is the *Successive OverRelaxation (SOR)* method [20, 21].

The iteration scheme (3.1) is generally recast as

$$u^{(n+1)} = Hu^{(n)} + W^{-1}b \tag{3.2}$$

where

$$H = I - W^{-1}A \tag{3.3}$$

As examples, for the JOR and the SOR methods,

$$H^{JOR} = I - \omega D^{-1}A \tag{3.4}$$

$$H^{SOR} = (D + \omega L)^{-1}(D(1 - \omega) - \omega U) \tag{3.5}$$

where U is the strict upper triangle of A.

The convergence of the iterative scheme (3.2) depends only on H. A necessary and sufficient condition for convergence, is that the spectral radius (largest of the moduli of the eigenvalues) of H be

$$\rho(H) < 1 \qquad (3.6)$$

It is well known [20] that condition (3.6) is satisfied by H^{SOR} for $0 < \omega \leq 2$ in a large class of systems for which A is Symmetric Positive Definite (SPD). If A is not SPD, the original system

$$Au = b \qquad (3.7)$$

can be rewritten as

$$A^T Au = A^T b \qquad (3.8)$$

where A^T is the transpose of A. Since $A^T A$ is SPD for any real, non-singular matrix, the SOR method is convergent in a large class of systems.

The rate of convergence of the iterative scheme (3.2) is also determined by the updating matrix H. In particular, the asymptotic rate of convergence is

$$R(H) = -\log(\rho) \qquad (3.9)$$

3.2   Partial Random Synchronicity

The main difference between stationary iterative methods and the type of updating done by swarms, is in the lack of synchronicity and order of execution in swarms. Stationary methods update identically at each step. Non-stationary iterative methods in use for numerical solutions do not update identically but still update according to an order which physically could be realized only by a synchronization and/or by centralized control. Hence, even non-stationary methods do nor represent physically the mode of operation of a swarm.

To specify the kind of updating done by swarms, consider first the possible cases. Divide the updates in updating cycles. An updating cycle (UC) ends when all the units have updated at least once since the end of the previous UC. According to the following three properties, there can be eight distinct types of UC.

(A) *Asynchronicity.* No two units can update simultaneously. (Partial synchronicity is not allowed)
(R) *Repetitiveness.* Any unit may update more than once.
(D) *Disorder.* The updating order varies (randomly) from one UC to another.

Eight types of UC are obtained from the eight possible triplets of properties. (A or not-A, R or not-R, D or not-D). The classic iteration methods (Sec. 3.1) use either parallel (Jacobi and JOR) or sequential (Gauss-Seidel and SOR) updating. Parallel updating is the (not-A, not-R, not-D) case, and sequential updating is the (A, not-R, not-D) case. The swarm updating is the opposite of the latter case. In fact, in a swarm, during an UC, any unit may update more than once

(R); also it may update simultaneously with any number of other units (not-A); and, in general, the order of updating, the number of repeated updates, and the number/identity of units updating simultaneously are all events that occur at random (D) during any UC. We call the swarm type of updating *Partial Random Synchronicity (PRS)*.

Note also that while swarm updating models a system with no central control, the parallel and/or sequential updating of the classic iteration methods model physical systems that are centrally controlled. This is obvious in the parallel case. In the sequential case, in principle, each unit could update autonomously; however, in order to keep the order, a leader must be assumed. Electing a leader autonomously is generally possible [22] only under special topologies and conditions. So, typically, the degree of order necessary for sequential updating, requires a centralized controller.

Another important factor in an updating scheme is the communication delay. This is of special importance in distributed computing systems [18]. In a typical distributed computing model a set of processors operate with separate clocks. Each processor p_i updates at the sequence of times $\{t_i : i = 1, 2, ...\}$. Other processors p_j, generally, update at other sequences of times $\{t_j : i = 1, 2, ...\}$. Considering the set of the time sequences for all processors in the system, at any one of these times one or more processor is updating. Thus, the model is (not-A). It is also clear that, in this model, repetition of updates may occur in a UC. The model is (R). Typically, however, the model is (not-D). The processors operate in their own time sequences but generally do not operate at random times. Randomness, in this model, occurs in the updating values. Each processor updates by using values residing in other processors. Access to these values may have delays (communication delays) and these delays maybe at random. In fact, each processor, whenever it updates, may use values from other processors obtained at any previous time. Because of this randomness in the communication delays, such systems are said to be running "Asynchronous Iterative Algorithms" [18]. The asynchronicity here refers to the randomness in the communication delays. Actually several processes may be updating at the same time. So, in our terminology, these systems are (not-A).

In the swarm model considered in this paper, communication delays are neglected. It is assumed, in fact, that each unit updates using the values that other units have obtained at their latest updating step. We neglect communication delays because, in a broad range of cases, the presence of communication delays does not invalidate the convergence of a process which converges without communication delays. This is the result of the Asynchronous Convergence Theorem [18].

3.3   Swarm Factorization

Given two $N \times N$ matrices A and B we define $A_{B@i}$ to be the matrix A with the i-th row substituted by the i-th row of B. More generally, we define $A_{B@\{k\}}$ to be the matrix A with the set $\{k\}$ of rows substituted by the corresponding rows of B. In particular $I_{A@i}$ is the identity matrix with the i-th row substituted by the i-th row of A. The matrices $I_{A@i}$ update only one component of a vector v in the product $I_{A@i}v$. Hence they are a representation for the action of a unit of a linear swarm.

Definition 2. *We define the "asynchronous conjugate" of a $N \times N$ matrix A, to be the matrix A'''*

$$A''' = I_{A@N}I_{A@(N-1)}.....I_{A@2}I_{A@1} \tag{3.10}$$

Replacing H with H''' in the iteration scheme (3.2) corresponds to replacing parallel updating with sequential updating. It is easy to see, for example, that H^{SOR} is the asynchronous conjugate of H^{JOR}.

More generally,

Definition 3. *We define the "p-th asynchronous conjugate" of a $N \times N$ matrix A, to be the matrix*

$$A'''_p = [I_{A@N}I_{A@(N-1)}.....I_{A@2}I_{A@1}]_p \tag{3.11}$$

where $[]_p$ denotes the p-th permutation of the product enclosed in $[]$. Clearly the possible permutations are $N!$; we call the set of these permutations *the asynchronous set of A*. For the permutation corresponding to the sequential update (3.10) we drop the subscript p for simplicity.

To see how this applies to the partial random synchronicity of swarms, note that:

(1) A random complete update cycle (as defined in sect. 3.2) is obtained by substituting H, in the updating scheme (3.2), with a random element of the asynchronous set of H.
(2) A repeated update of a component u_j is obtained by inserting a factor $I_{H@i}$ in a complete UC.
(3) Simultaneous updates of subsets of components are obtained by inserting, in a complete UC, a factor $I_{H@\{k\}}$ where $\{k\}$ is a subset of positive integers no larger than N. This applies also if the UC is not complete but is missing any or all of the factors $I_{H@m}$, where m is an element of $\{k\}$. In fact, in this case, the insertion of the factor $I_{H@\{k\}}$ completes the UC.

These three operations describe the partial random synchronicity (PRS) characteristic of swarms (sect. 3.2). The next section considers the convergence of iterative schemes which update with PRS.

4   Convergence of PRS Iterations

Accurate predictions of the convergence of non-stationary iterative methods are difficult to make, but useful conditions can often be obtained. The effect on convergence of the three PRS operations is considered in turn. (Assume throughout that complete UC do take place, even without central control; this is very plausible when updates occur at random, such as in a swarm.)

Table 1. Spectral radii conditions.

Case	$\rho(H)$	$\rho(H''')$
(i)	< 1	< 1
(ii)	< 1	≥ 1
(iii)	≥ 1	< 1
(iv)	≥ 1	≥ 1

4.1   Random Updating Order

Starting from the stationary iterative scheme (3.2), the convergence condition (3.6) holds. A random updating order (without considering simultaneous and/or repeated updates in a UC), replaces this condition with a slightly stricter one, as follows . First, note that examples from Jacobi iterations and the Gauss-Seidel counterpart show that the cases of Table 1 are all possible.

For case (i) both parallel updating and sequential updating converge. When random updating order is substituted for sequential updating order by replacing the sequential UC with another member of the asynchronous set (defined in sect. 3.3) of H, generally the spectral radius changes. However, the elements of the asynchronous set fall into two classes: even and odd permutations. The spectral radii for all the members of one class are identical. This can be easily proven from the fact that the spectral radius of the product of two matrices is independent of the order in which they are multiplied (see, e.g., [20]). The spectral radius of the even class is $\rho(H''')$. For the odd class, it can be easily calculated as $\rho(H_p''')$ where p is any odd permutation. In this way, *the convergence of cases (i) and (iii) is maintained* for random updating order, with only the added condition

$$\rho(H_{odd}''') < 1 \tag{4.1}$$

Clearly cases (ii) and (iv) will not converge even with random updating order. But it will be seen below that repetitions of updating within a UC can lead to convergence in these cases too.

4.2   Repeated Updating

Repeated updating has the most significant effect. In fact, it can lead to convergence (or to the loss of it) in all four cases of Table 1. Begin by considering the insertion (at any random position) of a single $I_{H@i}$ in the product H_p''' so as to obtain the product

$$I_{H@N}I_{H@(N-1)}..I_{H@i}...I_{H@2}I_{H@1} \tag{4.2}$$

By cycling permutations, the inserted factor can be repositioned at the beginning of the product without affecting the spectral radius, i.e.,

$$I_{H@i}I_{H@N}I_{H@(N-1)}.....I_{H@2}I_{H@1} = I_{H@i}H_p''' \tag{4.3}$$

Considering the *max* norm ($\|A\|_\infty \equiv \max(\sum_{j=1}^N |a_{i,j}|)$), we have

$$\|I_{H@i}\|_\infty \geq 1 \tag{4.4}$$

And if

$$\|I_{H@i}\|_\infty = 1 \qquad i = 1, 2, ..N \tag{4.5}$$

we have,

$$\left\|I_{H@i}H_p'''\right\|_\infty \leq \|I_{H@i}\|_\infty \left\|H_p'''\right\|_\infty = \left\|H_p'''\right\|_\infty \tag{4.6}$$

Therefore, when (4.5) holds, the insertion of a single $I_{H@i}$ in the product H_p''' does not increase the max norm of H_p'''.

If H_p''' converges, $\rho(H_p''') < 1$, but there is no such restriction on $\left\|H_p'''\right\|_\infty$. However, in a large class of cases of practical importance, the stricter convergence condition

$$\left\|H_p'''\right\|_\infty < 1 \tag{4.7}$$

also applies. Thus, from (4.6), $\rho(\ I_{H@i}H_p''') < 1$.

By applying again the argument, (4.3) to (4.7), to the insertion of a matrix $I_{H@j}$ in the product $I_{H@i}H_p'''$ we can see that , if H_p''' converges (with the stricter condition (4.7)), the random insertion of a number of matrices $I_{H@i}$ ($i = 1, 2...N$) in H_p''' maintains its convergence. Note that (4.5), by itself, does not imply the convergence of either H_p''' or H , but it does not exclude the convergence of either (since the spectral radius is never larger than any norm).

Thus, under rather general conditions (i.e., (4.5) and (4.7)), repeated updating maintains convergence in case (i) and case (iii). Moreover, and more importantly, convergence can be achieved also in cases (ii) and (iv), i.e., when sequential updating without repetitions does not converge. This follows from (4.6) when the strict inequality applies. Examples can be easily constructed (see Appendix). The significant result is that *repetitions within the UC can lead to convergence*.

4.3 Partially Synchronous Updating

The modes of updating considered in the previous two sections update one unit at each time step. Now we consider updating more than one unit per time step. This is partial synchronicity (the synchronous case is the limit when all the units update in one time step). Consider then simultaneous updates of subsets of components (operation (3) sect. 3.3); it may be assumed that there are no repetitions since the effect of repetitions can be treated as in sect. 4.2. After substituting in H_p''' the factors $I_{H@i}$, with $I_{H@\{k\}}$, we may examine the spectral radius ρ of the resulting partially synchronous matrix $H^{(ps)}$. In general $\rho(H^{(ps)})$ depends on the set $\{k\}$ and on where $I_{H@\{k\}}$ is inserted. In any case though, for large enough systems, $\rho(H^{(ps)})$ can be regarded, in practice, as a continuous function of the number of elements in the set $\{k\}$. As this number goes from zero to the number of units in the swarm, $\rho(H^{(ps)})$ goes from $\rho(H)$ to $\rho(H_p''')$. This fact by itself, i.e. without knowing the actual value of $\rho(H_p''')$, is significant since it affects the convergence of case (iii) (see Table 1). In fact, if the set $\{k\}$ contains more than a critical number of elements n_c ($1 \leq n_c \leq N$) there will be no convergence.

Determining n_c analytically is not simple but the existence of n_c is guaranteed by the continuity of $\rho(H_p''')$ and it can be verified numerically. The existence of this threshold for convergence is an important effect for the design of swarms. Increasing n beyond the threshold n_c describes a transition from a larger degree of synchronous updating to a larger degree of asynchronous updating. Thus, the fact that the convergence is achieved only beyond a certain threshold, means that a swarm can achieve convergence by reducing its amount of synchronism. The implications of this result are discussed below.

4.4 PRS Updating

Combining the results of sect. 4.1-4.3, we see that swarm updating (partial random synchronicity, sect. 3.2), *under quite general conditions, does not restrict the convergence of synchronous and/or sequential iterative schemes.* This is a main result. Moreover, some significant new behavior is possible for swarms, which is not for synchronous and other centralized schemes of updating: *(1) swarms can converge when synchronous and other centralized schemes do not; (2) swarms can converge as their degree of partial synchronicity diminishes.* Both results characterize swarms as systems capable of producing order by "disordered" action. This is a feature of swarms that distinguish them from other forms of group behavior.

5   Conclusion

A swarm operates as a map in the general sense that it determines the time evolution of a system by expressing its state as a function of its previous state. Iterating the map corresponds to the system moving through time in discrete updates. The swarm iterates the map "physically", i.e., the state being updated is the physical (e.g., dynamical) state of the swarm itself.

Many maps giving rise to rich phenomena, such as chaos and bifurcations, are non-linear maps. In contrast, the key feature of the swarm maps (i.e., the unpredictable reaching of a fixed point) is not in the non-linearity but in the partial random synchronicity (PRS) of the swarm iterating process. Also, a swarm is not a random iteration algorithm of an Iterated Function System (IFS) (see, e.g., [23]) since the matrices $I_{A@i}$ are not contraction maps, for (4.4). Hence, Elton's ergodic theorem [24] cannot be applied.

In this paper we have shown that, under a broad range of conditions, PRS linear maps have the property of reaching the same fixed points as their synchronous counterpart in comparable times (rates of convergence are discussed in Appendix) and under not much stricter conditions. Moreover, swarms can reach fixed points unreachable by synchronous and/or centralized updating.

5.1   Applications

From the results (sect.4) it is clear that swarms can be applied to the "physical" solution of a very broad class of effects, e.g., most phenomena which can be modeled by linear systems of equations. This is the case, e.g., of many systems described by differential/difference equations. Thus, the design problem of making swarms do prescribed tasks that reduce to the solution of linear systems becomes, at least in principle, feasible. In fact, apart from modeling by linear systems of equations, the feasibility of forming arbitrary patterns can be simply illustrated. While the description of realistic applications of swarm convergence is left to another publication, a simple example of how a swarm can be designed to reach a desired arbitrarily complex pattern is as follows.

Consider the updating rule (3.2); it can be recast as

$$u^{(n+1)} = Hu^{(n)} + (I - H)u^{(w)} \tag{5.1}$$

where $u^{(w)}$ is the "wanted" pattern, i.e. the pattern to be formed by the swarm. The swarm does not know $u^{(w)}$; it knows only the "guiding vector" $v = (I - H)u^{(w)}$. More precisely, each unit i of the swarm knows only its component of the guiding vector, v_i . The swarm knows also its updating rule. In a nearest neighbor type of swarm, this means knowing H_{ii}, $H_{i,i+1}$, and $H_{i,i-1}$. In the simple example considered here $H_{ii} = 0$, and $H_{i,i+1} = H_{i,i-1} \equiv$ a random number x_i ($0 < x_i < 0.5$). So each unit i of the swarm knows only two numbers: x_i and v_i. These two numbers are generally totally unrelated to the final value that the unit i will reach, i.e., $u_i^{(w)}$. And the unit i can sense only the swarm components u_i(that is itself) and (its nearest neighbours) u_{i+1} and u_{i-1}. This is all the information accessible to each unit of the swarm. Clearly no unit of the swarm can come to know in advance the "wanted" pattern $u^{(w)}$ which it will eventually contribute to form by reaching its final value $u_i^{(w)}$. Also, the goal of the swarm is inaccessible to any observer of a subset of units of the swarm. And even if the whole swarm were to be observed, there is still no guarantee (from the assumed knowledge of v and H) of being able to tell what $u^{(w)}$ is going to be, since this would require knowledge of the ordering of the units and the solution of $u^{(w)} = (I - H)^{-1}v$, which may not be possible, in general, or at least before the swarm reaches its goal.

Figure 1 shows results for this simple example. Figure (1a) is the desired pattern that the swarm has to form. Figure (1b) is the initial pattern: the swarm units are all in the same state with $u_i = 0$. Figure (1c) is a representation of the "guiding vector" v. Each component of v is represented by a gray value. It may be possible to vaguely discern the wanted pattern in v. It is clear, however, even for this very simplistic choice of H, that the wanted pattern is quite different from the guiding vector.

Figures 1(d–f) illustrate the swarm self organization into the final pattern, figure 1(f). Figure 1(d) represents the state of the swarm after 10 iterations (starting from the initial state 1(b)) and figure 1(e) after 20 iterations. After 100 iterations (figure 1(f)) the swarm has essentially reached the wanted pattern. In this example the amount of synchronicity is kept at a low level of 3.6% to show clearly that synchronism is not required to converge to the stationary state.

The example does not show how a swarm can form patterns by motion. All the units have a fixed location and are ordered in a linear sequence (the units are

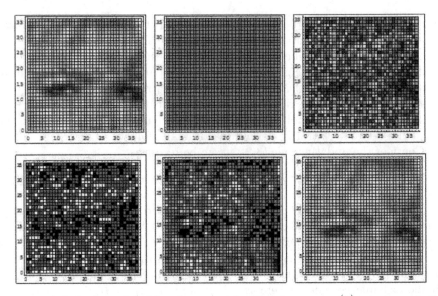

Fig. 1. Labels from top left (a) to bottom right (f). (a) pattern $u^{(w)}$ to be formed; (b) initial pattern; (c) "guiding vector" v; (d-f) patterns formed by the swarm after 10, 20 and 100 iterations (only 3.6% of units updated synchronously at each iteration).

the pixels, ordered from top left to bottom right). The purpose of this example is simply to show that arbitrarily sophisticated patterns can be formed with the Partial Randomly Synchronous updating method of swarms. Applications to realistic swarm robotics problems require a separate publication.

5.2   Summary and Comments

Starting from a definition of a swarm as a special type of self-updating vector (Definition 1) we have seen the relation of swarm updating to the classic stationary iterative methods (3.1). Next we have used these methods to make them applicable to swarms . This extension required to take into account the essential feature of the swarm, i.e. its partial random synchronicity in updating the state of its units (3.2). We have seen that these properties correspond mathematically to specific operations on matrices derived from the synchronous update matrix (3.3). The essential step in deriving these matrices is the factorization of the sequential update matrix into the product of simple matrices derived from the rows of the synchronous update matrix. We have seen that *the swarm converges (4.3) to the synchronous solution under not much more restrictive conditions than in sequential updating.* Since, as is well known, the sequential updating matrix converges for a large class of practically relevant matrices (e.g., tridiagonal, symmetric, positive definite), the conditions for swarm convergence turn out to be quite general. Moreover, *the swarm converges in cases when the synchronous and/or sequential updating do not. And the swarm can undergo a transition from non convergence to convergence as its degree of partial synchronicity diminishes, i.e., as it gets more "disordered".* The rate of convergence has been tested with numerical examples (see Appendix). It is comparable to that of synchronous updating; and it is generally faster than some basic swarm algorithms.

Several points are worth commenting. First, the objection maybe raised as to whether considering "Partial Random Synchronicity" in swarm updating is really necessary. Wouldn't a synchronous but stochastic model be equivalent in describing natural systems? To answer this question, the point to clarify is the difference between "synchronous and stochastic" on one hand, and "deterministic and non (or partially) synchronous" on the other. The difference between the two cases is best understood by first specifying the sense in which we take the term "stochastic". There are several ways of introducing randomness in a system besides updating in random order. The randomness maybe in the rules applied to the updating or in the possible outcomes of the rules.

The first case is what is done for example in probabilistic iterated function systems (IFS) [23]. In probabilistic IFS a vector evolves via a set of maps; at each time step a map is chosen, probabilistically, from a set of possible maps. So the probabilistic IFS evolution is defined by a set of maps and by a probability distribution of choosing them. At each time step a map is chosen according to the probability distribution. This is a "synchronous stochastic" case of evolution.

The second case is typical of probabilistic cellular automata (CA). In probabilistic cellular automata [25] the state vector, at each time steps, evolves according to fixed rules which produce a new state vector from the previous one. The rules are based on the state of the neighbors of each unit and don't change from step to step as in the case of probabilistic IFS. But, the outcome of the rules is not unique; rather it is distributed according to some distribution of values. So, the same rule, from the same initial state vector, would in general produce (slightly) different outcomes, randomly. This is also a case of "synchronous stochastic" evolution.

But, is the swarm evolution reducible to one of these cases, in which either the evolution rule or the outcome of the evolution rule is stochastic ? The answer is no for the following reason. Suppose we try to describe the swarm as a synchronous system. We can think that at each time step a map is applied to the swarm vector with the following probabilistic rule:

$$\{p : R; (1 - p) : I\} \tag{5.2}$$

Which means, with probability p, apply updating rule R (e.g. a difference equation updating matrix), and, with probability $(1 - p)$ do nothing (the rule I stands for "Identity"). This is a synchronous stochastic description of the probabilistic IFS type. (We must exclude the probabilistic CA type since the outcomes in the swarm updating are "deterministic" in the sense that the same rule produces the same outcome). But, is the rule (5.2) really the same as the swarm updating?

It all depends on how one takes the meaning of "apply". If "apply" refers collectively to all the components, then the updating according to (5.2) is indeed of the probabilistic IFS type, but it is not of the swarm updating type. If, on the other hand, "apply" refer to applying the rule individually to each component, then (5.2) indeed describes the swarm and it is different from the probabilistic IFS type of updating.

So, the key difference between swarms and the other systems considered above is not in the synchronicity. The rule (5.2), which can be used to describe the swarm, is applicable synchronously to all the units at each step; so one can create, e.g., a synchronous simulation of the swarm (and in fact this is what is done in the calculations in the Appendix). But this synchronous simulation models units that update with Partial Random Synchronicity since each unit, at each time step, may or may not update.

The key difference is not even in "probabilistic" versus "deterministic". One might in fact consider probabilistic as well as deterministic swarms– rule R in (5.2) could be chosen to be probabilistic in its outcome. This is not essential. The key difference is in *collective* versus *individual* updating. Notice that individual updating does not require that the units obey different rules. The units may obey the same identical rule (as in (5.2) above) which may also be applied synchronously. But if the rule is applied independently for each unit, rather than collectively for all units, the result is a system that updates with Random Partial Synchronicity (the Swarm updating method) unlike any of the other systems considered above.

Having mentioned the synchronous simulation of the swarm, we note that this type of simulation, in which the updating is done synchronously but with a rule of the type (5.2) applied individually to each component, is actually not implemented frequently (generally because of high computational time). Much more commonly, in order to represent independently updating units, a sequential type of updating is carried out. For example, in Particle Swarm Optimization (PSO) [3], each particle is updated in turn. Each particle follows the same rule, resulting in different outcomes for different particles because of different conditions and because the rule is probabilistic. Still, no two particles update simultaneously. They do not operate on independent clocks. They obey a "centrally imposed" sequential order of updating. Since PSO is not meant to represent any physical system this is not a problem. But for models of actual swarms, this mode of updating would not be valid.

On the other hand, the validity of the swarm mode of updating (PRS) is not really an issue. In fact, partial randomly synchronous updating is simply a fact in many natural systems (and especially biological systems). And carrying out PRS updating simulations is not difficult. But, as far as I can tell, these simulations are not so common. The reason is that the distinction between collective and individual updating is often not considered. The point is that for most systems there is not a clear connection between simulations and analytical results, so that one often remains to wonder if a result is general or due to a particular simulation and/or system.

Attempts at elucidating this issue have been carried out for Asynchronous Cellular Automata (ACA). As pointed out in [26] there are several description of "asynchronicity" for CA. These different descriptions lead in general to qualitatively different results. In step-driven asynchronous updating, the types of updating considered correspond to the asynchronous and repetitive updating considered here in sections 4.1 and 4.2. There is, however, no counterpart of the partially synchronous updating (Sect. 4.3). All the different updating of ACA are carried out one unit at a time. So, no partial synchronicity is possible. But, partial synchronicity is of course fundamental in swarms and it is the reason for the synchronous/asynchronous transition.

Even though ACA updating does not contain the partial synchronicity characteristic of swarms, the results for ACA point out clearly that synchronous and asynchronous updating lead to qualitatively different results. This had been noted already ten years ago [27] in connection with Artificial Life studies using CA. In [27] two famous CAs were compared: Conway's "game of life" and the Immune Network model. The former is a synchronous CA and the latter is asynchronous. The crucial factor in the different behavior of the two systems was identified as the synchronous vs. asynchronous updating. In fact, it was concluded that, in this case, asynchrony induces stability in CA. This agrees qualitatively with our results for swarms.

To sum up this comment on stochastic and deterministic updating: first of all, swarms cannot be considered special cases of CA, neither asynchronous nor probabilistic. Swarms generalize CA in several features regarding the updating rules and in particular in the PRS mode of updating. The effects observed in swarms depend fundamentally (and not trivially due to simulation methods) on the mode of updating. Second, the fact that swarms converge, under broad conditions, to the same stationary states as their synchronous counterparts, is not obvious. In fact it has been shown for CA that, although the stationary states for asynchronous and synchronous updating must the same [26], these states have, in general, totally different basins of attraction. This means that, starting from a given initial configuration, synchronous and asynchronous updating may lead to totally different stationary states. And there are examples of stationary states that may not be at all reachable with any asynchronous updating method. Hence, the result on swarm convergence derived here is relevant.

From another point of view, we may look at the results obtained here as of relevance to justifying (or not) some types of simulation methods. In a sense, we have considered a (large) class of simulations (PRS updating simulations) and have shown that we can predict the results of this class of simulations on the basis of analytical results for the corresponding synchronous or sequential systems. The class of simulations considered applies to systems described by, e.g., difference equations but evolving individually. For these systems, analytical predictions on convergence exist (based on the spectral radius of the updating matrix) when the systems evolve *collectively*. What we have seen is that such predictions can be extended to include systems simulated by evolving them *individually*. We have also been able to see how the individual updating of the swarms may lead to unexpected convergence. So if in a simulation of the swarm type it is found, contrary to intuition, that the system converges when it should not, it is not to be concluded automatically that there is something wrong with the simulation. Updating independently helps the convergence (in some cases).

Acknowledgement

The author thanks the referees for many valid comments and suggestions. He is also grateful to the organizers, E. Sahin and W. Spears, and other participants in the workshop for numerous stimulating discussions.

References

1. Beni, G., Wang, J.: Swarm Intelligence. Proc. 7th Ann. Meeting of the Robotics Society of Japan (in Japanese), (1989) 425–428.
2. Bonabeau, E. ,Dorigo, M., Theraulaz, G.: *Swarm Intelligence: From Natural to Artificial Systems*. New York: Oxford Univ. Press, 1999.
3. Kennedy, J., Eberhart, R.C.: *Swarm Intelligence*. San Mateo, CA:Morgan Kauffman, 2001.
4. Parrish, J.K., Hamner, W.M., Eds.: *Animal Groups in Three Dimensions*. Cambridge,U.K.: Cambridge University Press, 1997.
5. Camazine, S., Deneubourg, J-L., Franks, N. R., Sneyd, J., Theraulaz, G., Bonabeau, E.: *Self-Organization in Biological Systems*. Princeton, NJ: Princeton Univ. Press, 2001.
6. Liu, Y., Passino, K.M., Polycarpou, M.M.: Stability analysis of one-dimensional asynchronous swarms. Proc. Amer. Contr.Conf., Arlington, VA, (2001) 716–721.
7. Liu, Y., Passino, K.M., Polycarpou, M.M.:Stability analysis of one-dimensional asynchronous mobile swarms. Proc.Conf. Decision Contr., Orlando, FL. (2001) 1077–1082.
8. Liu, Y., Passino, K.M., Polycarpou, M.M.: Stability analysis of one-dimensional asynchronous swarms. IEEE Trans. Automat. Contr. 48 (2003) 1848–1854.
9. Gazi, V., Passino, K. M.: Stability of a one-dimensional discrete-time asynchronous swarm. Proc.Joint IEEE Int. Symp. Intell. Contr/IEEE Conf. Contr.Appl., Mexico City, Mexico, (2001) 19–24.
10. Gazi, V.:Passino, K. M.: Stability Analysis of Social Foraging Swarms. IEEE Trans.Syst. Man and Cybern -B 34 (2004) 539–557.
11. Liang, P., Beni, G.: Robotic Morphogenesis. Proc. Int. Conf. Robotics and Automation, 2, (1995) 2175–2180.
12. Turing, A. M.: The Chemical Basis for Morphogenesis. Phil. Trans. Royal Soc. London, B 237 (1952) 37–72.
13. Beni, G.: Research Perspectives in Swarm Intelligence: the reconfiguration problem. Proc. Int. Symposium on System Life, Tokyo, Japan, July 21–22 (1997).
14. Beni, G.: Distributed Robotic Systems and Swarm Intelligence. Journal of the Robot Society of Japan (in Japanese), 10, (1992) 31–37.
15. Beni, G., Hackwood, S.: Stationary Waves in Cyclic Swarms. Proc. IEEE Int. Symposium on Intelligent Control, Glasgow (1992) 234–242.
16. Beni, G., Liang, P.: Pattern Reconfiguration in Swarms–Convergence of a Distributed Asynchronous and Bounded Iterative Algorithm. IEEE Trans. Robotics and Autom., 12 (1996) 485–490.

17. Axelsson, O.: *Iterative Solution Methods*, Cambridge,U.K.:Cambridge University Press,. 1994.
18. Bertsekas,D.P., Tsitsiklis, J.N.: *Parallel and Distributed Computation*,Englewood Cliffs, N. J. 1999.
19. Huang, Q., Beni, G.: Stationary Waves in 2–Dimensional Cyclic Swarms. IEEE/TSJ International Conference on Intelligent Robots and Systems, Yokohama, Japan, (1993) 433–440.
20. Young, D. M.: *Iterative Solutions of Large Linear Systems*, Academic Press. 1971
21. Stoer, J., Bulirsch, R., Introduction to Numerical Analysis 2nd Ed., Springer-Verlag. 1971.
22. Tel,G.: *Introduction to Distributed Algorithms*, Cambridge,U.K.: Cambridge University Press. 1994
23. Barnsley, M.: *Fractals Everywhere*, New York, NY: Academic Press. 1988.
24. Elton, J.:An Ergodic Theorem for Iterated Maps. Journal of Ergodic Theory and Dynamical Systems, 7, (1987) 481–488.
25. Wolfram, S.: *A New Kind of Science*, Wolfram Media (2002) p. 591.
26. Schonfisch, B., deRoos, A.:Synchronous and Asynchronous Updating in Cellular Automata. Biosystems, 51 (1999) 123–143.
27. Bersini, H., Detours, V.: Asynchrony induces stability in cellular automata based models, in: Brooks, R.A., Maes, P., (Eds.) *Artificial Life IV*. MIT Press, MA, (1994) pp 382–387.

Appendix

Rate of Convergence

General Considerations. The rate of convergence of the iterative scheme (3.2) is determined by the spectral radius of the updating matrix H , as in (3.9). From the features of convergence of the swarm iterative method (Section 4) it is clear that the rate of convergence for the swarm is also determined by the spectral radii of H, and H_p'''. For the sequential case, the rate determining matrix is H_p'''. For the partially synchronous case, the determining matrices are both H and H_p''' in varying degree depending on the amount of synchronicity. The more synchronous is the updating the more determining H becomes. Thus, we do not expect the swarm iteration (PRS) to be faster than H_p''' (in terms of number of updates) nor faster than H (in terms of clock time) but to be of comparable speed both in number of updates and in clock time. Compared with other types of swarm updating, the PRS swarm updating is expected to be generally faster. Analytical results for rates of convergence are not straightforward in the case of swarms because of the random nature of the updating. So, in order to compare rates of convergence we consider numerical examples.

Comparisons with JOR and SOR. The swarm is assumed to consist of 100 units ($N = 100$). In (3.7) we choose A to be a block tridiagonal (actually Toeplitz, Symmetric, tridiagonal) matrix with10×10 diagonal blocks S, and 10×10 off-diagonal blocks T , where S is a tridiagonal matrix with diagonal elements a, and off diagonal elements c; and $T = cI_{10}$ where I_{10} is the identity

Table 2. Parameters for six numerical examples.

Examples	ω	c	$\rho(JOR)$	$\rho(SOR)$
I and II	1	-1	0.959	0.921
III	1	1	0.959	0.921
IV	1	-0.75	0.72	0.518
V	1	0.9	0.864	0.746
VI	1.33	0.9	1.48	0.33

matrix of rank 10. For the numerical results of this subsection we use $a = 4$ and the parameter values given in Table 2.

For any of these values the matrix A is SPD. Since the matrix is also block tridiagonal, JOR is also guaranteed to converge (for $0 < \omega \le 1$). Note that in case VI the JOR method does not converge (consistently with $\omega > 1$) as can be seen from $\rho(JOR) > 1$.

Although the value of the vector b does not affect the rate of convergence of SOR or JOR, which depends only on the iteration matrix, two values of b are given here to check the spread in the numerical accuracy of the results. For both cases the values of the b components are chosen arbitrarily to be significantly different. For cases I,III,IV,V,and VI, the vector b is chosen with zero components except as follows : $b_2 = b_9 = b_{91} = b_{99} = 1$. For case II the vector b is chosen with zero components except as follows: $b_1 = 2; = b_i = 1$ for $i = 2, 3, 11, 21, 31, 41, 51, 61, 71, 81, 91$. The initial value of the solution is taken to be: $u(0) = 0$. The relaxation parameter is set to the (non optimal) value $\omega = 1$, except for case VI. In case VI, the relaxation parameter is optimized by the well known [20] relation: $\omega_{best} = 2/(1+\sqrt{1 - \rho^2(J)}\,)$ where $\rho(J)$ is the Jacobi spectral radius. Apart from this case, SOR and JOR reduce to the Gauss-Seidel and Jacobi methods respectively. So, in these examples, the rate of convergence is generally not optimized. In fact, we are interested only in comparing the rates of convergence of the swarm PRS updating with the classic methods and with other swarm methods. The results are given in Table 3 for the six representative cases of the parameters shown in Table 2.

The values shown in Table 3 are number of iterations (in hundreds of single unit updates) required to reach a solution which differs less that 2.5% from

Table 3. Numerical results for six indicative cases. Swarm (Asyn) is randomly repeated SOR, i.e., using members of the asynchronous set of JOR . Swarm (PRS) updates with partial random synchronicity from JOR. This is the actual swarm updating method (sect. 4).

Method	I	II	III	IV	V	VI
SOR	41	40	13	4	7	5
JOR	79	78	20	7	11	NA
Swarm(Asyn)	81.4	85.0	21.0	8.8	13.0	10.0
Swarm(PRS)	79.2	85.6	20.9	8.6	11.5	11.1

the exact solution. The latter two methods include randomness; the results are averaged over five runs. The Swarm (Asyn) row gives results for totally asynchronous Swarms, whereas Swarm (PRS) includes partially synchronous updating. The latter numerical results are for an average number of 50 (i.e., half the total number) of units updating synchronously.

As discussed previously, in case VI, we would expect the convergence to disappear above a critical number of simultaneously updating units. This is indeed the case for approximately above 80% of the units updating simultaneously. On the other hand, by comparing Swarm (Asyn) with Swarm (PRS) we see that the simultaneous update of up to an average of 50% of the units does not affect significantly the convergence rate. From Table 3 it is clear that the Swarm methods have a rate of convergence comparable to JOR which is typically, as in this case, about half as fast as SOR. Still, the results confirm the fact that the swarm updating is capable of reaching the solution in a number of updates comparable to that of classic iteration algorithms for synchronous and/or sequential systems. Comparisons with LAQOR and the gradient methods are available from the author.

Swarm Convergence When Other Methods Fail

We give an example of swarm convergence in cases where synchronous methods, such as Jacobi or JOR, and sequential methods, such as Gauss-Seidel and SOR, do not converge.

Consider a block diagonal matrix with the block

$$A = \begin{bmatrix} 2.3 & 1.0 & 2.0 \\ -1.0 & 2.3 & -2.0 \\ -2.0 & 2.0 & 2.3 \end{bmatrix} \tag{A1}$$

From this matrix, form the Jacobi matrix :

$$H = \begin{bmatrix} 0 & -0.4348 & -0.8696 \\ 0.4348 & 0 & 0.8696 \\ 0.8696 & -0.8696 & 0 \end{bmatrix} \tag{A2}$$

Then, from H, form the aynchronous set of H and calculate the spectral radius of H_p''' for both even and odd permutations p. The spectral radii for H, $H_{p(even)}'''$, $H_{p(odd)}'''$ turn out to be: 1.304, 1.063, and 2.180, respectively. Hence neither Jacobi, nor Gauss-Seidel methods converge; nor does the swarm(Asyn) method. But the swarm(PRS) method, which includes repetitions in the UC, converges. The key to convergence are the sequences of swarm unit updates

$$I_{H@3}I_{H@2}I_{H@3} \quad \text{and} \quad I_{H@3}I_{H@1}I_{H@3} \tag{A3}$$

Such sequences are prevented in sequential schemes. But it is precisely these sequences which, working as an "effective" contraction with spectral radius 0.756, lead to convergence.

Subject Index

Author Index

Lecture Notes in Computer Science

For information about Vols. 1–3257

please contact your bookseller or Springer